Y0-BRJ-436

DATE DUE

VOLUME 627

JANUARY 2010

THE ANNALS

of The American Academy of Political
and Social Science

PHYLLIS KANISS, *Executive Editor*

Beyond Admissions: Re-thinking College Opportunities and Outcomes

Special Editors:

MARK C. LONG
University of Washington

MARTA TIENDA
Princeton University

Los Angeles | London | New Delhi
Singapore | Washington DC

Origin and Purpose. The Academy was organized December 14, 1889, to promote the progress of political and social science, especially through publications and meetings. The Academy does not take sides in controverted questions, but seeks to gather and present reliable information to assist the public in forming an intelligent and accurate judgment.

Meetings. The Academy occasionally holds a meeting in the spring extending over two days.

Publications. THE ANNALS of The American Academy of Political and Social Science is the bimonthly publication of the Academy. Each issue contains articles on some prominent social or political problem, written at the invitation of the editors. These volumes constitute important reference works on the topics with which they deal, and they are extensively cited by authorities throughout the United States and abroad.

Membership. Each member of the Academy receives THE ANNALS and may attend the meetings of the Academy. Membership is open only to individuals. Annual dues: $94.00 for the regular paperbound edition (clothbound, $134.00). Members may also purchase single issues of THE ANNALS for $18.00 each (clothbound, $27.00). Student memberships are available for $52.00.

Subscriptions. THE ANNALS of The American Academy of Political and Social Science (ISSN 0002-7162) (J295) is published six times annually—in January, March, May, July, September, and November—by SAGE Publications, 2455 Teller Road, Thousand Oaks, CA 91320. Telephone: (800) 818-SAGE (7243) and (805) 499-0721; Fax/Order line: (805) 375-1700; e-mail: journals@sagepub.com. Copyright © 2010 by The American Academy of Political and Social Science. Institutions may subscribe to THE ANNALS at the annual rate: $743.00 (clothbound, $839.00). Single issues of THE ANNALS may be obtained by individuals who are not members of the Academy for $133.00 each (clothbound, $151.00). Single issues of THE ANNALS have proven to be excellent supplementary texts for classroom use. Direct inquiries regarding adoptions to THE ANNALS c/o SAGE Publications (address below). Periodicals postage paid at Thousand Oaks, California, and at additional mailing offices. POSTMASTER: Send address changes to The Annals of The American Academy of Political and Social Science, c/o SAGE Publications, 2455 Teller Road, Thousand Oaks, CA 91320.

All correspondence concerning membership in the Academy, dues renewals, inquiries about membership status, and/or purchase of single issues of THE ANNALS should be sent to THE ANNALS c/o SAGE Publications, 2455 Teller Road, Thousand Oaks, CA 91320.Telephone: (800) 818-SAGE (7243) and (805) 499-0721; Fax/Order line: (805) 375-1700; e-mail: journals@sagepub.com. *Please note that orders under $30 must be prepaid.* SAGE affiliates in London and India will assist institutional subscribers abroad with regard to orders, claims, and inquiries for both subscriptions and single issues.

Printed on acid-free paper

THE ANNALS

Editorial Office: 3814 Walnut Street, Fels Institute for Government, University of Pennsylvania, Philadelphia, PA 19104-6197.
For information about membership* (individuals only) and subscriptions (institutions), address:
SAGE Publications
2455 Teller Road
Thousand Oaks, CA 91320

For SAGE Publications: Allison Leung (Production) and Sandra Hopps (Marketing)

From India and South Asia, write to:
SAGE PUBLICATIONS INDIA Pvt Ltd
B-42 Panchsheel Enclave, P.O. Box 4109
New Delhi 110 017
INDIA

From Europe, the Middle East, and Africa, write to:
SAGE PUBLICATIONS LTD
1 Oliver's Yard, 55 City Road
London EC1Y 1SP
UNITED KINGDOM

*Please note that members of the Academy receive THE ANNALS with their membership.
International Standard Serial Number ISSN 0002-7162
International Standard Book Number ISBN 978-14129-8686-1 (Vol. 627, 2009) paper
International Standard Book Number ISBN 978-14129-86878-4 (Vol. 627, 2009) cloth
Manufactured in the United States of America. First printing, January 2010.

For a full list of the databases in which articles appearing in *The Annals* can be found visit http://ann.sagepub.com and click on theAbstracting/Indexing link on the left-hand side.

Information about membership rates, institutional subscriptions, and back issue prices may be found on the facing page.

Advertising. Current rates and specifications may be obtained by writing to The Annals Advertising and Promotion Manager at the Thousand Oaks office (address above). Acceptance of advertising in this journal in no way implies endorsement of the advertised product or service by SAGE or the journal's affiliated society(ies). No endorsement is intended or implied. SAGE reserves the right to reject any advertising it deems as inappropriate for this journal.

Claims. Claims for undelivered copies must be made no later than six months following month of publication. The publisher will supply replacement issues when losses have been sustained in transit and when the reserve stock will permit.

Change of Address. Six weeks' advance notice must be given when notifying of change of address. Please send the old address label along with the new address to the SAGE office address above to ensure proper identification. Please specify name of journal.

THE ANNALS

OF THE AMERICAN ACADEMY OF
POLITICAL AND SOCIAL SCIENCE

Volume 627   January 2010

IN THIS ISSUE:

Beyond Admissions: Re-thinking College Opportunities and Outcomes

Special Editors: MARK C. LONG
MARTA TIENDA

FORKCOMING

Field Experiments in Comparative Politics and Policy
Special Editors: DONALD P. GREEN and PETER JOHN

Exploring Culture and Poverty
Special Editors: MICHÈLE LAMONT, DAVID HARDING, and MARIO SMALL

Beyond Admissions: Lessons From Texas

By
MARK C.LONG
and
MARTA TIENDA

Policy Context

The use of affirmative action in college admissions has been controversial for decades. The nomination and confirmation of Sonia Sotomayor as a U.S. Supreme Court Justice refocused media attention on the criteria selective postsecondary institutions use to admit students. Was she given preferential consideration for being Puerto Rican; for growing up poor; or because she excelled in high school, despite achieving lower test scores than other applicants? As her stellar professional career attests, administrators at both Princeton University and Yale University Law School saw in her application a gifted student whose intellectual promise warranted admission.

The Supreme Court has repeatedly been asked to decide the constitutionality of racial and ethnic preferences in college admissions. In its 1950 *Sweatt v. Painter* decision, the Court ruled that a separate law school for blacks in Texas was not equal to the whites-only University of Texas Law School and, thus, did not meet the "separate but equal" requirements of the Court's 1896 decision in *Plessy v. Ferguson*. Justice Lewis F. Powell Jr. wrote the

Mark Long is an associate professor of public affairs at the Daniel Evans School at the University of Washington. His research focuses on the effects of affirmative action and alternative college admissions policies on college entry; the effects of college financial aid on household savings; the effects of high school course-taking and school and college quality on test scores, educational attainment, labor market outcomes, family formation, and other behaviors; and the economics of nursing labor markets.

Marta Tienda is the Maurice P. During '22 Professor in Demographic Studies and professor of sociology and public affairs at Princeton University. Her current research interests include equity and access to higher education and the causes and consequences of child migration and immigrant integration in new destinations. She is co–principal investigator of the Texas Higher Education Opportunity Project.

DOI: 10.1177/0002716209348716

lead opinion in the 1978 *Regents of University of California v. Bakke* decision, which affirmed the constitutionality of a narrowly tailored consideration of race as one factor among many in order to produce a diverse class. However, in *Hopwood v. Texas* (1996), which challenged the University of Texas Law School's use of affirmative action, the Fifth Circuit Court of Appeals ruled that the *Powell* decision was not binding, and their decision led to a statewide ban on the use of race-based admissions. This decision was subsequently overturned by the Supreme Court's 2003 decision in *Grutter v. Bollinger*, which reaffirmed Justice Powell's diversity rationale in the *Bakke* case.

Shortly after the landmark *Grutter* decision, critics vowed continued challenges to affirmative action policies while legal scholars focused on Justice Sandra Day O'Connor's aspiration that 25 years hence race preferences would no longer be necessary. As the children of baby boomers graduate from college in unprecedented numbers, intensified competition for access to the most selective institutions also sustains angst about race preferences in access to college. Yet, a preoccupation with admissions neglects equally, if not more, important considerations in achieving campus diversity and narrowing gaps in educational attainment—namely, the circumstances that motivate students to attend and succeed in college. Opponents of race preferences continue to focus on the criteria postsecondary institutions use in their admissions decisions, which deflects attention from two fundamental choices that precede and follow those acts: individual students' decisions whether to apply and, if admitted, whether to enroll. A better understanding of this process is crucially needed in order to provide opportunities for talented, ambitious youth from disadvantaged environments, such as Judge Sotomayor, to succeed.

Texas Higher Education Opportunity Project: Data

Since its inception, the Texas Higher Education Opportunity Project (THEOP) has sought to understand the determinants of college-decision making in broad terms—plans to attend, decisions to apply, enrollment behavior, and academic performance. THEOP was developed to evaluate the effects of a bold policy experiment: the elimination of affirmative action in Texas and the establishment of the Top Ten Percent Law guaranteeing admission to any Texas public university for Texas high school seniors who graduated in the top decile of their high school class.[1] THEOP was additionally designed to address myriad questions about college-going behavior.

THEOP collected two types of data that are used in the articles in this volume: (1) a two-cohort longitudinal survey representative of sophomores and seniors enrolled in 105 Texas public high schools as of 2002 and (2) administrative data for nine Texas universities, differing in the selectivity of their admissions, collected over a 10-year period that spanned three admission policy regimes. The senior cohort in the survey data were followed for three waves (2002, 2003, and 2006) with 13,803 students in the first wave, while the sophomore cohort were interviewed in 2002 and 2004 with 19,969 participants in the first wave. The administrative data contain records collected by the universities at the time students applied to their institutions, as well as students' transcript files, which can be linked to the application records.[2] Thus, in addition to permitting analysts to exploit the "natural experiment" afforded by the change in admission regime, these data were designed to address a broad range of questions related to college-decision making more generally, from application through enrollment, college performance, and graduation.

Beyond Admissions: Articles in This Volume

The articles in this volume are intended to advance scientific knowledge about the circumstances that influence postsecondary outcomes—from attendance to completion. However, at the same time, they go beyond a pure focus on admissions to also examine topics that few prior studies have analyzed systematically, such as major selection by foreign-born students, high school–specific application rates, and trends in institutional feeding patterns. The unique survey and administrative data also permit novel approaches to questions of general concern in higher education communities, such as persisting racial and gender gaps in collegiate academic achievement, the consequences of school segregation on college choice, and the emergence of college aspirations among diverse population groups.

To date, studies based on the restricted use data files have generated three key insights that have broad implications for diversification of postsecondary campuses. First, the *high schools students attend* are highly decisive for predicting who pursues postsecondary education, irrespective of the admission regime in place. Second, despite public controversy about criteria used in admission decisions, it is *application behavior* that holds the key to diversification of college campuses along socioeconomic, geographic, and demographic lines. In fact, uniform admission plans (such as percentage plans) have the potential to broaden access primarily by expanding the *geographic* reach of high school feeding patterns. Third, campus diversity is at best an interim goal for the broader vision of opening the pathways to leadership, as Justice O'Connor envisioned. Answering the questions of whether, to what extent, and how that goal is being met requires evidence that *academic performance* and *graduation rates* do not reproduce in the labor market the inequities that institutional admission officers seek to correct by broadening access to their campuses. Rather, enabling students to actualize their college intentions and boosting application rates will likely contribute more to campus diversification than race-sensitive policies.

This volume is organized into four sections. The first, which considers the circumstances that orient students to postsecondary education, underscores the importance of emphasizing precursors to college attendance as the first step in campus diversification. Drawing on Pierre Bourdieu's notion of "habitus," Eric Grodsky and Catherine Riegle-Crumb explore the existence of a college *habitus* based on whether students make a conscious decision to attend college. Their results show that sophomores with a college *habitus* are highly likely to apply to a four-year college. Although students with college-educated parents are more likely to report a lifelong expectation to attend college, both advantaged and disadvantaged students benefit from a college *habitus*. Their study underscores the importance of early awareness of college and, in particular, the need to orient students to college early in their scholastic careers.

Butler revisits the claim that high school racial segregation becomes self-perpetuating via students' college preferences, making two important extensions in light of the changing demography of the college-age population. First, he extends the initial racial formulation to a multiethnic context and expands the college choice framework by considering the ethnic composition of the nearest two- and four-year institutions in addition to students' first choice. Empirical analyses based on the senior cohort show a strong association between the ethno-racial composition of high schools and first college preference, even after taking into account socioeconomic attributes of students and their schools. However, for Hispanics the relationship between the racial composition of a student's high school and the composition of the student's college is completely explained by the characteristics of nearby colleges (most importantly, the racial composition of nearby colleges). That is, Hispanic students who attend predominantly Hispanic high schools likely also have nearby colleges that are predominantly Hispanic, and this explains the positive relationship between high school and college segregation.

Section two illustrates the salience of high school attended for college-going behavior. Angel Harris and Marta Tienda reinforce and strengthen claims about the centrality of application behavior in diversifying college campuses, particularly in states such as Texas with rapidly growing minority populations. By computing high school–specific application rates over time, they disentangle shifts in campus diversity resulting from secular demographic change and behavioral responses to the uniform admission regime. Simulations of gains and losses of black, Hispanic, Asian, and white students at each stage of the college pipeline reveal that the changes in the size and composition of high school graduation cohorts were primarily responsible for restoring diversity at the University of Texas at Austin (UT) and Texas A&M University (TAMU). They argue that application and enrollment decisions of individual students are highly consequential for the ethno-racial composition of college campuses, often more than the highly controversial use of race preferences in admission decisions.

Focusing on the admission guarantee for students who graduate in the top 10 percent of their high school class, Mark Long, Victor Saenz, and Tienda ask whether that guarantee changed the high school–sending patterns to the Texas public flagships, as envisioned by the architects of the legislation. Using administrative data for both UT and TAMU, they examine changes in the geographic origins of enrollees over an 18-year period. Historically, TAMU drew from a broader range of high schools than UT. However, after the Top Ten Percent Law went into effect, sending patterns to UT changed. Representation of enrollees from the dominant feeder schools declined, while enrollees from high schools located in rural areas, small towns, and midsize cities grew. They attribute the changed feeding patterns to the transparency of the law, which eliminates guesswork about eligibility for admission for a known set of graduating seniors.

Section three considers variation in choice of fields of study by race, ethnicity, gender, and nativity. In their articles, Lisa Dickson and Milagros Nores focus on the relatively understudied phenomenon of the sorting of minorities, immigrants, and women among major fields of study in college. Dickson extends prior research on this subject, which mainly focuses on graduation majors, by considering initial major choice and switching patterns. She finds that individual variation in academic preparation accounts for a relatively small share of the race-ethnic and gender differences in intended field of study (first choice) and graduation majors. Gender gaps in major choice are larger than ethnic gaps, and women are significantly more likely to switch away from science and engineering majors than men, although ethnic differences in these outflows show Asians more likely to persist compared with other groups. Comparisons of students' first and graduation majors suggest that the underrepresentation of blacks and Hispanics in the sciences and engineering fields reflects lower graduation rates rather than unequal participation in these fields while enrolled.

An additional consideration relates to college tuition, which at public postsecondary institutions differs substantially for in-state and out-of-state students, including foreign students. For example, at Texas Tech, in-state student residents paid approximately $6,800 for tuition during the 2008-2009 academic year, compared with more than $15,000 for non-Texas students. Nores considers whether a state law allowing non-U.S. citizens to pay in-state tuition influences choice of college major. Before the law was passed, foreign-born students were more likely than Texas residents to pursue science, engineering, and math majors. However, as Nores documents, after the Texas legislature broadened access to in-state tuition for non-citizen students who met strict residency requirements, there was a behavioral shift in the propensity of non-citizens to pursue majors associated with lower economic returns, notably humanities and social sciences.

The final section focuses on race, ethnic, and gender variation in collegiate academic performance—grades, persistence, and graduation—and the circumstances that generate and maintain achievement gaps in college. Fletcher and Tienda demonstrate the enduring influence of high school quality on collegiate academic performance. Specifically, they estimate high school fixed-effects specifications to evaluate group differences in first- and sixth-semester grade point average (GPA) and fourth-year graduation for enrollees at four Texas public institutions that differ in admissions selectivity. When comparisons are restricted to students who confront similar precollegiate educational inputs, as occurs for students who attend the same high schools, Hispanic-white and black-white achievement gaps are largely eliminated, and often reversed.

Conger and Long then examine gender gaps in college grades, credits earned, persistence, and graduation, gaps that have aroused considerable attention as women continue to overtake men in college enrollment and completion rates. Comparing enrollees in four-year institutions in Texas and Florida, the authors trace women's advantage in first-semester grades and credits to their better high school grades. They show that gender disparities in achievement widen over time. Although high school academic achievement partly explains why gender achievement gaps widen through college careers, sex differences in course-taking and majors explain a larger share of the disparities in college performance in subsequent years.

Finally, Eric Furstenberg evaluates the effect of attending a more selective college on college performance measured by college graduation and GPA in the first and sixth semesters. He uses the Top Ten Percent Law (which causes a discrete jump in college selectivity for students whose class rank percentile is just above the top 10 percent threshold) as an instrumental variable to identify the causal effect of institutional selectivity on performance. Unlike prior research on this relationship, Furstenberg finds a large negative effect of attending a more selective institution on both college grades and the likelihood of graduation.

The concluding essay by Bridget Long fleshes out novel insights and future research directions.

Notes

1. This guarantee was weakened in 2009 by the Texas legislature when it voted to allow the UT to restrict the share of automatically admitted freshmen to 75 percent of the incoming class beginning in the 2010-2011 academic year. Because 81 percent of the 2008-2009 applicant cohort qualified for automatic admission, this cap will likely eliminate applicants ranked near the cut-point in favor of those ranked higher.

2. A broader description of these data and of the papers that have used these data can be found at http://theop.princeton.edu/.

PART ONE

Precursors: College Intentions and Applications

Those Who Choose and Those Who Don't: Social Background and College Orientation

BY
ERIC GRODSKY
and
CATHERINE RIEGLE-
CRUMB

Empirical research on the decision to attend college is predicated largely on the assumption that students make conscious, utility-maximizing decisions about their educational careers. For many students this may not be the case; in fact, the authors find that a large share of students assume from a young age that they will attend college, exhibiting what might be called a college-going *habitus*. Consistent with critical arguments about how social class is reproduced, the authors find that white, native-born children of college-educated parents are more likely to take college for granted than their less advantaged peers. Students with a college-going *habitus* are more likely than others to apply to a four-year college by spring of their senior year in high school. Although social origin accounts for some of the association between *habitus* and college application, both advantaged and disadvantaged students appear to benefit from a college-going *habitus*.

Keywords: K-12 schooling; sociocultural; social traits; cultural capital

How do students choose whether or not to attend college? Much of the empirical work in sociology and virtually all of the empirical work in economics that addresses this question is predicated on a model of individual utility maximization. Presumably, students weigh the financial and psychic costs of college attendance against the benefits they expect to enjoy as a consequence of attending college and, if the benefits exceed the costs, they attend. Although some models of the college choice process assume that students operate with perfect information, many are more realistic in their assessment of what students know and how certain they are in their expectations.[1]

Contrary to this literature, we argue that many students do not really choose at all; they have always *assumed* that they will attend college. For these students, the decision is not whether but *where* to attend. Other students, however, do choose. They are the students who conform to the models of college choice common in the literature:

DOI: 10.1177/0002716209348732

many if not most of them decide whether or not to attend college based on material resources, personal constraints, and academic achievement.

Building on the insights of Pierre Bourdieu (1984) and other scholars working in the cultural reproduction framework, we estimate a model of college *habitus* based on whether students claim to have made a (self-) conscious decision to attend college. We suggest that students with a lifelong expectation of continuing their education past high school hold a different *habitus* than those who make a more proximate conscious decision to go to college. By *habitus*, we mean a largely unconscious constellation of preferences, behaviors, and styles of self-presentation shaped during childhood (Bourdieu and Passeron 1990). Although enduring, *habitus* is also subject to change over the life course, particularly as people come into contact with environments (or, in the language of Bourdieu, "fields") inconsistent with their worldviews. There is a strong class component to *habitus* but also substantial variation across individuals in the same social class. *Habitus* bounds behavior by leading actors to reject pathways they view as highly unlikely to lead to success.

Analyzing data collected by the Texas Higher Education Opportunity Project (THEOP) from students who were high school sophomores in Texas in 2002, we find that, consistent with a reproductionist frame, parental education, race/ethnicity, and nativity predict college-going *habitus*.[2] This relationship is partly but not fully mediated by student secondary school achievement, suggesting that the pathway from social origins to *habitus* is only partly manifested through the high school accomplishments of potential college matriculants. Furthermore, college-going *habitus* is associated with college application behavior among high school seniors. Contrary to reproductionist expectations, however, we find that the association between *habitus* and college application is substantially, though not

Eric Grodsky is an assistant professor of sociology at the University of Minnesota. His research interests include sociology of education and social stratification. He researches the influence of divergent high school academic qualifications on postsecondary pathways and how institutional practices impact matriculation, persistence, and time to degree. His current research examines the effects of divergence in high school academic qualifications on postsecondary pathways.

Catherine Riegle-Crumb is an assistant professor of curriculum and instruction and a faculty research associate at the Population Research Center at the University of Texas at Austin. Her research interests include gender and racial/ethnic inequality in educational trajectories from high school through college, with focus on the fields of science, technology, engineering, and mathematics. She is currently co-principal investigator on a National Science Foundation grant exploring how academic preparation in high school impacts the college careers of minority and majority students.

NOTE: This research uses data from the Texas Higher Education Opportunity Project (THEOP) and acknowledges the following agencies that made THEOP data available through grants and support: the Ford Foundation, the Andrew W. Mellon Foundation, the William and Flora Hewlett Foundation, the Spencer Foundation, the National Science Foundation (NSF Grant # SES-0350990), the National Institute of Child Health & Human Development (NICHD Grant # R24 H0047879), and the Office of Population Research at Princeton University. We thank Angel Harris, Mark Long, Marta Tienda, and an anonymous reviewer for comments on earlier drafts.

completely, independent of social origins. Disadvantaged youth, although less likely to evidence a college-going *habitus*, benefit from a college-going *habitus* as much as their more advantaged peers. Finally, we find no evidence that secondary school characteristics are associated with either college-going *habitus* or the probability of applying to college independent of student characteristics.

Social Origins and Higher Education

Rates of college attendance among high school graduates in the United States have never been higher. Within two years of their graduation, 72 percent of students who completed high school in 1992 had attended some sort of college or university, an increase of almost 25 percentage points over the class of 1972. Among sophomores in 2002 who had completed a high school diploma or certificate of attendance by 2006, 78 percent had attained some college education by 2006.[3] At the same time, the baccalaureate degree completion rate declined from 51 to 45 percent between the high school graduating classes of 1972 and 1992 (Bound, Lovenheim, and Turner 2007). Much of the rise in college attendance over the past few decades has been driven by increases in the rates of attendance among women as well as students with modest levels of secondary school achievement who are less college ready and thus less likely to complete a degree (Bound, Lovenheim, and Turner 2007; Buchmann and DiPrete 2006).

Changes in college-going rates partly reflect increases in the economic returns to higher education (or alternatively declines in the earnings power of high school graduates and dropouts). Whether a cause or consequence of the college-for-all myth, more and more Americans believe that a college education is essential for labor market success. Changes in the educational expectations of recent cohorts of high school students illustrate the spread of the college-for-all myth. Between 1980 and 2002, the share of high school seniors expecting to attend college rose from 43 to 85 percent but did so differently among different demographic groups. The increase was twice as great among children of parents who had not completed a bachelor's degree as among children with college-educated parents and substantially outpaced the actual growth in college attendance (Goyette 2008). This and other similar patterns have attenuated the relationship between social origins and educational expectations among high school students.

Homogenization of educational expectations coupled with rising college attendance rates would seem to undermine claims of reproduction theorists that education in general (and postsecondary education in particular) plays a pivotal role in perpetuating intergenerational social inequalities. Educational attainment is far from fully determined by social origins, however. In fact, prior academic achievement is largely independent of social origins and is a strong predictor of educational attainment (Hearn 1984, 1991). Even net of academic achievement, however, social origins continue to influence whether and where students attend college (Grodsky 2007; Roksa et al. 2007; Turley 2006). We argue that reproduction theory continues to inform our understanding of the role education plays in perpetuating social advantage and disadvantage (Stevens, Armstrong, and Arum 2008). Although college expectations are widely held by high school students (Goyette 2008), expectations evolve at different stages in students' primary and secondary school careers. Students who have always believed that they will attend college are fundamentally different from those who make a conscious decision at some point in middle or high school to attend college. Focusing on expectations of students at the end of high school misses this critical distinction by combining early and late adopters of a college orientation into a single group.

School domains are heavily classed, with assumptions and styles of conduct and communication driven by the middle-class norms of the teachers schools employ (Lareau 2003). In addition to being classed, schools legitimate social inequality by nurturing what some call the myth of meritocracy: everyone (or at least almost everyone) can succeed if that individual only tries. Originally formulated by Young (1958) as a combination of intelligence and effort, the ideology of meritocracy provides the underlying justification for social inequalities that arise during and through schools. Students are taught to accept the evaluations of their teachers and other educators through grades on individual assessments or courses as a legitimate basis for sorting. In the schools' narrative, failure reflects shortcomings of the student, either in effort, cognitive skill, or a combination of the two.

College for all is a softer, more disingenuous version of meritocracy, offering the possibility that even students who have not performed at the highest levels can still attend college if they eventually improve their performance. The high enrollment levels in remedial classes at community and four-year colleges attest to the strength of the college-for-all myth and the extent to which American educators and the general public are willing to postpone uncomfortable assessments of merit to achieve the veneer of universal educational opportunity.

Almost everyone in high school believes he or she will attend a baccalaureate college. Roughly 40 percent will actually do so in the first few years after high school, with an additional 30 percent going on to a subbaccalaureate college.[4] Some students decide to attend college by weighing the costs and benefits of attendance relative to other options, while others simply assume that college is in their future. We suggest that the *habituses* adopted by privileged youth differ from those adopted by less advantaged students. Even though the *expectation* of college attendance is almost universal, economically advantaged students are more likely to take this belief for granted than their less privileged classmates. In particular, students who are white, native-born, and from better-educated families are more likely to fall into a reproductionist mode of college choice by not really deciding whether to go to college. They simply assume from a young age that it will be so. Minority youth and those from less well-educated families, on the other hand, trace their college expectations back to a more recent time. Such students are more likely to develop their college-going expectations as a result of their interactions with others during middle or secondary school, which become pivotal fields of influence.

In addition to being more temporally proximate, we argue that the college expectations of these students may be more sensitive to school climate, or what some have called the "college-going culture" or "organizational *habitus*" of the school. According to McDonough (1997, 156), organizational *habitus* "refers to the impact of a social class culture on individual behavior through an intermediate organization, in this case, the high school." In her study of four California high schools, McDonough finds that organizational *habitus* "made possible different individual [college attendance] decisions by bounding the search parameters: different schools offered different views of the college opportunity structure" (p. 156).

McDonough (1997) assumes school *habitus* to reflect that of the modal enrolled student. Even if college decisions are structured by individual and high school *habitus*, they may still be rational or consistent with a utility-maximizing pathway. Privileged students may in fact be more likely to complete college and enjoy the rewards of a bachelor's degree than otherwise similar disadvantaged students. However, her perspective (and ours) suggests that standard models of college choice based on students and their parents *consciously* evaluating the costs and benefits of college attendance are partly misguided. Any analysis by privileged students of the costs and benefits of attending college is necessarily *ex ante* if they have always believed that they will attend college or, in the case of McDonough's work, attend high schools where it is a given that students will continue on to a selective four-year institution.

Along the same lines, the possession of a college-going *habitus* may also change students' behavior in ways that increase their likelihood of making a successful transition from secondary to (and even through) tertiary education. A college-going *habitus* takes for granted that the goal of college is both proper and attainable without serious consideration of the alternatives and is similar to Morgan's (2005) notion of prefigurative commitment to postsecondary education. Prefigurative commitment is someone's orientation toward a future goal, whether arrived at by conscious deliberation, socialization, or a mixture of the two. Like prefigurative commitment, a college-going *habitus* may increase the likelihood that students engage in behaviors that increase their probability of attaining their goals, which Morgan describes as preparatory commitment. In the case of college attendance, preparatory commitment likely includes taking advanced coursework in high school, earning high grades, and taking a Scholastic Aptitude Test (SAT) or American College Testing (ACT) exam and their precursors (PSAT/PACT).

Surprisingly little past research has applied Bourdieu's notion of *habitus* to this critical transition. The research that has built on Bourdieu's insights to understand social stratification has largely focused on the choices *among colleges* made by students continuing their education at the tertiary level (Karen 2002; McDonough 1997; Reay 1998; Reay, David, and Ball 2005). This work finds that social inequality is partly reproduced through the postsecondary choices students make, the resources available to them to help them make those choices, and their experiences in college. We seek to extend this literature back beyond the decision of what type of college to attend to its precursor, namely, the decision of whether to attend college at all.

Data

We use the first and second waves of the sophomore survey collected by THEOP. In the base year (2002), THEOP drew a stratified, clustered sample of 108 public high schools and sought to collect data from all sophomores and seniors enrolled in each sampled school in March 2002. After eliminating ineligible schools, THEOP achieved a school participation rate of 93.3 percent. In-class surveys were the primary means of data collection, but students attending schools that did not allow THEOP to conduct in-class surveys and those THEOP was unable to reach during school hours were surveyed by mail. Seventy-three percent of sophomores who attended participating schools completed a survey (THEOP 2003). All student-level measures are based on student reports.

Of the 19,969 students who participated in the base-year survey, we exclude 1,377 who were not presented with the question on which we base our measure of college-going *habitus* (either because they indicated they did not expect any education past high school or because they terminated the interview before getting to this screener question) and an additional 226 respondents who failed to answer the *habitus* question. Of those with valid data for our *habitus* measure, another 3,038 (15.2 percent of the sample) failed to provide information about parent education.[5]

With the exception of the measures of last grade earned in each of four subjects (described below), we use listwise deletion to address item nonresponse. This procedure leaves us with 12,522 observations for most of the analyses of college-going *habitus*. While we doubt missing values are missing completely at random, ordinary least squares (OLS) regression is fairly robust to violations of this assumption (Allison 2002). We experimented with models based on multiply imputed data as well as models using dummy substitution rather than listwise deletion. These strategies increased our sample size to more than 18,000, but they yielded substantively identical results to those we present here.[6]

In 2004, THEOP attempted to resurvey a stratified random sample of 3,000 base-year respondents with adequate permissions and identifying information. Students were surveyed by phone in the spring of 2004, when most of them would have been high school seniors. The final response rate was around 72 percent, resulting in an analytic sample of 2,038 students. We use dummy substitution to deal with missing values on prior grades and listwise deletion otherwise. We use base-year characteristics for all independent variables in the senior-year equations. We estimate all models with sample weights that adjust for unequal probabilities of selection and, in the case of the senior follow-up, sample attrition. Standard errors of the estimates are adjusted for clustering at the (base-year) school level.

Measures

Our measure of *habitus* is based on student responses to the following question: "When did you *first think* about going to college?" Students could indicate that they had "always wanted to go to college" or had first thought about going to college during elementary school, middle school, freshman year, sophomore year, or never. Our measure collapses these latter categories to create a dichotomous indicator that distinguishes students with an enduring college *habitus* (who always expected to go to college) from those who likely made a conscious decision during the course of primary and secondary school. Students who indicated that they either would *like to* or *expected* to go no further than high school graduation (about 8 percent of respondents) were not asked when they first thought about going to college and therefore are excluded from analysis.

While we would have preferred a measure of *habitus* composed of several concordant items, the measure available to us has a few desirable properties. First, even if subject to recall error, this item taps the presumption of college attendance. Students who always thought that they would go to college evidence a different college choice process than students who can recall a time when they decided that college was in their future. Second, the measure has strong construct validity, as we will demonstrate below. That is, our measure behaves in ways that are largely consistent with our theoretical expectations (Cronbach and Meehl 1955).

Measures of social origin include student race/ethnicity, nativity, citizenship, whether the student lives with both parents, parent education, whether each parent was employed at any time in the month leading up to the survey, and whether the primary language the student speaks to her or his parents is English. Students' race/ethnicity is based on a single question combining racial and ethnic origin and recoded into white, African American, Mexican/Mexican American/Chicano, other Latino, Asian/Pacific Islander, and other. Parent education is based on the higher level completed by parents in two-parent families and the sole parent/guardian otherwise. We recode parent education to distinguish among those with less than a high school education, a high school diploma, any postsecondary schooling but less than a bachelor's degree, and a bachelor's degree or more.[7] Statistical analyses control for student's sex.

To distinguish students with relatively uninformed postsecondary expectations from those engaged in activities to increase their likelihood of successfully completing a postsecondary degree, we also adjust for measures of postsecondary preparation. These measures of preparatory commitment include the student's most recent grade in math, English/language arts, social studies, and science; whether the student has taken the PSAT or PACT; and whether the student completed or was at the time of the survey enrolled in algebra II. Grades were collected on an ordinal scale and recoded to the approximate grade point value for each level on a 4-point scale.[8]

To evaluate the role of college-going *habitus* in actual college-going behavior, we estimate the association between *habitus* and other student and school characteristics with the probability that a student applies to at least one 4-year college by the spring of her or his senior year of high school. This latter measure is derived from the wave-two sophomore survey. Parallel analyses of the probability of applying to *any* college yielded substantively identical results, largely due to the concentration of 4-year institutions among the colleges to which students had applied at the time of survey. Of the colleges to which students reported applying, roughly 90 percent granted baccalaureate degrees.

We rely on two sets of measures to capture elements of organizational *habitus* related to college attendance. Unfortunately, these data are only available for students attending public schools in Texas, resulting in a loss of 14 secondary schools, or about 15 percent of all schools in the sample. But because these private schools are comparatively small, their exclusion reduces the sample of students by only about 2 percent. The first set of measures reflects the preparatory commitment of students attending each of the schools for which we have data. To ensure that these proxies reflect properties of the school rather than the students in our sample, we base each of these measures on the outcomes of the graduation cohorts two years ahead of respondents in our analytic sample. The high school's four-year graduation rate is based on school reports to the Texas Education Agency (TEA) and represents the percentage of first-time 1997-1998 high school freshman who completed high school in the 2001-2002 school year. We also include estimates of the percentage of students who plan to attend college and the percentage of students taking advanced placement (AP) courses. These indicators reflect variation in the college-going culture of the different high schools that students attend. Our second set of measures reflects actual college attendance decisions made by students who graduated from each public high school in the 2001-2002 school year (the year in which our sample members were sophomores). TEA reports the number of graduates from each public high school attending each public college in Texas by graduating cohort. We coded colleges as elite four-year colleges (Texas A&M University and the University of Texas at Austin), four-year colleges more generally, and two-year colleges (including community and junior colleges as well as technical colleges offering only associates degrees or certificates). For each high school, we then estimated the percentage of 2002 graduates pursuing each postsecondary pathway in the year following their high school graduation (2002-2003).

This second set of estimates speaks directly to the supposed product of a school's college-going culture. If there is such a thing as a college-going culture, or organizational *habitus*, it should exert its influence at the school level, leading students attending more collegiately focused schools to enjoy a greater likelihood of college attendance than otherwise similar students attending schools with lower levels of organizational *habitus*. However, these estimates only reflect the college attendance of students in the year after high school graduation at public institutions in the state of Texas. A large share (and perhaps even the majority) of high school graduates who attend college will do so the year after graduating and in the state in which they completed high school, but many college attendees chose private or out-of-state institutions, and still others will delay attendance for a year or more.[9]

Findings

Table 1 presents results from the linear probability model predicting the likelihood of possessing a college-going *habitus*. Each model is weighted using the sample weights, and standard errors are adjusted for clustering within secondary

TABLE 1
Linear Estimates of the Probability of Having
a College-Going *Habitus*

	Socioeconomic Status	Ethnicity/Nativity	Achievement
Female	.194°°°	.193°°°	.169°°°
	(.014)	(.014)	(.014)
Mother/female guardian present	.068°	.069°	.039
	(.028)	(.028)	(.023)
Father/male guardian present	.004	−.006	−.017
	(.016)	(.018)	(.018)
Worked last month			
Mother/female head	.004	−.001	.001
	(.015)	(.016)	(.016)
Father/male head	.083°°°	.076°°°	.052°°
	(.018)	(.018)	(.018)
Parental education			
Less than high school	−.067°°	−.045	−.033
	(.025)	(.027)	(.025)
Some college/AA	.085°°°	.080°°°	.054°°°
	(.017)	(.016)	(.015)
Bachelor's	.190°°°	.174°°°	.120°°°
	(.021)	(.019)	(.020)
Graduate/professional	.244°°°	.223°°°	.162°°°
	(.020)	(.018)	(.017)
Race/ethnicity			
African American		−.062°°	−.012
		(.021)	(.022)
Mexican/Chicano		−.077°°°	−.044°
		(.019)	(.021)
Other Latino		−.071°°	−.047
		(.027)	(.028)
Asian/Pacific Islander		.067°	.035
		(.026)	(.026)
Other		−.006	.015
		(.054)	(.055)
Nativity			
Born in U.S.		.062°	.072°°
		(.025)	(.024)
Citizen		−.017	.010
		(.025)	(.022)
Non-English parent		.029	.028
		(.018)	(.019)
Most recent grade			
English/language arts			.042°°°
			(.007)

(continued)

TABLE 1   (continued)

	Socioeconomic Status	Ethnicity/Nativity	Achievement
Math			.030°°°
			(.006)
History/social studies			.024°°°
			(.007)
Science			.016°
			(.008)
Took algebra II			.088°°°
			(.018)
Taking algebra II			.076°°°
			(.012)
Took the PSAT/PACT			.047°°°
			(.012)
Constant	.156°°°	.150°°°	−.172°°°
	(.036)	(.041)	(.050)
n	12,522	12,522	12,522
r^2	.09	.10	.14

$°p < .05.$ $°°p < .01.$ $°°°p < .001.$

schools. Estimates of average marginal effects based on logistic regression models are substantively identical to estimates we report in this article and are available upon request from the first author. Model 1, labeled "SES" (socioeconomic status) reveals a striking gender difference in college-going *habitus*. Girls are about 19 percentage points more likely than boys to have always believed that they would attend college (give or take 3 percentage points).[10] This difference in the college choice process, with girls much less likely to "choose" to go to college than boys (and more likely to assume that they will do so), may help account for the emerging gender gaps in postsecondary participation and completion (Buchmann and DiPrete 2006; Conger and Long 2009 [this volume]).[11] Although secondary and postsecondary grades appear to account for a sizeable share of the gender gap in enrollment and persistence (Conger and Long 2009), those differences in academic preparation (or preparatory commitment to college) may be at least partly endogenous to early formation of a college-going *habitus*.

The probability of having a college-going *habitus* is insensitive to the presence of a father or male guardian, but is sensitive to patterns of paternal employment; children of fathers who worked in the month before the survey are about 8 percentage points more likely to have always believed that they would eventually attend college than children of fathers who did not work in the previous month (±3.6 percentage points).

Parental education exerts an enormous influence on the timing of college aspirations. Compared to children of parents who completed high school but never attended college, students whose parents completed a bachelor's degree or more are around 20 percentage points more likely to have a college-going *habitus* (give or take about 4 percentage points). Children of parents who failed to complete high school, by contrast, are about 7 percentage points less likely than children of high school graduates to hold a lifelong expectation of postsecondary attendance (±5 percentage points).

Net of parental employment and education, we still find modest racial/ethnic differences in the probability of always expecting to attend college. African American students are around 6 percentage points less likely than non-Hispanic white students to hold a deep-seated college *habitus* (±4 percentage points), while Latino students are around 7 to 8 percentage points less likely to do so (give or take about 5 percentage points). Although the native-born are about 6 percentage points more likely to assume from a young age that they will attend college (±5 percentage points), citizenship is inconsequential net of nativity. This is potentially problematic, because students who are not U.S. citizens face many additional barriers to college entry and persistence than do citizens. Non-citizens are among the most disadvantaged students in a college-for-all world; even if they adequately prepare themselves for college, they have many fewer options for financing their education compared with citizens (Abrego 2006).

Finally, as one would anticipate, children who have always believed that they would attend college also tend to perform better in school and to take more advanced math classes and are more likely to take the PSAT or PACT (Table 1, column 3, labeled "achievement"). In Morgan's (2005) terms, these students are transforming the prefigurative commitment they exhibit by their temporally unbound college expectations into preparatory commitment, or action in the service of their educational goals. These actions mediate the association between background characteristics and college *habitus*, but substantial ascriptive differences remain. Even net of preparatory actions, girls are almost 17 percentage points more likely to assume that they will attend college relative to boys (±3 percentage points). Likewise, children of parents with at least a college education remain around 14 percentage points more likely to have always assumed that they would attend college compared with children of high school graduates (give or take about 4 percentage points), even after adjusting for the advantages children of highly educated parents enjoy in academic preparation and high school achievement.

The importance of a college-going culture

Turning to the role of organizational *habitus*, school fixed-effects models (not shown) suggest that less than 1 percent of the variance in college-going *habitus* is associated with differences among schools net of individual controls. We modeled measures of school preparatory commitment and college attendance patterns separately, restricting our sample to the 11,841 sample members attending schools for which we had valid information on these indicators (a loss of about 5 percent of the sample). We also included all individual-level controls in each model.[12] We find virtually no evidence to support the contention that variation in the college-going culture of the schools our sample members attend contributes

TABLE 2
Linear Estimates of the Probability of Having
a College-Going *Habitus*

	Preparatory Commitment	College Attendance
4-year grad rate (1997-98 freshman)	−.0003	
	(.0016)	
% taking AP course	.0007	
	(.0008)	
% college plans	.0005	
	(.0004)	
% grads attending 4-yr college		−.0003
		(.0008)
% grads attending 2-yr college		.0004
		(.0005)
% grads attending UT/A&M		.005*
		(.003)
Constant	−.186	−.196**
	(.153)	(.054)
n	11,841	11,841

NOTE: All random-effects models adjust for the full set of individual-level predictors for habitus: socioeconomic status, race/ethnicity, nativity, and academic achievement. The sample sizes for these regressions are slightly less that the sample sizes in Table 1 due to items missing data at the school level.
*$p < .05$. **$p < .01$.

to their college-going *habitus*. Coefficients for these organizational attributes (shown in Table 2) are very small in magnitude and, with the exception of proportion of students applying to an elite college, fail to attain statistical significance.

Habitus and the decision to apply to college

Thus far, we have demonstrated the fairly substantial relationship between social origin and college-going *habitus*, on one hand, and the tenuous relationship between schools and college-going *habitus*, on the other. But does college-going *habitus* translate into action, or is it, like college aspirations, an optimistic belief shared by an increasingly large fraction of high school youth? If *habitus* does influence the decision to apply to a four-year college, does it attenuate the relationship between social origins and educational attainment? Is *habitus* a resource that benefits all students equally, or does it only serve to advance children of the advantaged? To answer these questions, we estimate a series of linear probability models predicting whether sample members report applying to any four-year college by the spring of their senior year in high school. Again, estimates of average marginal effect based on logistic regression models are substantively identical to estimates we report in this article and are available upon request from the first author.

The marginal association between college-going *habitus* and actual application behavior is substantial: students who always assumed that they would go to college are almost 18 percentage points more likely to apply to a baccalaureate-granting institution than those who make a conscious decision to attend (±5 percentage points; see Table 3). To more fully explore the overlap between the effects of *habitus* and social origins on college application behavior, we compare a model with the full set of social origin measures excluding *habitus* (column 3) with a model adding *habitus* (column 4). We find that the effects of social origins are powerful and change relatively little with the inclusion of *habitus* (less than 10 percent).[13] The association between *habitus* and application is reduced by almost a third with the inclusion of social origin measures. It appears that some but not all of the advantage a college-going *habitus* affords students results because advantaged students are significantly more likely to take college attendance for granted.

Few substantively or statistically significant racial/ethnic differences in the conditional probability of college application (Table 3, column 4) are evident; however, estimates from the final model reported in Table 3 suggest that racial/ethnic differences in application behavior are suppressed by differences in academic achievement and college preparatory commitment. Net of differences in secondary school academic experiences, African American and Mexican/Chicano students are about 10 percentage points more likely to apply to a four-year college than otherwise similar non-Hispanic white students.

Even adjusting for variation in socioeconomic origins, race/ethnicity, nativity, citizenship, and preparatory commitment, we find that students with a college-going *habitus* continue to enjoy a modest 6-percentage-point advantage in their probability of applying to a four-year college over those who make a conscious decision to attend (±4.6 percentage points). That the association between *habitus* and college application behavior is at least partly independent of both social origins and secondary school experiences undermines a strictly reproductionist interpretation of the role a college-going *habitus* plays in educational attainment.

The results of the models reviewed above suggest a modest, but persistent, influence of college-going *habitus* on application behavior. It is plausible, however, that the effects of *habitus* vary across social origins such that *habitus* benefits only more advantaged children. In models not shown, we also explored the possible interactive effects of *habitus* and social origins on college application patterns. We find little evidence of divergent effects of *habitus* across levels of parental education or race/ethnicity.

A final set of models revisits the question of whether or not organizational *habitus* influences college attendance patterns net of student attributes. Less than 1 percent of the variance in the probability of applying to a four-year college is attributable to differences between schools, net of social origins, race/ethnicity, academic achievement, and college-going *habitus*. Controlling for various measures of organizational *habitus* has relatively little bearing on the college-going *habitus* coefficient, as shown in Table 4.[14] Point estimates for our indicators of organizational *habitus* are very small in magnitude and not uniform in their significance. When coefficients do attain statistical significance, they are sometimes signed in counterintuitive ways.

TABLE 3
Linear Estimates of the Probability of
Applying to a Four-Year College

	Marginal	Ascription (No *Habitus*)	Ascription (*Habitus*)	Achievement
College-going *habitus*	.178°°°		.121°°°	.060°
	(.025)		(.021)	(.023)
Female		.079°	.061	.034
		(.038)	(.039)	(.033)
Mother/female guardian present		.090	.083	.029
		(.055)	(.053)	(.052)
Father/male guardian present		.065	.066	.040
		(.039)	(.037)	(.030)
Worked last month				
Mother/female head		.039	.038	.039
		(.032)	(.031)	(.028)
Father/male head		.022	.014	−.034
		(.041)	(.039)	(.037)
Parental education				
Less than high school		−.092	−.094	−.059
		(.064)	(.067)	(.051)
Some college/AA		.145°°	.134°	.109°
		(.054)	(.055)	(.043)
Bachelor's		.257°°°	.232°°°	.189°°°
		(.042)	(.040)	(.038)
Graduate/professional		.300°°°	.278°°°	.199°°°
		(.047)	(.046)	(.038)
Race/ethnicity				
African American		−.012	.005	.097°
		(.045)	(.043)	(.040)
Mexican/Chicano		.034	.051	.104°°
		(.039)	(.037)	(.034)
Other Latino		.040	.052	.055
		(.064)	(.064)	(.056)
Asian/Pacific Islander		.138°	.128°	.080
		(.065)	(.064)	(.048)
Other		−.123	−.123	−.059
		(.131)	(.133)	(.103)
Nativity				
Born in U.S.		−.046	−.053	−.028
		(.074)	(.072)	(.065)
Citizen		−.002	.006	.048
		(.073)	(.073)	(.068)

(continued)

TABLE 3   (continued)

	Marginal	Ascription (No *Habitus*)	Ascription (*Habitus*)	Achievement
English not primary language with parent		−.023	−.029	−.013
		(.045)	(.045)	(.041)
Most recent grade				
English/language arts				.013
				(.024)
Math				.043°
				(.017)
History/social studies				.071°°°
				(.019)
Science				.022
				(.016)
Took algebra II				.216°°°
				(.036)
Taking algebra II				.193°°°
				(.042)
Took the PSAT/PACT				.091°°
				(.027)
Constant	.538°°°	.302°°	.274°	−.178
	(.027)	(.108)	(.108)	(.133)
n	2,038	2,038	2,038	2,038
r^2	.03	.11	.12	.24

°$p < .05$. °°$p < .01$. °°°$p < .001$.

Discussion

Although the substantial majority of high school students expect to attend college, we contend that the trajectories they follow in forming those intentions matter. Some students go through life simply assuming they will attend college. They do not arrive at the application decision by carefully weighing the costs and benefits of a postsecondary credential but rather by default; attending college is something they always just assumed would occur. Other students, however, engage in a more (self-) conscious process of educational choice. They recall a time when they decided to attend college, suggesting that such a pathway was not a foregone conclusion. They either had not formed expectations about their educational futures up to that decision point or had expected to attain less than a college education.

Building on the work of Bourdieu and others in the educational reproduction literature, we anticipated that parental education, student race/ethnicity, nativity, and citizenship would contribute substantially to the probability that students

TABLE 4
Linear Estimates of the Probability of
Applying to a Four-Year College

	Random Effects	Preparatory Commitment	College Attendance
College-going *habitus*	.056°°	.056°°	.056°°
	(.024)	(.024)	(.024)
4-year grad rate 1997-98 freshman		−.008°°	
		(.003)	
% taking advanced placement (AP) course		.004°	
		(.002)	
% college plans		.001	
		(.001)	
% grads attending 4-yr college			−.004°°
			(.002)
% grads attending 2-yr college			−.005°°
			(.001)
% grads attending University of Texas at Austin/Texas A&M University			.002
			(.004)
Constant	−.208°	.122	.047
	(.086)	(.181)	(.153)
n	1,938	1,938	1,938

NOTE: All random-effects models adjust for the full set of individual-level predictors for habitus: socioeconomic status, race/ethnicity, nativity, and academic achievement. The sample sizes for these regressions are slightly less that the sample sizes in Table 3 due to items missing data at the school level.
°$p < .05$. °°$p < .01$. °°°$p < .001$.

assumed from a young age that they would attend college, which we argue indicates a college-going *habitus*. We also suggested that these background characteristics would operate through the college-going *habitus* to influence the probability that students actually attend a four-year college or university, taking application as an indicator of attendance. Borrowing from McDonough's (1997) insights into organizational *habitus* and the work of others on the importance of a "college-going culture," we expected between-school variation in the probability of having a college-going *habitus* and applying to college across schools, net of student characteristics. Empirical results only partly support our expectations.

We find that social origins do exert a substantial degree of influence on the probability of adopting a college-going *habitus* (Table 1). Native-born children of college graduates living in households in which the male head is employed enjoy a substantially higher probability of having a college-going *habitus* than other children. Conditional on social origins, preparatory commitment (as measured by academic performance, course taking, and taking the PSAT or PACT) is also associated with a college-going *habitus*.

Race/ethnicity is not very strongly associated with the probability of having a college-going *habitus* conditional on other social origin characteristics (and even less so conditioning on preparatory commitment). Likewise, we find little evidence to support the notion that a college-going culture, or organizational *habitus*, contributes to the timing of students forming their postsecondary educational expectations (Table 2). Linear probability models account for a modest 14 percent of the variance in college-going *habitus*. Possessing a college-going habitus is influenced, but far from determined, by social origin characteristics.

Habitus does exert some influence on the probability that students apply to a baccalaureate-granting institution during their senior year of high school, suggesting that the construct is more than merely symbolic in its importance. Students with a college-going *habitus* are roughly 12 percentage points more likely to apply to a four-year college than others after conditioning on social origin characteristics and about 5 percentage points more likely to do so conditioning on preparatory commitment. Interestingly, the advantages parents pass on to their children are largely independent of children's college-going *habitus*. Conditioning on social origins reduces the direct effect of *habitus* on college application, but adjusting for *habitus* does little to increase equality in the probability of applying to a four-year college across race/ethnicity or levels of parental education. Even net of preparatory commitment, the advantage children of college-educated parents enjoy over otherwise similar children of high school graduates is roughly three times the advantage those with a college-going *habitus* hold over students who make a conscious decision somewhere along the road to attend college.

Although the effect of a college-going *habitus* on application behavior is modest, its potential importance should not be understated. First, conditioning on academic preparation understates the contribution of *habitus* to college application behavior to the extent that a college-going *habitus* leads students to work harder in school. Academic performance is to some degree endogenous to *habitus*. Second, the fact that *habitus* works largely independently of social class origins opens up the possibility that *habitus* may have the potential to undermine rather than reinforce social inequalities. Regardless of social origins, students seem to experience a fairly uniform positive return to assuming from a very young age that they will eventually attend college. Future research should explore further the characteristics leading to a college-going *habitus* and the means by which *habitus* contributes to the college application process.

Organizational *habitus* has little bearing on students' college application decisions. In fact, school-level indicators of high school preparatory commitment have contradictory influences on college application behavior, but the net association between the attendance behavior of earlier cohorts of students and application behavior of our sample members is negative (Table 4). We do not make much of these negative coefficients both because of their magnitude and the trivial share of variance in the probability of applying to a four-year college across high schools after conditioning on student attributes. That said, the evidence we present undermines claims that organizational *habitus* is an important component of student postsecondary enrollment decisions.

These findings temper claims about the importance of organizational *habitus* in patterns of postsecondary attendance, but our evidence is tentative. First, as noted at the outset of this article, we have relatively few empirical studies of any sort on which to build to understand how *habitus* shapes postsecondary outcomes. Second, we rely on a single-item indicator of student college-going *habitus*. Assuming the indicator is valid, it is still much less reliable than a set of indicators would be. As a result, we likely overstate standard errors in models predicting individual college-going *habitus* (including standard errors around organizational *habitus* coefficients) and understate the influence of college-going *habitus* on college application behavior. Finally, we have a relatively small sample of schools on which to base our evaluation of the role of organizational *habitus* (n = 77). A larger sample of schools would provide more power to identify the association between organizational *habitus* and individual outcomes.[15]

Conclusion

Many theories of educational stratification assume students make conscious decisions about their educational futures, weighing the costs and benefits of alternative pathways. In the case of postsecondary attendance, however, this is not necessarily so. Many students believe from a young age that they will attend college as a natural part of their development. They do not consciously weigh the costs and benefits of that decision any more than they weigh the costs and benefits of attending primary or middle school. Students with what we term a college-going *habitus* take for granted that they will continue their formal education past high school.

That the decision to attend college is for many students a nondecision need not imply irrationality. Given the degree to which the college-for-all ethos has penetrated our culture and the substantial economic returns to postsecondary credentials and course taking, attending college may be quite rational, at least in a bounded sense. Likewise, most students with a college-going *habitus* probably engage in a conscious process in deciding *where* to apply to college and where ultimately to attend. The application and attendance processes may be affected by organizational *habitus* in ways consistent with McDonough (1997) that we do not observe statistically.

That said, we believe that if researchers want to understand how students go about deciding whether to end their education at high school, they must adjudicate between students who consciously make such a decision and those who do not. As a matter of policy, encouraging a college-going culture may be more important in the early years, fostering the evolution of a college-going *habitus* among children, than during the secondary school years. Practices to encourage such an orientation among students may be as simple as normalizing college attendance by making

college a more familiar concept to students, particularly those from less socioeco-
nomically advantaged families.

Yet many students enter college inadequately prepared, with little understanding
of the level of preparation and work necessary to successfully complete a degree.
Sowing the seeds of a college-going *habitus* may therefore have mixed effects,
encouraging preparatory commitment and improving educational outcomes among
some, while fostering the evolution of naively optimistic postsecondary beliefs
among others. Improving the organizational *habitus* of primary schools without
giving students greater opportunities to learn and encouraging them to rise to
more demanding academic challenges may simply postpone the time at which
individual students must confront the incompatibility of their educational expectations and academic skills.

On a theoretical level, our findings offer mixed support to reproductionist theories of educational stratification. Social origins do contribute to variation in the
probability of adopting a college-going habitus. Children of more highly educated parents enjoy a markedly higher probability of taking their college attendance for granted rather than making a conscious decision to attend. Variation in
preparatory commitment mediates only a small share of the origin-*habitus* relationship we observe.

However, a college-going *habitus* is not restricted to the children of the most
educated parents. The social origin characteristics we observe, while limited,
account for a fairly modest share of the variance in the probability of possessing
a college-going *habitus*. Models of college application that allow for the interaction of *habitus* and social origin characteristics do not improve prediction above
models restricted to main effects. College-going *habitus* appears to enhance the
probability of applying to a four-year college for more and less advantaged students in similar ways, leaving open the possibility that increases in college-going
habitus among disadvantaged youth could undermine social stratification. Rather
than a strictly reproductive force, *habitus* may also act to enhance the capacity of
disadvantaged students to resist social reproduction along the lines advocated by
Giroux (1983).

Several scholars have warned against an overly rigid reading of Bourdieu's work
on the association between *habitus* and social class. In fact, it is not surprising
that *some* disadvantaged students possess a college-going *habitus* and enjoy its
subsequent benefits. Without occasional working-class success stories, the system
by which schools reproduce class might be seen by some as illegitimate. Our
reading of Bourdieu, however, is that these success stories should be sufficiently
unusual as to perpetuate the myth of the meritocracy without permitting any meaningful degree of social mobility. They are not. Advantage is reproduced through
college-going *habitus*, but not very effectively. Many disadvantaged students
assume from a young age that they will attend college. This college-going *habitus*
has the same conditionally modest beneficial effect on applying to a four-year
college for advantaged and disadvantaged students alike.

Bourdieu's insights into social stratification have produced a wealth of scholarship. There have been relatively few empirical studies of how his insights apply

to higher education and almost no studies using representative samples and quantitative techniques. We find that Bourdieu's insights into *habitus* have merit as they apply to assumptions about educational attainment, but that college-going *habitus* can serve simultaneously to enhance and undermine social reproduction. Although we find little evidence in support of claims about the importance of organizational *habitus* or a "college-going culture" for students' postsecondary careers, we recognize that our indicators of these constructs are imperfect. Given the very small share of between-school variation in either college-going *habitus* or the conditional probability of attending college, however, we think efforts to enhance the organizational *habitus* of secondary schools with the goal of increasing baccalaureate college attendance may be misplaced.

Notes

1. For reviews of the contemporary literature on college choice see Perna (2006) and Grodsky and Jackson (2009).

2. The model we have in mind is similar to that proposed by Perna (2006) in its emphasis on social context but different from Perna in its focus on *habitus*. Perna conceives of *habitus* as providing the context in which students make utility-maximizing decisions. We suggest that *habitus* is a substitute for utility-maximizing choice, at least at the stage of the choice process in which students decide whether or not to attend college at all.

3. Authors' calculations based on Table 6 in Bozick and Lauff (2007).

4. Authors' calculations based on students who participated in the Educational Longitudinal Study and graduated high school in 2004.

5. Item nonresponse increased fairly monotonically over the survey instrument, and unfortunately, the parent education items appeared near the end of the survey.

6. Results are available on request.

7. Among students participating in the second wave of the survey, 38 percent reported a different level of parent education in wave two than they did in wave one. Results using both measures, however, are substantively similar and statistically indistinguishable.

8. Analyses using dummy coding for the each grade measure failed to improve model fit over the interval/ratio coding.

9. Bozick and DeLuca (2005) found that only about 20 percent of students from the high school class of 1992 who attended college delayed their matriculation more than seven months after completing high school.

10. Margins of error reflect 95 percent confidence intervals.

11. Of course, one would need to control for gender differences across cohorts to build an argument that part of the growing gender gap is attributable to college *habitus*. We are exploring these gender differences further in another paper.

12. One might worry that individual-level measures of achievement, including grades, taking algebra II, and taking the PSAT or PACT are endogenous to organizational *habitus*. In models not shown, we removed the achievement measures and found results virtually identical to those presented here.

13. When using multiple imputation, the coefficients on habitus are increased by 10 to 15 percent, and the parental education coefficients are attenuated but are still moderate to large in size and statistically significant.

14. Each model in Table 4 also controls for the full set of individual-level predictors: social origins, race/ethnicity, nativity, and preparatory commitment. Models excluding measures of preparatory commitment yielded virtually identical results.

15. We should note, however, that our sample of 77 schools is appreciably larger than the sample of 4 schools on which McDonough (1997) based her work.

References

Abrego, Leisy J. 2006. "I can't go to college because I don't have papers": Incorporation patterns of Latino undocumented youth. *Latino Studies* 4:212–31.

Allison, Paul D. 2002. *Missing data*. Vol. 136 of *Quantitative applications in the social sciences*, ed. Michael S. Lewis-Beck. Thousand Oaks, CA: Sage.

Apple, Michael, and Lois Weis. 1983. Ideology and practice in schooling: A political and conceptual introduction. In *Ideology and practice in schooling*, ed. Michael Apple and Lois Weis, 3-33. Philadelphia: Temple University Press.

Bound, John, Matt Lovenheim, and Sarah Turner. 2007. Understanding changing college completion rates. In *Population Studies Center research reports*. Ann Arbor: University of Michigan Institute for Social Research.

Bourdieu, Pierre. 1984. *Distinction: A social critique of the judgment of taste*. Translated by Richard Nice. Cambridge, MA: Harvard University Press.

Bourdieu, Pierre, and Jean-Claude Passeron. 1990. *Reproduction in education, society and culture*. Translated by Richard Nice. London: Sage.

Bozick, Robert, and Stefanie DeLuca. 2005. Better late than never? Delayed enrollment in the high school to college transition. *Social Forces* 84 (1): 531-54.

Bozick, Robert, and Erich Lauff. 2007. *Education longitudinal study of 2002 (Els: 2002): A first look at the initial postsecondary experiences of the high school sophomore class of 2002*. Washington, DC: National Center for Education Statistics, Institute of Education Sciences, U.S. Department of Education.

Breen, Richard, and John H. Goldthorpe. 1997. Explaining educational differentials: Towards a formal rational action theory. *Rationality and Society* 9 (3): 275-305.

Buchmann, Claudia, and Thomas DiPrete. 2006. The growing female advantage in college completion: The role of family background and academic achievement. *American Sociological Review* 71 (4): 515-41.

Conger, Dylan, and Mark C. Long. 2009. Why are men falling behind? Gender gaps in college performance and persistence. *The Annals of the American Academy of Social and Political Science* (This Volume).

Cronbach, Lee J., and Paul E. Meehl. 1955. Construct validity in psychological tests. *Psychological Bulletin* 52:281-302.

Giroux, Henry A. 1983. Theories of reproduction and resistance in the new sociology of education: A critical analysis. *Harvard Educational Review* 53 (3): 257-93.

Goyette, Kimberly A. 2008. College for some to college for all: Social background, occupational expectations, and educational expectations over time. *Social Science Research* 37 (2): 461-84.

Grodsky, Eric. 2007. Compensatory sponsorship in higher education. *American Journal of Sociology* 112:1662-1712.

Grodsky, Eric, and Erika Jackson. 2009. Social stratification in higher education. *Teachers College Record* 111 (10).

Hearn, James C. 1991. Academic and nonacademic influences on the college destinations of 1980 high school graduates. *Sociology of Education* 64 (3): 158-71.

Hearn, James C. 1984. The relative roles of academic, ascribed, and socioeconomic characteristics in college destinations. *Sociology of Education* 57 (1): 22-30.

Horvat, Eric McNamara. 2003. The interactive effects of race and class in educational research: Theoretical insights from the work of Pierre Bourdieu. *Perspectives on Urban Education* 35 (2).

Kane, Thomas J., and Cecilia Elena Rouse. 1995. Labor-market returns to two and four year college. *American Economic Review* 85 (3): 600-614.

Karen, David. 2002. Changes in access to higher education in the United States: 1980-1992. *Sociology of Education* 75:191-210.

Lareau, Annette. 2003. *Unequal childhoods: Class, race, and family life*. Berkeley: University of California Press.

McDonough, Patricia M. 1997. *Choosing colleges: How social class and schools structure opportunity*. Albany: State University of New York Press.

Morgan, Stephen L. 2005. *On the edge of commitment: Educational attainment and race in the United States*. Stanford, CA: Stanford University Press.

Perna, Laura W. 2006. Studying college access and choice: A proposed conceptual model. *Higher Education: Handbook of Theory and Research* 21:99-157.

Reay, Diane. 1998. "Always knowing" and "never being sure": Familial and institutional habituses and higher education choice. *Journal of Education Policy* 13 (4): 519-29.

Reay, Diane, Miriam E. David, and Stephen Ball. 2005. *Degrees of choice: Social class, race, gender and higher education*. Sterling, VA: Trentham.

Roksa, Josipa, Eric Grodsky, Richard Arum, and Adam Gamoran. 2007. Changes in higher education and social stratification in the United States. In *Stratification in higher education*, ed. Y. Shavit, R. Arum, and A. Gamoran, 165-91. Stanford, CA: Stanford University Press.

Stevens, Mitchell L., Elizabeth A. Armstrong, and Richard Arum. 2008. Sieve, incubator, temple, hub: Empirical and theoretical advances in the sociology of higher education. *Annual Review of Sociology* 34:127-51.

Texas Higher Education Opportunity Project. 2003. *Texas Higher Education Opportunity Project (THEOP) baseline survey methodology report*. Princeton, NJ: Princeton University.

Turley, Ruth N. Lopez. 2006. Social origin and college opportunity expectations across cohorts. *Social Science Research* 36:1200-1218.

Young, Michael. 1958. *The rise of the meritocracy*. Harmondsworth, UK: Penguin.

Ethno-Racial Composition and College Preference: Revisiting the Perpetuation of Segregation Hypothesis

By
DONNELL BUTLER

Braddock's perpetuation hypothesis argues that racial segregation is self-perpetuated over the life cycle and across institutional settings. Studies examining the relationship between segregation and college choice consistently show that black students who attend segregated schools are more likely to choose predominantly black colleges over predominantly white colleges. This study extends previous research by considering not only blacks but also Hispanics, Asians, and whites. Consistent with Braddock's claim, results show a positive association between the ethno-racial composition of schools and first college preference for all demographic groups considered. However, this association disappears for blacks and Hispanics after controlling for the ethno-racial composition of the nearest two- and four-year colleges. These findings indicate that geographic context better explains the perpetuation of segregation than same-group preferences.

Keywords: college choice; high school; segregation; race; ethnicity; Texas

The Supreme Court declared in 1954 that "separate educational facilities are inherently unequal" in its landmark *Brown v. Board of Education* decision. The Court reasoned that segregated schools engendered a sense of inferiority among minority students that reduced their

Donnell Butler recently earned his PhD from Princeton University. His dissertation research examined the consequences of racial and ethnic segregation in high school on students' preferences for and experiences with racial and ethnic diversity in college.

NOTE: This research was supported by grants from the Ford, Mellon, Hewlett, and Spencer Foundations and NSF (Grant # SES-0350990), with institutional support from the Office of Population Research, Princeton University (NICHD Grant # R24 H0047879). With gratitude, I acknowledge the suggestions of Marta Tienda, Mark Long, Sunny Niu, Dawn Koffman, and the participants of the 2008 THEOP research workshop. Please direct all correspondence to Donnell Butler, Office of Population Research, Princeton University, 228 Wallace Hall, Princeton, NJ 08544; e-mail: djbutler@princeton.edu.

DOI: 10.1177/0002716209348738

motivation to learn and thus deprived them of equal educational opportunities. Partly owing to court-ordered desegregation, the percentage of black students who attended a majority nonwhite public school fell from 76 to 63 percent between 1968 and 1980, but by 2005, it rose again to 73 percent (Orfield and Lee 2007). School segregation has proven resistant to change due to parental aversion to integrated schools (Mickelson, Bottia, and Southworth 2008; Renzulli and Evans 2005; Saporito and Lareau 1999), the rise of ethnic-themed charter schools (Gootman 2009; Rimer 2009), and federal court decisions overturning school integration programs (Editorial Board 2007; Orfield et al. 1997).

Early studies of racial segregation focused solely on blacks, who for much of American history were denied access to property and space through legal and social institutions. Today, segregation is no longer an issue only for blacks. Hispanics surpassed non-Hispanic blacks as the largest minority population in 2003, and concurrently they became the most segregated minority population in schools: the percentage of Hispanics in majority nonwhite public schools rose from 55 percent in 1968 to 78 percent in 2005 (Orfield and Lee 2007; U.S. Census Bureau 2005a). Although high school students are a generation removed from de jure segregation and America is more ethno-racially diverse now than ever before, schools are as segregated as ever.

Braddock (1980) argued that racial segregation is self-perpetuated across institutional settings and life cycle stages both because spatial distribution of resources constrains choices and because individuals raised in segregated settings develop preferences for segregated environments. Such preferences reflect a general uneasiness in unfamiliar settings and a desire to avoid anticipated hostile reactions that might occur during interracial contact (Braddock 1980; Braddock and McPartland 1989). Presumably, young people who attend segregated high schools will choose to attend a segregated college and subsequently work and live in segregated environments as adults.

Studies that invoke Braddock's perpetuation hypothesis to understand college choice consistently find a strong association between segregated high school attendance and preferences for postsecondary institutions with large minority populations, such as Historically Black Colleges and Universities (HBCUs) (Braddock 1980; Wells 1995). Existing studies are based on students who graduated from high school in the 1970s and 1980s. There is less evidence about whether and how high school segregation is associated with college preferences for the growing Hispanic population or students graduating from high schools in the current millennium. This study investigates whether there is a positive association between students' high school ethno-racial composition and the ethno-racial composition of their first college preference. Are students who attend high schools with a large proportion of classmates who share their race or ethnicity more likely to prefer colleges with a large proportion of classmates who share their race or ethnicity?

Three circumstances warrant revisiting Braddock's perpetuation of segregation hypothesis at this time. First, the change from de jure to de facto school segregation and the "resegregation" of blacks in schools presents a different social context from the one originally theorized by Braddock. In addition, changing demographics complicate Braddock's concept of segregation as a black-white phenomenon. Braddock identified a segregated school as one where blacks constituted 50 percent of the student body or greater. This operational measure of segregation does not have the same meaning in a modern multi-ethnic context. Second, although blacks and Hispanics share similarities, such as high poverty rates, low levels of wealth, and the social ills associated with both (Massey and Denton 1993; Oliver and Shapiro 1997), the two groups are very different with regard to their experiences as ethno-racial groups in America. The dissimilarity in arrival history and government classification contributes to differences between blacks and Hispanics with regard to identity formation and stigmatization from the white majority (De Genova and Ramos-Zayas 2003; Omi 2001). Third, recent research on college choice options and geography suggests that characteristics of nearby colleges might explain self-perpetuated segregation in college choice better than same-group preference (Cohen and Brawer 2002; Tienda and Niu 2006a; Turley 2009).

College represents a unique opportunity for minority students raised in segregated settings to break the cycle of segregation by selecting a diverse college and gaining access to a wider variety of experiences, knowledge, and social networking opportunities. For many years, HBCUs provided essential postsecondary opportunities for black students denied admission to many postsecondary institutions (Pascarella, Smart, and Stoecker 1989). Hispanic-Serving Institutions (HSIs) were not founded as such but emerged because of regional demographic growth and migrant settlement patterns (Benítez 1998). Consequently, unlike HBCUs, HSIs often lack the rationale, mission, and practices designed to serve the specific educational needs of Hispanic students (Benítez 1998; Hubbard and Stage 2009).

Evidence about benefits to attending minority-serving institutions (MSIs) is mixed, partly due to the lack of systematic evidence for HSIs comparable to that available for HBCUs. Allen (1992) finds that black students in the 1980s achieved higher grade point averages when attending black colleges versus predominantly white colleges. Notwithstanding the potential benefits of attending MSIs, according to Bowen and Bok (1998), blacks who attended predominantly white selective colleges are more likely to graduate than blacks who attended less selective colleges. Furthermore, several studies claim that diverse college campuses enhance students' critical thinking, perspective-taking ability, intercultural competence, and civic engagement (Chang, Astin, and Kun 2004; Gurin et al. 2004; Zhao 2002). Students who attend diverse colleges also have access to a wider variety of job opportunities through social networks that they would not acquire at an MSI (Wells and Crain 1994). Presumably, diverse colleges prepare students for leadership in a globalized workplace and increasingly diverse society (Harrison, Price, and Bell 1998; Milem 2003).

The following section presents a conceptual framework that uses previous research to develop three hypotheses to test and expand Braddock's perpetuation of segregation hypothesis. After discussing the survey data, I present an analysis plan and report the findings. Results offer limited support for Braddock's perpetuation of segregation hypothesis for all groups considered. The association between ethno-racial composition of high school and first college preference disappears for both blacks and Hispanics after controlling for the ethno-racial composition of the nearest two- and four-year colleges. In light of these findings and rising high school segregation levels, the conclusion discusses the implications of the findings for future research and policymaking.

Conceptual Framework

Originally proposed by Hossler and Gallagher (1987), the three-stage college choice model provides a framework for understanding how students make the decision to enroll in a college. Cabrera and La Nasa (2000) synthesized the considerable research using this framework to identify three cumulative stages—namely, predisposition, search, and choice—as inputs and enrollment decisions as outputs. This study concentrates on the early stages of the choice process, when students choose where to apply, as opposed to the later stages of the choice process, when students decide where to matriculate.

Racial differences in college preferences

Existing research on ethno-racial composition of college is largely based on the experiences of black students. Braddock's (1980) study that proposed the perpetuation of segregation hypothesis is based on a randomly selected sample of 253 black undergraduates from two predominantly black and two predominantly white colleges in Florida in 1973. He finds a large positive association between attending a desegregated college and graduating from a high school with less than 50 percent black students. Braddock concludes that the "data provide supporting evidence for the self-perpetuating tendencies of early school desegregation" (p. 183) but acknowledges the difficulty in generalizing the results beyond blacks in Florida.

Selection bias and retrospective reporting weaken his self-perpetuation argument. Because the study selected students from among the undergraduate black population at four colleges, it is difficult to know whether students actively sought colleges based on the ethno-racial composition of their high school or whether majority-white colleges were more likely to admit students who attended majority-white high schools. One reason majority-white colleges would admit students from majority-white high schools is that greater numbers are likely to qualify for admission compared with graduates from predominantly black schools. Aside from the dichotomous measure of desegregated high schools, Braddock's study lacked any additional school-level measures of academic quality or college-going traditions that might be associated with successful admission.

Drawing on intergroup contact theory, Braddock suggested that students from majority- or all-black schools would avoid predominantly white colleges because they lacked experiences to counterbalance stereotypes regarding interracial differences. Braddock suggested these students may underestimate their academic abilities

due to "traditional myths and stereotypes concerning black-white intellectual differences" and "overanticipate the amount of overt hostility to be encountered or
underestimate their skill at coping with strains in future interracial situations"
(Braddock 1980, 181).[1]

In Texas, for example, black and Hispanic students, even those at the top of
their class, are less likely than whites to prefer and attend colleges with highly
competitive admissions standards (Niu, Tienda, and Cortes 2006). Despite their
potential for success at predominantly white colleges, high-achieving black and
Hispanic students who attend segregated schools might, as Braddock suggested,
underestimate their ability to compete at selective colleges, which tend to be predominantly white. Furthermore, black and Hispanic students from segregated
high schools might also be steered toward colleges by the desire to continue their
education amongst their friends. Among a sample of 1,539 incoming freshmen at
four colleges, black and Hispanic students reported that the college preferences
of peers are a significant factor in their college choice decision (Cho et al. 2008).

Relatively few studies of high school students directly address whether campus ethno-racial composition influences college choice, and most of those that do
are qualitative. Using data from group and individual interviews of 158 black
college-bound students, counselors, and parents at twenty Los Angeles high
schools, Tobolowsky, Outcalt, and McDonough (2005) find that some black students avoided predominantly white institutions based on a fear of racial isolation,
while others sought these schools in search of experiences with diversity that mirrored the real world. Their study does not distinguish between whether high
school ethno-racial composition generates the observed differences in these student motivations.

Based on group interviews with seventy black high school students in five
urban cities, Freeman (1999) finds that knowing a graduate or current student of
an HBCU is the most consistent predictor of HBCU matriculation. She also finds
that black students who attended predominantly white private high schools are
motivated to consider HBCUs by a desire to "search for their roots [or find] a
connection to the African American community" (p. 99). Alternatively, black
students who attended predominantly black high schools are motivated to consider predominantly white colleges to experience different cultures. These findings provide a counterfactual to the perpetuation of segregation hypothesis.

Nearest college characteristics

Frenette (2004) claims that distance to college deters enrollment because of
relocation costs, particularly for economically disadvantaged students. Black and
Hispanic students are more likely to be economically disadvantaged than either
white or Asian students and therefore might be more inclined to attend a nearby
college. Furthermore, existing research shows that the demographic composition
of high schools reflects that of the local community (Cohen and Brawer 2002,
47). It is conceivable, therefore, that claims about self-perpetuated segregation
in college choices might largely reflect the characteristics of nearby colleges rather
than a preference for segregated settings.

Using a nationally representative sample, Turley (2009) finds that living near a college increases the likelihood of applying. In particular, she claims that college proximity exerts a large influence on postsecondary choices for students whose parents wanted their child to live at home while attending college. Among Texas high school students, Desmond and Turley (2009) find that Hispanics are more likely than other demographic groups to live at home while attending college. Using the same sample of Texas high school students, Tienda and Niu (2006a) show that students who consider the school's distance from home an important factor in their college decision were more likely to enroll at less selective public colleges (e.g., community colleges) than students who did not rank this criterion highly.

Hypotheses

Braddock's core argument is that individuals raised in segregated settings will avoid interracial settings and prefer segregated settings, because they lack diversity experiences to counterbalance myths and stereotypes related to interracial differences. Those stereotypes lead individuals to fear hostile or uncomfortable reactions that they anticipate in interracial settings. Although Braddock's perpetuation of segregation hypothesis was theorized for blacks in the 1970s and 1980s, I extend his hypothesis to all contemporary ethno-racial groups because his proposed explanatory mechanism (i.e., fear of hostile or uncomfortable reactions in interracial settings) should operate for other groups as well. Therefore, I measure ethno-racial composition as the high school or college share that is the same race or ethnicity as the respondent.

The studies reviewed above suggest the following testable hypotheses:

Hypothesis 1A: Following Braddock, high school ethno-racial composition is positively associated with ethno-racial composition of first college preference for black students.

Hypothesis 1B: As suggested by Toblowsky, Outcalt, and McDonough (2005) and Freeman (1999) (i.e., black students who attend segregated schools seek integrated cultural experiences), high school ethno-racial composition will be negatively associated with ethno-racial composition of first preference college choices for black students.

Hypothesis 2A: If Braddock's hypothesis extends across ethno-racial groups, then high school ethno-racial composition will be positively associated with ethno-racial composition of first preference college choices for Hispanic, white and Asian students.

Hypothesis 2B: If Toblowsky, Outcalt, and McDonough's (2005) and Freeman's (1999) findings extend across ethno-racial groups, then high school ethno-racial composition will be negatively associated with ethno-racial composition of first-preference college choices for Hispanic, white, and Asian students.

Hypothesis 3: If distance to postsecondary institutions is a more important consideration than the ethno-racial composition of the student body, then characteristics of nearby colleges—proximity, selectivity, and ethno-racial composition—will attenuate or eliminate any association between the ethno-racial composition of students' high schools and their first college preferences.

Data and Methods

Empirical analyses use the senior cohort survey data from the Texas Higher Education Opportunity Project (THEOP), administered in spring 2002 to a representative sample of 13,803 Texas public high school students.[2] For purposes of the present analysis, I impose two constraints on the baseline sample. First, I restrict the study sample to the 7,636 white, black, Hispanic, and Asian high school seniors who reported a first college preference. Further restricting the sample to seniors with complete information for all variables used in the analysis reduces the analysis sample to 7,016 seniors.

I used a listwise deletion approach to handle missing data but confirmed that findings are similar to those obtained using multiple imputation (five imputations) for data missing at random following a strategy outlined by Scott Lynch (2003) and Paul Allison (2007).[3] Tabulations that compare the mean and standard deviations of the study sample with the analysis sample reveal no differences. These diagnostics, which are available on request, suggest that the analysis sample adequately represents the white, black, Hispanic, and Asian Texas public high schools seniors who have a first college preference.

The THEOP survey data offer several unique advantages for this research. First, the data contain student- and school-level characteristics most often associated with college choice decisions. Second, students are asked about their college preferences *before* they enrolled, which reduces selection bias inherent in studies of college enrollees that examine college choice decisions retrospectively. Third, these data include information about the ethno-racial composition of both the students' high schools and their college preferences. High schools and college preferences were assigned Texas Education Agency (TEA) and Integrated Postsecondary Education Data System (IPEDS) codes. Institutional attributes (e.g., ethno-racial composition) from TEA, Common Core of Data (CCD), and IPEDS were then appended to the individual records in the study. Finally, the data are representative of recent high school seniors from a state with a diverse population and a variety of postsecondary institutions.

Texas as a research setting

The state of Texas is a favorable research site due to its diverse high school student population. The ethno-racial composition of the Texas public elementary and secondary schools in 2005-06 was 45 percent Hispanic, 37 percent non-Hispanic white, 15 percent black, and 3 percent other (Texas Education Agency 2007). Texas has had a long history of residential segregation but also includes five of the ten metropolitan areas (El Paso, Odessa-Midland, San Antonio, Laredo, and Galveston–Texas City) that experienced the largest declines in residential segregation over the 1980 to 2000 period (U.S. Census Bureau 2005b).

Table 1 shows how ethno-racial composition varies by race and ethnicity across the high schools attended and colleges preferred by Texas high school seniors in

TABLE 1
Distribution of Texas Public High School Seniors by School and
College Preference Ethno-Racial Composition Strata (in Percentages)

Ethno-Racial Composition Strata	White ($n = 3,557$)	Hispanic ($n = 2,202$)	Black ($n = 885$)	Asian ($n = 373$)	Strata n
High school					
Median percentage same group	70	78	28	19	
Predominantly same group (>75%)	34	58	11	0	2,491
Majority same group (>50%-75%)	54	8	2	0	2,164
Integrated (>25%-50%)	9	13	28	0	984
Minority same group (≤25%)	4	21	60	100	1,377
First college preference					
Median percentage same group	74	22	15	16	
Predominantly same group (>75%)	48	13	23	0	2,263
Majority same group (>50%-75%)	46	14	1	0	1,888
Integrated (>25%-50%)	5	20	3	5	600
Minority same group (≤25%)	1	53	73	95	2,265

SOURCE: 2002 THEOP, Senior Baseline Survey.
NOTE: Statistics are weighted to population level using weights provided with the THEOP data; n = unweighted group sample size.

this sample. The typical Hispanic student attends a high school that is 78 percent Hispanic, and the typical white student attends a high school that is 70 percent white. By comparison, the average Asian and black student attends a high school with 19 percent and 28 percent, respectively, of their same-race peers. More than half (58 percent) of Hispanic students attend predominantly (i.e., greater than 75 percent) Hispanic high schools, but 21 percent attend high schools where they constitute less than one-fourth of enrolled students. Most white students attend high schools that are majority (i.e., from 50 to 75 percent) white. Despite blacks' relatively small population in Texas, 11 percent of black students attend predominantly black high schools. Thus, despite high levels of de facto school segregation, Texas high schools exhibit extensive variation in demographic composition.

Texas also hosts a wide assortment of postsecondary institutions. A diverse set of in-state college options is essential, because 92 percent of college-bound high school graduates attend college in-state (Niu, Tienda, and Cortes 2006, 262). There are 9 HBCUs and 38 HSIs among the 143 institutions of higher education in Texas (Hispanic Association of Colleges and Universities 2009; Texas Higher Education Coordinating Board 2008; U.S. Department of Education 2009). Black and Hispanic students in Texas who would prefer an ethno-racially homogeneous college campus have a fair selection of prominent HBCUs, including Prairie View

A&M University (PVAMU) and Texas Southern University (TSU), and HSIs, including University of Texas–Pan American and University of Texas at El Paso. Table 1 shows that the typical black or Hispanic student prefers a college composed of 15 percent and 22 percent, respectively, of classmates with the same ethno-racial origin. Nonetheless, one-quarter of black and Hispanic students name colleges in which their own ethno-racial group is in the majority as their top choice.

Measures and descriptive statistics

The dependent variable is the proportion of the student body at the respondent's first college preference that is the same race or ethnicity as the respondent. The survey asked students, "Please think about the colleges/universities that you are likely to attend, and order them by your preference. For each, enter the name and the state . . ." Students were instructed to list up to five colleges or universities and to answer questions about each college related to applying, admittance, financial aid, and scholarships. The following example describes the construction of the variable referred to as "proportion same ethno-racial group." If State University (SU) is 45 percent Hispanic, 37 percent non-Hispanic white, 15 percent black, and 3 percent Asian, then I code first college preference proportion same ethno-racial group as .45 for all Hispanic respondents who named SU as their first college preference. As Table 2 shows, the first college preference percent for "same ethno-racial group" is highest for whites (73 percent) and lowest for Asians (14 percent). Hispanics and blacks, on average, preferred colleges composed of approximately one-third of classmates with similar ethno-racial backgrounds.

The primary explanatory variable to test the perpetuation of segregation hypothesis is the proportion of the student body that is the same race or ethnicity as the respondent. As shown in Table 2, whites and Hispanics, on average, attend high schools with about two-thirds of classmates from the same race or ethnicity. High school percentage same ethno-racial group is significantly lower for blacks (27 percent) and lowest for Asians (10 percent).

The statistical analyses control for variables that previous studies show to correlate with high school ethno-racial composition or that influence students' college decision-making process. Table 2 provides summary statistics of the variables used in the multivariate models for each ethno-racial group. These variables include high school socioeconomic and academic characteristics, family socioeconomic status, student academic achievement, and distance of college preference from home. Most of these characteristics differ by ethno-racial group, as indicated in the right-most column of Table 2.

High school proportion same ethno-racial group might simply reflect the socioeconomic status of the school because schools with high concentrations of black or Hispanic students also tend to have high concentrations of economically disadvantaged students (Orfield and Lee 2005). Therefore, I include a variable to control for high school socioeconomic status, based on the proportion of students in the

TABLE 2
Group-Specific Means or Percentages for
Variables Used in the Regression Analysis

	White	Hispanic	Black	Asian	Differences[a]
First college preference					
% same group	72.7	35.4	30.7	14.3	W > H | B > A
High school characteristics					
% same group	67.0	64.4	27.0	10.1	W | H > B > A
Size (# of students)	1,604	1,941	1,893	2,507	
	(1,040)	(903)	(1,181)	(1,170)	
% qualified for subsidized lunch	20.2	48.6	34.2	17.6	H > B > W | A
% passing state algebra tests	35.4	31.0	34.0	41.1	
Attend feeder school	16.1	3.8	3.8	24.9	A | W > H | B
Attend Longhorn/ Century school	1.8	27.7	27.6	4.6	H | B > A | W
Student characteristics					
Parent with BA degree	56.9	20.7	35.1	60.9	A | W > B > H
Parents own home	87.4	78.6	57.8	82.0	W > A | H > B
Class rank: top 10 percent	21.9	15.4	12.6	47.5	A > W > H | B
Class rank: second decile	23.7	18.7	17.7	18.8	
Male	42.8	39.1	32.9	49.3	A | W > B
Foreign-born	3.9	21.1	8.3	47.3	A > H > B > W
English not primary with friends	0.2	9.2	1.8	4.6	H | A | B > W
Nearest college characteristics					
Distance to nearest 4-year college (miles)	15.5	11.7	11.0	8.5	
	(15.0)	(11.7)	(11.8)	(7.3)	
Distance to nearest 2-year college (miles)	14.8	12.7	8.2	8.5	W > B
	(15.5)	(14.8)	(9.6)	(8.8)	
Nearest 4-year college is highly selective[b]	4.6	2.5	1.7	3.6	
% same group at nearest 4-year college	58.6	42.1	28.6	11.6	W | H > A
% same group at nearest 2-year college	65.1	51.3	20.2	5.0	W > H > B > A
Unweighted group sample size (n)	3,557	2,202	885	373	

SOURCE: 2002 THEOP, Senior Baseline Survey.
NOTE: Statistics are weighted to population level using weights provided with the THEOP data. Standard deviations for means appear in parentheses.
a. Statistically significant ($p < .05$) mean differences between ethno-racial groups are reported in this column.
b. Most or highly selective classification is based on students tests scores, high school rank, and college acceptance rate (Source: Barron's Guide, 2003).

high school who qualify for free or reduced-price lunch. Because economically disadvantaged and minority students are more likely to attend larger schools (Cotton 1996), empirical models control for the number of students in the school. Students of color, on average, attend larger high schools, but the variance is so great that there is no statistically significant difference from white students.

Social scientists deem high schools with large minority populations of lower quality due to fewer certified and experienced teachers and substandard educational resources. To control for education quality, the models include the proportion of students passing the state algebra exams because, among all high school subjects, taking algebra is the most consistent predictor of college access and choice outcomes (Choy et al. 2000; Gamoran and Hannigan 2000).

Graduates from high schools that send large numbers of freshmen to the Texas public flagship universities are more likely than students from economically disadvantaged schools to consider a larger breadth of college choices including selective colleges both in- and out-of-state (Niu and Tienda 2008; Niu, Tienda, and Cortes 2006). Generally, feeder high schools are made up of mostly white students from families with high incomes and college degrees; this situation results in a combined concentration of economic resources, knowledge, and social networks that expand students' college choice options (Wolniak and Engberg 2007). Therefore, models include a dichotomous variable for feeder high school, which is defined as the 20 high schools with the most students admitted in 2000 to the two Texas public flagships—University of Texas at Austin (UT-Austin) and Texas A&M University (TAMU) (Tienda and Niu 2006b). Among high school seniors in Texas, Asians (25 percent) and whites (16 percent) are most likely to attend feeder high schools. Less than 4 percent of Hispanics and blacks attend feeders.

Lawmakers and administrators at the Texas flagships devised two strategies to increase college access for high-achieving students who attend high-minority and economically disadvantaged schools—the Texas Top Ten Percent Law and Longhorn or Century scholarships. The Texas Top Ten Percent Law currently guarantees admission to any Texas public postsecondary institution to all seniors who graduate in the top 10 percent of their high school class (Texas Higher Education Coordinating Board 1998).[4] UT-Austin and TAMU provide Longhorn Opportunity and Century scholarships, respectively, to students who graduate in the top decile of their class from a subset of economically disadvantaged high schools with low college-going traditions. Niu and Tienda (2008) find that access to Longhorn or Century scholarships increases the likelihood of including UT-Austin or TAMU among students' college preferences. Therefore, the model includes a THEOP-defined dichotomous variable that identifies high schools targeted for Longhorn Opportunity or Century scholarships. More than one-half of students who attend Longhorn Opportunity or Century schools are either Hispanic or Black.

College choice research consistently finds that family socioeconomic status influences the college search and choice process but differs by ethno-racial origin (Freeman and Thomas 2002; Teranishi et al. 2004). To model family background,

I include two dichotomous control variables to measure (1) whether a student has at least one parent with a bachelor's degree and (2) whether the student's parents own their home. Asian (61 percent) and white (57 percent) students are most likely to have college-educated parents. Both groups are more likely than black students (35 percent) to have a parent with a bachelor's degree. Hispanic students (21 percent) are the least likely to have college-educated parents. Furthermore, to control for variation in student academic achievement that is related to college choice, I constructed a dichotomous variable that identifies whether the student ranked in the top or second decile of their high school class. Asian students are most likely to rank in the top decile (48 percent), followed by whites (22 percent); Hispanic (15 percent) and black (13 percent) students are least likely to do so.

Based on previous research examining the relationship between background characteristics and college choice, I also include dichotomous variables for gender, foreign birth, and English language use among friends. Men make up 49 percent of the Asian students in the sample, 42 percent of whites, and 39 percent of Hispanics. Only 32 percent of the black students in the sample are men. Because the sample is restricted to students who report a likelihood of attending a college and thus a college preference, this finding—although disconcerting—is in line with national trends regarding the gender gap among blacks in college aspirations and enrollment (Brunn and Kao 2008; KewalRamani et al. 2007).

Finally, as described in the conceptual framework section, recent studies suggest that the characteristics of nearby colleges might explain evidence of perpetuated segregation in college choice. Accordingly, my analysis includes covariates for nearby college proximity, selectivity, and ethno-racial composition. To measure college selectivity, I use a modified Barron's selectivity classification scheme of postsecondary institutions that was appended to the THEOP data (Barron's College Division 2002; Niu, Tienda, and Cortes 2006). Less than 5 percent of Texas students identify a most or highly competitive college as their nearest college option. The same-group ethno-racial composition of the nearest four-year college is greatest for whites (59 percent) and Hispanics (42 percent), followed by blacks (29 percent) and Asians (11 percent). A similar distribution, albeit with a greater same-group share for whites and Hispanics, corresponds for two-year colleges. The ethno-racial composition of both nearest four-year and two-year colleges reflects the ethno-racial composition of the high schools that Texas students attend.

Analysis plan

To test Braddock's perpetuation of segregation hypothesis, I estimate ordinary least squares (OLS) regression models that assess the association between students' high school ethno-racial composition and the ethno-racial composition of their first college preference, controlling for several variables that influence postsecondary behavior.[5] Given the significant ethno-racial differences in proportion same ethno-racial group in Texas high schools and colleges, as well as previous research on the confluence of ethno-racial origin, high school ethno-racial

TABLE 3
First College Preference: Mean Percentage Same Race/Ethnicity by
High School Ethno-Racial Composition Strata (in percentages)

High School Ethno-Racial Composition Strata	White ($n = 3,557$)	Hispanic ($n = 2,202$)	Black ($n = 885$)	Asian ($n = 373$)	Strata n
Predominantly same group(>75%)	74	46	52	—	2,491
Majority same group(>50%-75%)	73	34	65	—	2,164
Integrated (>25%-50%)	70	**22**	**27**	—	984
Minority same group(≤25%)	**63**	**15**	**27**	14	1,377

SOURCE: 2002 THEOP, Senior Baseline Survey.
NOTE: Statistics are weighted to population level using weights provided with the THEOP data; n = unweighted group sample size. Values in bold are significantly different ($p < .05$) from predominantly same group strata within ethno-racial group.

composition, and other covariates of interest, I do not assume uniform associations among the demographics groups. Therefore, I estimate the models separately for whites, blacks, Hispanics, and Asians. Because students selected for the study are not sampled independently, but instead are clustered within particular high schools, I estimate the models in this article using Stata 10 survey commands, which produce accurate standard errors for both sampling design and clustering (Stata Corp 2003).[6]

Findings

Table 3 presents the average ethno-racial composition of Texas high school seniors' first college preference stratified by students' high school ethno-racial composition for each group. On average, white students who attend predominantly (i.e., greater than 75 percent) white high schools select a first-preference college that is 11 percentage points more white than white students who attend minority (i.e., 25 percent or less) white high schools (74 and 63 percent, respectively). Hispanics students who attend predominantly Hispanic high schools prefer colleges that have three times the proportion of Hispanic classmates as the colleges preferred by minority Hispanic high school attendees (46 and 15 percent, respectively). Among blacks, students in predominantly black high schools prefer colleges that have twice the proportion black as the colleges preferred by students attending both integrated (i.e., 25 to 50 percent same ethno-racial group) and minority black schools (52 and 27 percent, respectively). Because the population of Asian high school students is relatively small in Texas, they always represent a small minority of their high school.

Bivariate associations between the ethno-racial composition of high schools and first college preferences are positive for all ethno-racial groups, but the magnitude of the associations differ, as shown in model 1 of Table 4. These initial

TABLE 4
Effects of High School Ethno-Racial Composition on Ethno-Racial
Composition of Seniors' First College Preference: Group-Specific Estimates

	White	Hispanic	Black	Asian
Model 1 (baseline model)				
High school proportion same group	.123°°°	.451°°°	.320°°°	.235°°
	(.024)	(.050)	(.055)	(.069)
R^2	.028	.244	.049	.044
Model 2 (Model 1 + Other School Characteristics)				
High school proportion same group	.131°°	.407°°°	.354°°°	.246°°
	(.040)	(.101)	(.076)	(.074)
R^2	.047	.277	.058	.085
Model 3 (Model 2 + Student Characteristics)				
High school proportion same group	.130°°	.405°°°	.385°°°	.245°°
	(.039)	(.100)	(.076)	(.077)
R^2	.077	.318	.083	.179
Model 4 (Model 3 + Nearest College Characteristics)				
High school proportion same group	.065°	−.018	.166	.240°
	(.030)	(.058)	(.116)	(.115)
R^2	.101	.392	.112	.221

SOURCE: 2002 THEOP, Senior Baseline Survey.
NOTE: Statistics are weighted to population level using weights provided with the THEOP data. Standard errors appear in parentheses.
°$p < .05$. °°$p < .01$. °°°$p < .001$ (two-tailed tests).

findings support the extension of Braddock's perpetuation of segregation hypothesis beyond blacks. Previous studies find that high school socioeconomic status and feeder school status as well as family background and students' class rank influence the type of colleges that students prefer, and these attributes differ among demographic groups. Therefore, I estimate a series of nested models to purge the bivariate association of potentially confounding variables.

Multivariate results reported in Table 4 show that even when high school and student characteristics are taken into account (see model 3), support for Braddock's perpetuation of segregation hypothesis persists not only for blacks (hypothesis 1A) but also for Hispanics, Asians, and whites (hypothesis 2A). The findings do not support the alternative hypotheses (1B and 2B), as suggested by Toblowsky, Outcalt, and McDonough (2005) and Freeman (1999), namely, that students who attend segregated schools seek integrated cultural experiences.

Results from model 4 challenge Braddock's thesis, however. Controlling for nearest college characteristics eliminates the association between ethno-racial composition of high school and first college preference for both blacks and

Hispanics. For both white and Asian students, the association between high school and top college preference share of own group also shrinks when characteristics of nearby colleges are taken into account, but for both groups, it remains statistically significant. These findings support Hypothesis 3; the characteristics of nearby colleges rather than a preference for segregated settings in large part explains the observed perpetuated segregation in college choice. Nonetheless, Braddock's hypothesis fits the data for whites and Asians. The empirical models better explain the ethno-racial composition of first college preference for Hispanic ($R^2 = .392$) and Asian ($R^2 = .221$) than for white ($R^2 = .101$) and black ($R^2 = .112$) students.

Results for other covariates reveal a few noteworthy group-specific differences (available upon request).[7] Among white students, college-educated parents and same-group ethno-racial composition at the nearest two-year college is positively associated with the ethno-racial composition of first college preference. Among Hispanic students, the percentage of high school classmates who qualify for subsidized lunch as well as the same-group proportion at both the nearest two-year and four-year college also is positively associated with large Hispanic shares at their first college preference. Hispanic students with college-educated parents name colleges with lower shares of their own group as their first choice; these institutions also tend to be more selective. Conversely, white and black students with college-educated parents name colleges with higher shares of their own group as their first choice. Hispanic students who graduated in the top 10 percent of their class also identify top-choice colleges with lower shares of their own group compared with their lower-ranked counterparts. Conversely, Asian students ranked in the top 10 percent of their class identify top choice colleges with higher shares of their own group compared with their lower-ranked counterparts. That a significant positive association between same-group share at nearest four-year college and first college preference obtains for blacks but not other groups probably reflects the salience of historical black colleges in their preference list. This is likely the mechanism driving Braddock's claims about the perpetuation of segregation.

Whether the positive associations between the ethno-racial composition of high schools and top college choice actually represent *preferences* to attend institutions with same-race peers is an empirical question. To examine this possibility, I consider what factors students report are important in developing a choice set, such as peers, parents' opinions, as well as a desire for diversity. Using a scale of 1 = *not important* to 3 = *very important*, respondents were asked to rate the importance of various factors in choosing a college or university. Table 5 reports the item response means for students who attend high schools in which the percentage of their own-group classmates is greater than 50 percent and less than or equal to 50 percent.

Aside from demographic makeup, none of the other high school characteristics are associated with the ethno-racial composition of students' first college preference. One characteristic potentially associated with same-group share at first college preference is the presence of college-bound peers (Cho et al. 2008; Pope and Fermin 2003). To examine this possibility, I consider friends' college

TABLE 5
Item Response Means (3-Point Scale) of College Choice
Factors by High School Ethno-Racial Composition

College Choice Factors	High School Percentage Same Group Less Than 50%	High School Percentage Same Group Less Than or Equal to 50%
Friends plan to attend		
White	1.510	1.547
Hispanic	1.439	1.473
Black	**1.613**	1.395
Asian	—	1.557
Family attend(ed)	B > H | W	
White	1.276	1.253
Hispanic	1.197	1.197
Black	**1.458**	1.200
Asian	—	1.243
Ability to commute from home	H | B > W	H | A > W | B
White	1.386	1.510
Hispanic	1.908	1.908
Black	**2.115**	1.512
Asian	—	1.738
Ethno-racial mix of the students or faculty	B > H > W	B > H & B | H | A > W
White	1.353	1.432
Hispanic	1.611	1.710
Black	1.921	2.051
Asian	—	1.963

SOURCE: 2002 THEOP, Senior Baseline Survey.
NOTE: Statistics are weighted to population level using weights provided with the THEOP data; n = unweighted group sample size. Statistically significant (at $p < .05$) within-group differences between ethno-racial composition strata are highlighted in bold.

plans as one of several factors that students consider in choosing colleges. Among black students, friends' college plans are most important for those who attended majority-black schools. However, there are no other group differences in students' reported importance of friends' college plans.

Among students who attend schools where more than half of their classmates are of the same race or ethnicity, family attendance at college choice is more important for black students than for white and Hispanic students. In fact, family attendance at respondents' top choice is most important for black students who attended majority-black schools. A sizable number of their parents might have attended HBCUs, which have a long tradition of producing black graduates during a time when de jure segregation denied access to predominantly white postsecondary institutions for many black Americans (Allen 1992; Pascarella, Smart, and Stoecker 1989). Unlike blacks and whites, Hispanics are least likely to have a bachelor's degree from an American college due to more recent migration and lower rates of degree attainment (see Table 2). Consequently, Hispanic parents are least likely to influence their children toward a particular alma mater.

Another form of parental influence relates to steering children to remain at home while attending college. I observe that, among Hispanic students, men are less likely than women to prefer colleges with a greater same-group ethno-racial composition. Although Hispanic women might have a stronger preference for colleges with a greater proportion of Hispanic students, two other mechanisms might explain this result. One explanation is that Hispanic women exhibit a greater sense of family responsibility and thus prefer colleges near their home (Desmond and Turley 2009). A second is that parents have considerable influence over Hispanic women's college choices and disproportionately prefer nearby locations (Perez and McDonough 2008).

Due to spatial segregation of Hispanics and the location of HSIs in high-Hispanic-concentration areas, nearby preferred colleges are more likely to be HSIs. The greatest concentration of the Hispanic population in Texas is along the western and southern border, home to numerous HSI community colleges and three of the largest thirty-eight HSIs in Texas (i.e., UT–El Paso, UT–Pan American, and UT-Brownsville). The greatest concentration of the black population in Texas is along the eastern border and home to the only two public four-year colleges of the nine HBCUs in Texas (i.e., PVAMU and TSU). As shown in Table 5, among students who attended high schools where their own group made up a majority of the student body, the ability to attend college while living at home is a more important consideration for black and Hispanic students than for white students. However, among students who attend high schools where their group represents less than half of the student body, commuting to college from home is relatively more important for Hispanic and Asian students than for white and black students.

Recent polls find that a majority of students believe that colleges should do more to promote diversity and that diversity is one of the most important factors in choosing a college (Kujawski 2004; Watson 2007). Among students who attended high school where their own group represented less than half of the student body, the ethno-racial mix of the students or faculty is least important for whites relative to minority groups. The opposite obtains for graduates from high schools where their own group composes over half of the student body—for them, the ethno-racial mix of the students or faculty is most important for blacks, followed by Hispanics, and then whites. These findings suggest that diversity of postsecondary institutions is a more salient consideration for blacks.

The desire to live at home, however, might conflict with preferences for an ethnically diverse campus. The average distance to MSIs named as first college choices differs for blacks and Hispanics. Auxiliary tabulations show that the average distance to top-choice colleges that are designated MSIs is 196 and 84 miles, respectively, for black and Hispanic students who attend high schools where their own group is a majority. The distance gap to MSIs for blacks and Hispanics is even larger for students who attend high schools where their own group is not in

TABLE 6
Group-Specific Means or Percentages
for First College Preference Characteristics

	White	Hispanic	Black	Asian	Differences[a]
Distance (in miles) to first college preference	237.6 (369.8)	219.0 (368.4)	232.4 (321.1)	297.0 (433.4)	
First college preference is the nearest 2- or 4-year college to home	19.0	22.6	10.3	10.3	H > B | A

SOURCE: 2002 THEOP, Senior Baseline Survey.
NOTE: Statistics are weighted to population level using weights provided with the THEOP data. Standard deviations appear in parentheses.
a. Statistically significant ($p < .05$) mean differences between ethno-racial groups are reported in this column.

the majority. As shown in Table 6, Asians, on average, prefer colleges farther away, but they are not significantly different from other groups in this respect. Hispanic students (23 percent) and white students (19 percent) are most likely to name the nearest college as their top choice, but only one-tenth of black and Asian students prefer the nearest college. For black and Asian students who desire to attend college near home for economic or family reasons, their nearest college is more likely to be a predominantly white or Hispanic-serving institution.

For blacks and Hispanics, I observe a positive association between the proportion of same-group students at the nearest four-year college and the share of same-group students at their top college choice. Students' preference for the nearest college does not completely explain this finding because less than 20 percent of students prefer the nearest college (see Table 6). One potential explanation for the observed association is that students develop an affinity for colleges with characteristics similar to nearby colleges from years of indirect or direct exposure via guidance counselors, campus visits, or direct interaction with students or faculty. A second is that several colleges with similar ethno-racial compositions are likely to be relatively closer than more diverse institutions; thus, students may be opting for a college populated with many same ethnic peers rather than the nearest college. In the following section, I discuss potential explanations based on these findings.

Summary and Discussion

In light of rising school segregation (Orfield and Lee 2007), in this study, I aim to understand the relationship between high school ethno-racial composition and college preference. More specifically, I analyze a representative sample of recent Texas high school seniors to replicate and extend Braddock's perpetuation of segregation hypothesis, which claims that high school ethno-racial composition is positively associated with the ethno-racial composition of black students' first college preferences. Initial OLS regression results show that high school ethno-racial composition is positively associated with ethno-racial composition of first college preference for all demographic groups. However, after controlling for ethno-racial composition of the nearest four-year and two-year colleges, the association shrinks for whites and Asians and disappears for blacks and Hispanics. I also find that the ethno-racial composition of students' nearest four-year and two-year colleges reflects the ethno-racial composition of their high school. These findings suggest that a more compelling explanation for observed perpetuation of segregation in college choice is the ethno-racial composition of nearby colleges.

The top college named by students is the closest for less than 20 percent of Texas seniors, yet the positive association between own-group shares in high school and preferred college is statistically significant for blacks, Hispanics, and whites. A plausible explanation for this relationship is that several colleges with similar ethno-racial compositions are within commuting distance and that students prefer to attend one farther away rather than the nearest college. Of course, students do not often enroll at their preferred institution, either because they do not apply, are not admitted, or lack the resources needed to matriculate. Using a national sample of twelfth graders in 1992, Turley (2009) finds that the likelihood of applying to college increases with the number of colleges within commuting distance (i.e., 12 miles in urban areas and 24 miles in suburban areas). She also finds that the median number of colleges within commuting distance is nine for students in urban areas and three for suburban and rural students.

In this study, the nearest college serves as a proxy for the college choice set of nearby colleges. In addition to the number of college options, nearby colleges can serve as models for students when they are considering the type of college they wish to attend. The influence that nearby colleges can have on high school students ranges from active human interaction (e.g., mentoring and tutoring programs) to passive exploratory settings via campus visits. Consequently, students may develop a preference for characteristics (e.g., ethno-racial composition) of nearby colleges that they incorporate into their college choices, even among colleges farther from home. Future research could improve on this study by examining the characteristics of the full range of colleges within commuting distance and by asking students about the role of nearby colleges in their college choice decision-making process.

My results show that black students who attend majority-black high schools, along with all Hispanics and Asians, express a desire to live at home during college. However, unlike for Hispanics, the desire to commute to college from home for blacks and Asians does not result in naming the nearest college as their first college preference. Moreover, black students who attend majority-black high schools are willing to travel twice as far to attend an MSI. In addition to ethno-racial composition of nearby colleges, my study offers a second explanation alternative to Braddock's perpetuation of segregation hypothesis, namely, parental influence. Among whites and blacks, students with college-educated parents are most likely to prefer colleges with a greater percentage of same-ethno-racial-group students. Evidence that family alumni status is an important consideration for black students' preferences suggests that students may be guided to attend their parents' alma mater, many of which were likely HBCUs. This is an empirical question, however, that my data cannot address.

Both parental influence and ethno-racial composition of nearby colleges serve as potential mechanisms to explain findings that Hispanics prefer colleges closer to home and that female Hispanic students are more likely than male Hispanics to prefer colleges with a larger share of Hispanic students. The preference for nearby colleges could be a consequence of parental encouragement or a greater sense of family responsibility. In either case, because HSIs and high concentrations of Hispanics in Texas are similarly located, nearby preferred colleges are more likely to have a large share of Hispanic students. Future research that examines the role of parents and ethno-racial composition of nearby alternatives will contribute to understanding the mechanisms underlying the perpetuation of segregation. This research should also aim to build on limitations of this study by examining a nationally representative sample and paying close attention to other regions of the country and communities with different ethno-racial majorities, in particular those where Asians are in or near the majority. The inclusion of ethno-racial composition of nearby colleges into the model does not eliminate the positive association between the ethno-racial composition of students' high school and their first college preference for whites and Asians. Therefore, Braddock's perpetuation of segregation hypothesis warrants further exploration for these groups.

To summarize, I offer three possible explanations for the positive association between the demographic composition of students' high schools and their top college choice. First, the ethno-racial composition of nearby colleges mirrors that of the high schools (and the community). Second, parents who chose where to live based on their ethno-racial composition also orient their children toward colleges with a similar ethno-racial composition. Third, Braddock's self-perpetuation hypothesis is correct. Although most of the evidence presented supports the first explanation, the second and third cannot be completely ruled out. All three cases, however, represent different mechanisms that work to maintain de facto segregation across life cycles.

Notes

1. Wells and Crain (1994) report that an unpublished paper by Braddock affirmed his previous findings based on a representative national sample from the 1980 cohort of the High School and Beyond survey. In this later study, Braddock reportedly finds that "racial composition of a black student's high school exhibits a much larger effect on the racial makeup of the college he/she will likely attend than any of the other factors measured" (quoted in Wells and Crain 1994, 542).

2. Detail about the survey is available at http://www.theop.princeton.edu.

3. These multiple imputation results are available upon request.

4. The Texas legislature capped the number of automatic-admit students at the University of Texas at Austin only beginning with the 2010-2011 freshman cohort, but there was no cap during the years covered by my data.

5. McDowell and Cox (2004) argue that generalized linear models (GLM) with a logit link, binomial family, and robust standard errors, as suggested by Papke and Wooldridge (1996), are a better alternative

to OLS, because a proportion as a dependent variable has nonnormally distributed residuals, and the predicted values can fall outside of the expected range (0-1). They note, however, that use of this method would severely limit straightforward interpretation of a one-unit change in the independent variable on the dependent variable, as echoed by Hardin and Hilbe (2007). Regression diagnostics confirm the nonnormal distribution of the residuals. However, the predicted values are appropriately in range. Models using the suggested GLM approach are available from the author upon request. Findings are generally consistent between both GLM and OLS models. OLS models are more conservative in reporting significance of some associations. I present and describe results from the OLS tables in this paper for readability.

6. An alternative approach to clustering would be multilevel regression modeling; however, this study is not theoretically interested in making a distinction between within-school and between-school effects, which is one of the primary goals and benefits of multilevel modeling.

7. I do not present the full set of estimates in the interest of parsimony and to keep the focus on the association of interest. Results are available on request.

References

Allen, Walter R. 1992. The color of success: African-American college student outcomes at predominantly white and historically black public colleges and universities. *Harvard Educational Review* 62 (1): 26.

Allison, Paul. 2007. *Missing data: A two-day course on modern methods for handling missing data.* May 10. Princeton, NJ: Princeton University, Office of Population Research.

Barron's College Division. 2002. *Barron's profiles of American colleges: 25th edition 2003.* Hauppauge, NY: Barron's Educational Series Inc.

Benítez, Margarita. 1998. Hispanic-serving institutions: challenges and opportunities. *New Directions for Higher Education* 102:57-68.

Bowen, William G., and Derek Curtis Bok. 1998. *The shape of the river: Long-term consequences of considering race in college and university admissions.* Princeton, NJ: Princeton University Press.

Braddock, Jomills Henry, II. 1980. The perpetuation of segregation across levels of education: A behavioral assessment of the contact-hypothesis. *Sociology of Education* 53 (3): 178-86.

Braddock, Jomills Henry, II, and James M. McPartland. 1989. Social-psychological processes that perpetuate racial segregation: The relationship between school and employment desegregation. *Journal of Black Studies* 19 (3): 267-89.

Brunn, Rachelle, and Grace Kao. 2008. Where are all the boys? *Du Bois Review: Social Science Research on Race* 5 (1): 137-60.

Cabrera, Alberto F., and Steven M. La Nasa. 2000. Understanding the college-choice process. *New Directions for Institutional Research* 107:5-22.

Chang, Mitchell J., Alexander W. Astin, and Dongbin Kim. 2004. Cross-racial interaction among undergraduates: Some consequences, causes, and patterns. *Research in Higher Education* 45 (5): 529-53.

Cho, Su-Je, Cynthia Hudley, Soyoung Lee, Leasha Barry, and Melissa Kelly. 2008. Roles of gender, race, and SES in the college choice process among first-generation and nonfirst-generation students. *Journal of Diversity in Higher Education* 1 (2): 95-107.

Choy, Susan P., Laura J. Horn, Anne-Marie Nunez, and Chen Xianglei. 2000. Transition to college: What helps at-risk students and students whose parents did not attend college. *New Directions for Institutional Research* 107:45.

Cohen, Arthur M., and Florence B. Brawer. 2002. *The American community college.* 4th ed. San Francisco: Jossey-Bass.

College Division of Barron's Educational Series. 2002. *Barron's Profiles of American Colleges: 25th Edition.* Hauppauge, NY: Barron's Educational Series, Inc

Cotton, Kathleen. 1996. *Affective and social benefits of small-scale schooling.* Eric Digests, ED401088 1996-1two-00. Charleston, WV: ERIC Clearinghouse on Rural Education and Small Schools.

De Genova, Nicholas, and Ana Y. Ramos-Zayas. 2003. Latino racial formations in the United States: An introduction. *Journal of Latin American Anthropology* 8 (2): 2-16.

Desmond, Matthew, and Ruth N. López Turley. 2009. The role of familism in explaining the Hispanic-white college application gap. *Social Problems* 56 (2): 311-34.

Editorial Board. 2007. Resegregation now [Op-ed]. *New York Times*, June 29.

Freeman, Kassie. 1999. HBCs or PWIs? African American high school students' consideration of higher education institution types. *Review of Higher Education* 23 (1): 91-106.

Freeman, Kassie, and Gail E. Thomas. 2002. Black colleges and college choice: Characteristics of students who choose HBCUs. *Review of Higher Education* 25 (3): 349-58.

Frenette, Marc. 2004. Access to college and university: Does distance to school matter? *Canadian Public Policy/Analyse de Politiques* 30 (4): 427-43.

Gamoran, Adam, and Eileen C. Hannigan. 2000. Algebra for everyone? Benefits of college-preparatory mathematics for students with diverse abilities in early secondary school. *Educational Evaluation and Policy Analysis* 22:241-54.

Gootman, Elissa. 2009. State weighs approval of school dedicated to Hebrew. *New York Times*, January 12.

Gurin, Patricia, Eric L. Dey, Sylvia Hurtado, and Gerald Gurin. 2004. Defending diversity: Affirmative action at the University of Michigan. In *Defending diversity: Affirmative action at the University of Michigan*, ed. P. Gurin, J. S. Lehman, and E. Lewis, 97-188. Ann Arbor: University of Michigan Press.

Hardin, James W., and Joseph M. Hilbe. 2007. *Generalized linear models and extensions*. 2nd ed. College Station, TX: Stata Press.

Harrison, David A., Kenneth H. Price, and Myrtle P. Bell. 1998. Beyond relational demography: Time and the effects of surface- and deep-level diversity on work group cohesion. *Academy of Management Journal* 41 (1): 96-107.

Hispanic Association of Colleges and Universities. 2009. HACU member Hispanic-serving institutions (HSIs). http://www.hacu.net/assnfe/CompanyDirectory.asp?STYLE=2&COMPANY_TYPE=1,5&SEARCH _TYPE=0#Texas (accessed June 9, 2009).

Hossler, Don, and Karen S. Gallagher. 1987. Studying student college choice: A three-phase model and the implications for policymakers. *College and University* 62 (3): 207-21.

Hubbard, Steven M., and Frances K. Stage. 2009. Attitudes, perceptions, and preferences of faculty at Hispanic serving and predominantly black institutions. *Journal of Higher Education* 80 (3): 270-89.

KewalRamani, Angelina, Lauren Gilbertson, Mary Ann Fox, and Stephen Provasnik. 2007. *Status and trends in the education of racial and ethnic minorities*. NCES 2007-039. Washington, DC: National Center for Education Statistics, Institute of Education Sciences, U.S. Department of Education.

Kujawski, Laura. 2004. Students value diversity in high school and college. *PNN Online*, September 22.

Lynch, Scott. 2003. Missing data (Soc 504). Princeton University Sociology 504 Class Notes. http://www .princeton.edu/~slynch/SOC_504/missingdata.pdf (accessed July 23, 2008).

Massey, Douglas S., and Nancy A. Denton. 1993. *American apartheid: Segregation and the making of the underclass*. Cambridge, MA: Harvard University Press.

McDowell, Allen, and Nicholas J. Cox. 2004. How do you fit a model when the dependent variable is a proportion? Stata FAQs. http://www.stata.com/support/faqs/stat/logit.html (accessed April 4, 2009).

Mickelson, Roslyn Arlin, Martha Bottia, and Stephanie Southworth. 2008. School choice and segregation by race, class, and achievement. In *Education and the Public Interest Center: Education Policy Research Unit policy briefs*. http://epsl.asu.edu/epru/documents/EPSL-0803-260-EPRU.pdf (accessed January 15, 2009).

Milem, Jeffrey F. 2003. Educational benefits of diversity: Evidence from multiple sectors. In *Compelling interest: Examining the evidence on racial dynamics in colleges and universities*, ed. M. J. Chang, D. Witt, J. Jones, and K. Hakuta, 126-69. Stanford, CA: Stanford Education.

Niu, Sunny Xinchun, and Marta Tienda. 2008. Choosing colleges: Identifying and modeling choice sets. *Social Science Research* 37 (2): 416-33.

Niu, Sunny Xinchun, Marta Tienda, and Kalena Cortes. 2006. College selectivity and the Texas top 10% law. *Economics of Education Review* 25 (3): 259-72.

Oliver, Melvin L., and Thomas M. Shapiro. 1997. *Black wealth/white wealth: A new perspective on racial inequality*. New York: Routledge.

Omi, Michael A. 2001. The changing meaning of race. In *America becoming: Racial trends and their consequences*, vol. 1, ed. N. J. Smelser, W. J. Wilson, and F. Mitchell, 243-63. Washington, DC: National Academy Press.

Orfield, Gary, Mark D. Bachmeier, David R. James, and Tamela Eitle. 1997. Deepening segregation in American public schools: A special report from the Harvard Project on School Desegregation. *Equity & Excellence in Education* 30 (2): 5-24.

Orfield, Gary, and Chungmei Lee. 2005. *Why segregation matters: Poverty and educational inequality*. Cambridge, MA: Harvard University, The Civil Rights Project.

Orfield, Gary, and Chungmei Lee. 2007. *Historic reversals, accelerating resegregation, and the need for new integration strategies*. Los Angeles: University of California, Los Angeles, The Civil Rights Project.

Papke, Leslie E., and Jeffrey M. Wooldridge. 1996. Econometric methods for fractional response variables with an application to 401 (K) plan participation rates. *Journal of Applied Econometrics* 11 (6): 619-32.

Pascarella, Ernest T., John C. Smart, and Judith Stoecker. 1989. College race and the early status attainment of black students. *Journal of Higher Education* 60 (1): 82-107.

Perez, Patricia A., and Patricia M. McDonough. 2008. Understanding Latina and Latino college choice: A social capital and chain migration analysis. *Journal of Hispanic Higher Education* 7 (3): 249-65.

Pope, Myron L., and Baranda Fermin. 2003. The perceptions of college students regarding the factors most influential in their decision to attend postsecondary education. *College & University* 78 (4): 19-25.

Renzulli, Linda A., and Lorraine Evans. 2005. School choice, charter schools, and white flight. *Social Problems* 52 (3): 398-418.

Rimer, Sara. 2009. Immigrants see charter schools as a haven. *New York Times*, January 10.

Saporito, Salvatore, and Annette Lareau. 1999. School selection as a process: The multiple dimensions of race in framing educational choice. *Social Problems* 46 (3): 418-39.

Stata Corp. 2003. Stata statistical software: Release 10.0, survey data manual. College Station, TX: Stata Corp.

Teranishi, Robert T., Miguel Ceja, Anthony Lising Antonio, Walter R. Allen, and Patricia McDonough. 2004. The college-choice process for Asian Pacific Americans: Ethnicity and socioeconomic class in context. *Review of Higher Education* 27 (4): 527.

Texas Education Agency. 2007. Enrollment in Texas public schools 2005-06. Texas Education Agency Division of Accountability Research Reports. http://www.tea.state.tx.us/research/pdfs/enrollment_2005-06.pdf (accessed May 6, 2007).

Texas Higher Education Coordinating Board. 1998. *Report on the effects of the Hopwood decision on minority applications, offers, and enrollments at public institutions of higher education in Texas*. Austin: Texas Higher Education Coordinating Board.

Texas Higher Education Coordinating Board. 2008. *Texas higher education quick facts 2008*. http://www.thecb.state.tx.us/Reports/PDF/1096.PDF (accessed June 9, 2009).

Tienda, Marta, and Sunny Xinchun Niu. 2006a. Capitalizing on segregation, pretending neutrality: College admissions and the Texas top 10% law. *American Law and Economics Review* 8 (2): 312-46.

Tienda, Marta, and Sunny Xinchun Niu. 2006b. Flagships, feeders, and the Texas top 10% law: A test of the "brain drain" hypothesis. *Journal of Higher Education* 77 (4): 712-39.

Tobolowsky, Barbara F., Charles L. Outcalt, and Patricia M. McDonough. 2005. The role of HBCUs in the college choice process of African Americans in California. *Journal of Negro Education* 74 (1): 63.

Turley, Ruth N. López. 2009. College proximity: Mapping access to opportunity. *Sociology of Education* 82:126-46.

U.S. Census Bureau. 2005a. Annual estimates of the population by sex, race and Hispanic or Latino origin for the United States: April 1, 2000 to July 1, 2005. NC-EST2005-03. http://www.census.gov/popest/national/asrh/NC-EST2005-srh.html.

U.S. Census Bureau. 2005b. Chapter 6: Residential segregation of Hispanics or Latinos: 1980 to 2000. http://www.census.gov/hhes/www/housing/housing_patterns/ch6.html (accessed May 6, 2006).

U.S. Department of Education. 2009. List of HBCUs—White House initiative on historically black colleges and universities. http://www.ed.gov/about/inits/list/whhbcu/edlite-list.html (accessed June 9, 2009).

Watson, Jamal E. 2007. Poll: When choosing a college, high school students say diversity matters. *Diverse Issues in Higher Education*, December 10.

Wells, Amy Stuart. 1995. Reexamining social science research on school desegregation: Long- versus short-term effects. *Teachers College Record* 96 (4): 691-706.

Wells, Amy Stuart, and Robert L. Crain. 1994. Perpetuation theory and the long-term effects of school desegregation. *Review of Educational Research* 64:531-55.

Wolniak, Gregory C., and Mark E. Engberg. 2007. The effects of high school feeder networks on college enrollment. *Review of Higher Education* 31 (1): 27-53.

Zhao, Chun-Mei. 2002. Intercultural competence: A quantitative study of the significance of intercultural competence and the influence of college experiences on students' intercultural competence development. PhD diss., Department of Educational Leadership and Policy Studies, Virginia Polytechnic Institute and State University, Blacksburg, VA.

PART TW0

College Choice: Effects of Texas Top 10 Percent Law

Minority Higher Education Pipeline: Consequences of Changes in College Admissions Policy in Texas

By
ANGEL HARRIS
and
MARTA TIENDA

The authors uses administrative data for the two most selective Texas public institutions to examine the application, admission, and enrollment consequences of rescinding affirmative action and implementing the top 10 percent admission regime. The authors simulate the gains and losses associated with each policy regime and those from assigning minorities the corresponding rates for white students. Challenging popular claims that the Top Ten Percent Law restored diversification of Texas's public flagships, analyses that consider *both* changes in the size of high school graduation cohorts and institutional carrying capacity show that the uniform admission regime did *not* restore Hispanic and black representation at the University of Texas at Austin and Texas A&M even after four years. Simulations of gains and losses for Hispanics and blacks at each stage of the college pipeline across admission regimes confirm that affirmative action is the most efficient policy to diversify college campuses, even in highly segregated states like Texas.

Keywords: higher education; minority students; application rates; admission policy

The year following the 1996 *Hopwood* decision,[1] several Texas campuses, including the two flagship public universities, the University of Texas at Austin (UT) and Texas A&M University (TAMU), registered sharp declines in the number of black and Hispanic first-time freshmen (Barr 2002).[2] In response to the judicial ban on the use of race and national origin in college admissions decisions, the 75th Texas legislature passed H.B.588, the uniform admission law, which guarantees admission to any Texas public university to high school seniors who graduate in the top decile of their class. Popularly known as the Top Ten Percent Law, the uniform admission law was fully in force for the fall 1998 admission cohort.

H.B.588 sought to increase college access to a wide spectrum of the Texas population by attracting the very best students of every high school to the state's flagship universities (Holley and Spencer 1999; Montejano 2001). Initially, the law was praised as a race-neutral

DOI: 10.1177/0002716209348740

alternative to affirmative action because it both rewarded merit and broadened college access (Tienda and Sullivan 2009). Supporters claimed that the percentage plan helped restore diversity to the flagship campuses, albeit in part by removing the standardized test score barrier for minority students who achieve academic excellence at their high school (Alon and Tienda 2007). Over time, however, the Top Ten Percent Law remains as controversial as the affirmative action regime it replaced. Opponents argue that percentage-based admission regimes not only are a disguised form of affirmative action but that they also are unfair to high-achieving students ranked below the 90th percentile who graduate from competitive high schools. Although the landmark 2003 *Grutter*[3] decision reversed *Hopwood*, the Top Ten Percent Law remains in force until repealed or modified by the Texas legislature.[4] In effect, between the early 1990s and the present, judicial and statutory decisions produced four different college admission regimes in Texas (of which we compare three):

- Pre-*Hopwood:* affirmative action permitted (pre-1996);[5]
- *Hopwood:* Judicial ban on affirmative action (1997);
- Top Ten Percent Law with continued judicial ban (1998-2003);
- Post-*Grutter:* affirmative action permitted, Top Ten Percent Law remains in effect (2004–present).[6]

Because college admissions are highly scrutinized, publicly and legally, researchers also focus on this aspect of the postsecondary pipeline, and especially on the admission advantage enjoyed by minority applicants (Bowen and Bok 1998; Long and Tienda 2008). Yet, college administrators and legislators measure success in achieving campus diversity based on enrollment and, to a lesser extent, graduation rates. Despite their centrality in shaping the composition of entering classes, with few exceptions (e.g., Long 2004; Card and Krueger 2005; Brown and Hirschman 2006; Long and Tienda 2009; Koffman and Tienda 2008), application rates have been relatively ignored as a focus of inquiry. Partly this reflects data

Angel Harris is an assistant professor of sociology and African American studies at Princeton University. His research interests include social inequality, public policy, and education, with a focus on the social-psychological determinants of the racial achievement gap. His research examines the factors that contribute to differences in academic investment among African Americans, Latinos, Asian Americans, and whites.

Marta Tienda is the Maurice P. During '22 Professor in Demographic Studies and professor of sociology and public affairs at Princeton University. Her current research interests include equity and access to higher education and the causes and consequences of child migration and immigrant integration in new destinations. She is co–principal investigator of the Texas Higher Education Opportunity Project.

NOTE: This study was supported by grants from the Ford, Mellon, Hewlett, and Spencer Foundations and NSF (GRANT # SES-0350990). We gratefully acknowledge institutional support from the Office of Population Research (NICHD Grant # R24 H0047879) and programming assistance from Dawn Koffman. Direct all correspondence to Angel L. Harris, Department of Sociology, Princeton University, Princeton, NJ 08544; phone: (512) 471-1122; fax (512) 471-1748; e-mail angelh@princeton.edu.

constraints and partly the fact that litigation targets criteria used in institutional admissions decisions, not individual decisions to apply or, conditional on acceptance, to enroll.

Several recent studies have begun to fill this gap. For example, Long and Tienda (2009) show that the elimination of affirmative action and implementation of the top 10 percent plan not only impacts directly the most selective institutions but also produces substantial *indirect* effects at less selective institutions. Their analyses of administrative data show that average test scores of applicants to less selective institutions rose after affirmative action was banned, presumably because students with high test scores who did not qualify for the admission guarantee applied to a broader set of universities. Furthermore, as the share of top 10 percent applicants to highly selective UT rose, the average test scores of their applicant pool stagnated.

Although highly informative, Long and Tienda (2009) did not consider changes in the number of potential applicants (i.e., the size of high school graduation cohorts), which is highly relevant in a state experiencing above-average growth in its college-age population (Tienda and Sullivan 2009). To address this limitation, Koffman and Tienda (2008) analyzed administrative records for the top two flagships, making two important extensions. First, they disaggregated applicant pools according to the economic status of their high school, which is important in considering whether the uniform admission law broadens access across multiple criteria, as its architects envisioned. Second, they evaluated application behavior relative to the number of high school graduates in specific years. Their results showed that graduates from affluent schools are significantly more likely to seek admission at one of the public flagships compared with their peers who graduated from high schools that served students of low to moderate socioeconomic status. Importantly, they showed no change in the socioeconomic composition of applicants after the admission guarantees went into effect. Koffman and Tienda claimed that the admission guarantee did little to raise application rates to UT and TAMU from poor high schools.[7]

Building on these insights, this study asks about the consequences of the changes in Texas college admission policies for white, Hispanic, Asian American, and black students who graduated from Texas public high schools. Specifically, using more than a decade of administrative data for the two flagship campuses, we consider how students from these groups fared across the three of the four policy regimes in force since 1992.[8] To motivate the empirical analysis, we provide a brief overview of the changing demography of Texas higher education. Following a discussion of data and methods, we examine changes in each group's application, admission, and enrollment rates across the three policy regimes. The conclusion reconciles our findings with those of other studies using similar methods and discusses the implications of dismantling the Top Ten Percent Law for achieving campus diversity and educating the fastest growing demographic groups to meet the state's growing need for high-skill labor.

Our analysis is novel in two ways. First, we compute application rates by merging school-specific data on high school graduates with college applicants from those schools. This is important in light of the rapid growth of the college-eligible population in Texas (Western Interstate Commission for Higher Education [WICHE] 2008; Tienda and Sullivan 2009). Second, we simulate gains and losses for each group at each stage of the college pipeline under the three regimes analyzed. This exercise goes beyond conventional approaches that estimate admission and enrollment probabilities by quantifying the competition for seats at the Texas flagships. Despite popular claims that the Top Ten Percent Law has restored diversity to UT and TAMU (Wilgoren 1999), our results, which take into account both growing demand and the carrying capacity of the flagship public institutions, show that Hispanics and blacks are worse off relative to whites than they were under affirmative action.

Demography of Texas Higher Education

Owing both to high levels of immigration and high Hispanic birthrates, Texas is one of the nation's fastest growing and most rapidly diversifying states. Between 1994 and 2004, the number of diploma recipients rose 50 percent, from 163,000 to 244,000 (Tienda and Sullivan 2009; Tienda 2006). High school graduation rates improved by almost 11 percentage points from 1994 (pre-*Hopwood*) to 2003 (pre-*Grutter*)—rising from 56 to 67 percent (Swanson 2006); however, large differences remain between whites and disadvantaged minorities.[9] These gaps are particularly striking for Hispanics, many of whom do not complete high school. Nevertheless, the number of Hispanic high school graduates rose 78 percent during this period, boosting their share of Texas diploma recipients from 29 percent in 1994 to 35 percent by 2004 (Tienda and Sullivan 2009). Although white students are more likely to graduate from high school than are Hispanics, their share of the high school population has been shrinking. In 1994, whites earned 56 percent of diplomas awarded in Texas, but by 2004, their share dropped to 48 percent. Diversification of high school graduation cohorts continues, and the WICHE (2008, 107) reports that Hispanics earned 38 percent of diplomas in 2008, compared with 43 percent for whites.

Of course, not all high school graduates pursue postsecondary education, but even assuming constant shares of college-bound grads over time, the larger graduation cohorts imply intensified competition for access to the selective public institutions. Although Texas's postsecondary system expanded in response to growing demand, it failed to keep pace with demographic trends. Postsecondary enrollment rose 27 percent between 1994 and 2004, well below the 50 percent increase in the number of high school graduates during the same period. Texas differs from the nation and most states in another important respect that bears on the college squeeze—namely, the preponderance of two-year colleges within its postsecondary education system. At the national level, enrollment growth at two- and four-year institutions was relatively similar during this period—around 19 to 20 percent—but this was not the case in Texas, where two-year institutions registered a 37 percent enrollment increase (Tienda and Sullivan 2009; Texas

Higher Education Coordinating Board [THECB] 2005). Because critics of affirmative action and the Top Ten Percent Law invoke crowding and institutional carrying capacity as reasons for their opposition, it is particularly noteworthy that total enrollment at two-year institutions surpassed that of four-year public institutions in 1995, at least one year before the *Hopwood* decision (THECB 2005).

The change in Texas college admission regimes over a short period, coupled with appreciable increases in the number of college-eligible minorities, raises several questions about their representation in higher education. How did changes in admission regimes impact application, admission, and enrollment *rates* at UT and TAMU for black, white, Hispanic, and Asian students? Specifically, have minority-white gaps in application, admission, and enrollment rates improved under the top 10 percent regime? Finally, what are the enrollment implications of changes in application and admission rates for the four major racial groups? To address these questions, we simulate admission and enrollment changes in the post–affirmative action period under several scenarios about application and matriculation behavior for each group.

Data

For our analyses, we use publicly available data from the Texas Education Agency (TEA) about graduates from Texas public high schools and administrative data on applicants, admittees, and enrollees to UT and TAMU for the years 1993 to 2003. We exclude special and alternative schools from consideration on grounds that their students may differ systematically in their college-going behavior.[10] Therefore, analyses of application rates based on the TEA are restricted to 942 public high schools that were in operation throughout the observation period. Nearly 95 percent of Texas seniors graduate from public high schools, and this share has not changed since the early 1990s (WICHE 2008). We employed weights to account for variation in the size and ethnic composition of graduating classes across high schools.[11]

Institutional administrative files record the admission and enrollment status of all applicants to UT and TAMU, as well as students' demographic and achievement characteristics.[12] These include race and ethnicity, class rank, standardized test scores, year of application, and maternal education. School identifiers available on restricted use files permit us to append school attributes—such as size, public/private status, and share of students receiving free or reduced-price lunch—to student records.

Application Rates

Table 1 reports group-specific application rates to UT and TAMU for Texas public school seniors across the three policy regimes covered by our data. The large differences in application rates between Asians and other groups are striking,

TABLE 1

Average Application Rates to the University of Texas at Austin and Texas A&M from
Texas Public High School Seniors, 1993-2003 (in Percentages)

Policy (Years)	White	Asian	Asian-White	Hispanic	Hispanic-White	Black	Black-White
University of Texas at Austin							
Affirmative action (1993-1996)	7.19	30.76	23.57	3.61	−3.58	2.72	−4.47
No policy (1997)	6.56	29.79	23.23	2.77	−3.79	2.09	−4.47
Top 10 percent (1998-2003)	7.13	29.78	22.65	3.26	−3.87	2.48	−4.65
Texas A&M University							
Affirmative action (1993-1996)	9.48	11.77	2.29	3.23	−6.25	2.95	−6.53
No policy (1997)	9.30	14.27	4.97	2.74	−6.56	2.50	−6.80
Top 10 percent (1998-2002)	9.06	9.81	0.75	2.22	−6.84	1.88	−7.18

NOTE: Percentages are for the students enrolled in 942 public high schools in operation in Texas from 1993 through 2003.

particularly at UT. Taking account of large differences in group sizes provides more concrete perspective on the significance of the application gaps. During the period considered, Asian high school graduates constituted about 3 percent of all Texas high school graduates, but the Hispanic share rose from 28 to 34 percent. Although the Asian application rate is almost four times that of whites and more than eight times that of Hispanics, Asians represent a relatively small share of the college-eligible population.[13] Blacks represented between 12 and 13 percent of all high school graduates during the observation period, but given their low application rates, they represented about 514 and 770 of all public school applicants, respectively, in 1993 and 2003.

Of particular interest are the *changes* in application rates across the policy regimes and between institutions. UT application rates fell modestly for all demographic groups after affirmative action was rescinded but rebounded for all groups except Asians after H.B.588. Despite the modest rebound under the top 10 percent regime, Hispanic and black application rates remained below the levels observed during affirmative action; by contrast, the white application rate to UT returned to its pre-*Hopwood* level. Partly because the size of the graduation cohorts grew, the number of applications rose. For example, the 1993 white application rate of 7.2 percent implied roughly 6,600 students compared with 8,110 in 2003 (see WICHE 2003, appendix A).

Comparable data for TAMU differ in several important ways. First, compared with UT, the white application rate to TAMU is consistently higher by 2 or 3 percentage points and the Asian application rate appreciably lower. Thus, the Asian-white application gap ranges between 1 and 5 percentage points, well below the 23-point gap observed at UT. Second, Hispanic application rates were systematically lower than those observed at UT for each period, but black application rates were higher for all periods except during the top 10 percent regime. Third, application rates for all groups except Asians fell steadily during the observation period, rather than dropping and rebounding as occurred at UT. Asian application rates to TAMU actually rose in 1997 following the judicial ban on affirmative action; however, they plummeted nearly 5 points under the top 10 percent regime. In part, the steady drop in TAMU's application rates reflects a provision in the law that allows rank-eligible students to select their campus. It appears that an unintended consequence of the law is a shift in applications away from TAMU toward UT (Tienda and Sullivan 2009; Long and Tienda 2009).

Although the changes in application rates reported in Table 1 seem small, the numbers of black and Hispanic students are not trivial. Because the number of high school graduates increased by 50 percent between 1994 and 2004 (Tienda and Sullivan 2009), to provide a more intuitive assessment of the seemingly small changes in rates, we convert the application rates into numbers of students. Table 2 simulates the number of additional applicants under two hypothetical scenarios: (1) if each group's application rate remained at its affirmative action level and (2) if each group applied at the same rate as whites within policy regimes. For parsimony, we focus on the two underrepresented groups that benefited most from affirmative action and that presumably stood to gain most from the percent plan. These results show that the ban on race-sensitive admissions had a chilling effect on application behavior. Assuming no change in their application rates since affirmative action implies that an additional 380 Hispanics and 117 blacks would have sought admission to UT in 1997, the year that neither race nor class rank preferences were in force. An additional 221 Hispanics and 85 blacks would have applied to TAMU in 1997 had their application rates not dropped. Moreover, during the first four to five years of the top 10 percent regime, UT and TAMU would have gained an average of 243 and 691 Hispanic applicants per year, respectively, had their application behavior remained at the pre-*Hopwood* level. Similarly, UT and TAMU would have gained an annual average of 64 and 303 black applicants, respectively. These results are consistent with several other studies showing that admission policies impact application behavior in ways that alter the composition of the aggregate pool (Long 2004; Brown and Hirschman 2006; Long and Tienda 2009).

The second counterfactual—which assigns white application rates to blacks and Hispanics *within* policy regimes—implies that an additional 1,525 Hispanics and 768 blacks would have sought admission to UT annually under affirmative action. Owing both to growth in the college-eligible minority population and the larger disparities in application rates, the loss in potential applicants rises across successive policy regime. Under the top 10 percent policy, for example, UT's applicant pool would include an additional 2,604 Hispanics and 1,274 blacks if these groups applied at the same rate as white diploma recipients. The loss of

TABLE 2
Estimated Additional Applicants for Underrepresented Minorities under Two Scenarios

Policy (Years)	University of Texas at Austin		Texas A&M University	
	Hispanics	Blacks	Hispanics	Blacks
	If each group's application rates remained at affirmative action levels[a]			
No policy (1997)	380	117	221	85
Top 10 percent annual avg.	243	64	691	303
	If each group had whites' application rates under each policy regime[b]			
Affirmative action annual avg.	1,525	768	2,668	1,121
No policy (1997)	1,702	841	2,948	1,281
Top 10 percent annual avg.	2,604	1,274	4,683	2,023

NOTE: Data for TAMU exclude 2003.
a. The following formula was employed for each cell: Additional Applications = (GroupGrads × GrpAppRtAA − GrpApps), where GroupGrads are the group specific total number of high school graduates during the given policy regime, GrpAppRtAA is the group specific application rate during affirmative action, and GrpApps are the group specific total number of applicants from Texas public high schools during the same policy regime. Numbers were calculated from Texas Education Agency data.
b. The following formula was employed for each cell: Additional Applications = (GroupGrads × WhtAppRt − GrpApps), where WhtAppRt is the white application rate during the given policy regime.

potential additional Hispanic and black applicants at TAMU is substantially higher than for UT across all three policy regimes, which reflects the larger disparities in their application rates vis-à-vis whites. Specifically, the white-minority application gaps of roughly 7 percentage points translates into an annual loss of potentially 4,683 additional Hispanic applicants and potentially 2,023 blacks under the top 10 percent regime.

These estimates are likely to be conservative because the TEA data we used to compute school-specific denominators for application rates only include seniors from Texas public high schools. Although private schools account for about 5 percent of Texas high school seniors (WICHE 2003, appendix A, 137), they produce a disproportionate number of college applicants. In 1997, the year neither preference policy was in force, public school seniors accounted for approximately 80 percent of all applications received by UT and TAMU and approximately 70 percent of the applicants for both universities under the top 10 percent regime. The remainder of applicants to UT and TAMU were private school attendees, out-of-state students, international students, or nontraditional.

Admissions and Enrollment

Campus diversity depends not only on application rates but also on admission and enrollment rates. The former are constrained both by policy governing admission criteria and institutional carrying capacity, namely, the size of the freshman class that can be accommodated within existing physical and human capital resources. Most of the public controversies focus on the admission decision, but the decisions to apply and enroll are potentially more important determinants of campus diversity. Conditional on admission, financial aid and competing admission offers from private institutions also influence the ethno-racial composition of college campuses.

The top panel of Table 3 shows the percentage of applicants admitted to UT and TAMU across the three policy regimes. At both public flagships, whites' admission rate rose during the no-policy period but returned to affirmative action levels under the top 10 percent policy. At UT, Asian Americans' admission rates spiked in 1997 but fell under the uniform admission regime; still, Asian-origin students were more likely to be admitted under the top 10 percent policy compared with affirmative action. By contrast, Asian admission rates at TAMU declined steadily after affirmative action was rescinded. The repeal of affirmative action did not alter Hispanic admission rates at UT, possibly due to a drop in application rates of marginal students who hedged their bets. Compared with affirmative action, however, TAMU Hispanic applicants witnessed 10 and 15 percent drops in admission rates, respectively, in 1997 and under the top 10 percent regime. Finally, blacks' admission rates fell at both flagships after the repeal of affirmative action, and their admission rates stagnated at 1997 levels at TAMU but rebounded slightly at UT once the admission guarantee for top 10 percent graduates went into effect.

The second panel in Table 3 shows the ethno-racial composition of the admittee pools for the three policy regimes. The first two columns indicate that at UT the shift from affirmative action to the no-policy regime benefited Asians, whose share of admittees rose 3 percentage points, at the expense of Hispanics and blacks. As intended, the top 10 percent regime boosted the admit rate for blacks and Hispanics relative to 1997, but only blacks recovered their relative share of the admittee pool achieved under affirmative action. Based on the composition of the admittee pool, white applicants were the primary casualties under the Top Ten Percent Law; their share of admittees fell 4 percentage points as Asian and Hispanic representation inched up 1 and 2 percentage points, respectively, relative to the no-policy period.

Changes in the composition of TAMU's admission pools under the three regimes differ from UT in several ways. First, the white admission share increased steadily after affirmative action, averaging 77 percent under the top 10 percent policy. Second, although Asians benefited from the repeal of affirmative action, their share of admittees did not continue to rise, as at UT. Third, Hispanic and black representation in TAMU's admittee pool fell under both policies.

Because the Top Ten Percent Law is restricted to in-state applicants, these estimates likely overstate the consequences for Texas residents. To gauge this

TABLE 3

Admission and Enrollment Rates, and Share Admitted and Enrolled at the UT-Austin and TAMU across Three Admission Regimes

	Admissions						Yield					
	UT-Austin			Texas A&M University			UT-Austin			Texas A&M University		
	(Admitted / Applicants) × 100						(Enrolled / Admitted) × 100					
	Affirmative Action (1990-1996)	No Policy (1997)	Top Ten Percent (1998-2003)	Affirmative Action (1992-1996)	No Policy (1997)	Top Ten Percent (1998-2002)	Affirmative Action (1990-1996)	No Policy (1997)	Top Ten Percent (1998-2003)	Affirmative Action (1992-1996)	No Policy (1997)	Top Ten Percent (1998-2002)
Whites	71.7	83.2	71.4	73.9	79.9	74.0	59.1	64.0	61.7	61.8	57.4	64.6
Asians	74.3	84.4	77.5	73.2	72.4	66.1	60.8	64.0	63.3	38.3	32.2	36.5
Hispanics	74.9	75.4	67.7	86.2	76.2	70.8	54.5	64.3	60.2	50.3	46.5	51.7
Blacks	64.0	58.0	59.9	83.8	64.5	64.7	57.7	56.3	56.6	46.2	41.1	48.6
	Group Share of Total Admitted						Group Share of Total Enrollees					
Whites	.651	.656	.613	.730	.749	.766	.664	.668	.623	.782	.805	.822
Asians	.128	.160	.171	.052	.060	.057	.134	.163	.179	.034	.036	.035
Hispanics	.159	.124	.145	.144	.112	.109	.150	.127	.144	.125	.098	.094
Blacks	.040	.032	.039	.051	.036	.033	.040	.028	.036	.041	.028	.027
Totals	.978	.972	.968	.977	.957	.965	.988	.986	.982	.982	.967	.978
	Proportion of Total Admitted from In-State Public High Schools						Proportion of Total Enrollees from In-State Public High Schools					
Whites	.513	.497	.479	.612	.625	.645	.561	.551	.524	.696	.717	.729
Asians	.107	.132	.141	.042	.050	.047	.122	.147	.161	.031	.033	.032
Hispanics	.140	.106	.126	.119	.094	.093	.133	.111	.130	.109	.083	.083
Blacks	.036	.027	.035	.041	.031	.029	.037	.026	.034	.036	.025	.025
Totals	.796	.762	.781	.814	.800	.814	.853	.835	.849	.872	.858	.869

(continued)

TABLE 3 (continued)

	Group Share of Total In-State Public High School Admits						Group Share of Total In-State Public High School Enrollees					
Whites	.643	.650	.609	.745	.761	.779	.656	.657	.614	.793	.816	.827
Asians	.134	.172	.179	.051	.061	.057	.143	.175	.188	.035	.038	.036
Hispanics	.175	.138	.160	.145	.114	.112	.155	.132	.153	.124	.094	.094
Blacks	.045	.035	.045	.050	.037	.035	.043	.031	.040	.040	.029	.028
Totals	.997	.995	.993	.991	.973	.983	.997	.995	.995	.992	.977	.985

NOTE: Number of observations is 224,893 and 163,027 for UT-Austin and TAMU, respectively. Group share of total admitted = group specific admits / total admits; proportion of total admitted from in-state public HS = group-specific in-state public HS admits / total admits; group share of total in-state public HS admits = group-specific in-state public HS admits / total in-state public HS admits. For the analogous categories of enrollment, we replace the admitted information in the previous formulas with enrollment information.

possibility, the bottom two panels of Table 3 show the proportion of students admitted from Texas public high schools by race (panel 3) and the group shares admitted *among* applicants from Texas public high schools (panel 4). These distributions mirror those observed for all applicants, which is not surprising considering that about four in five of all students admitted to both universities hail from Texas public high schools. Despite the squeeze in admission rates due to growth in applications from Texas graduates, apparently both institutions' international and out-of-state students fill approximately 20 percent of seats at both flagships.[14]

The right panel of Table 3 provides parallel information for yield rates—namely, the percentage of admittees who enroll at each institution. For all groups except blacks, enrollment rates rose at UT after affirmative action was rescinded. Under the top 10 percent regime, however, yield rates for white and Hispanic admittees eroded slightly but held steady for blacks and Asians. Enrollment patterns at TAMU differ in that the percentage of admitted students who enrolled fell for all groups during the no-policy period and rebounded to levels slightly above those under affirmative action for whites, Hispanics, and blacks under the top 10 percent regime. Enrollment rates are based on small pools of Hispanics and blacks compared with whites. The second panel shows that representation of black and Hispanic freshmen at the public flagships was not restored to affirmative action levels under the top 10 percent regime—at least through 2003. At UT, Asian representation among first-time freshmen rose at the expense of all other groups, while TAMU's freshman pools became increasingly white. Campus diversity is largely driven by the high percentage of enrollees (about 85 percent) from in-state public high schools to both public flagships, as revealed by the lower two panels. The composition of enrollees based on the full pool and that based on in-state graduates is similar for both institutions and across policy regimes.

In sum, it seems that the shift in admission policy from affirmative action was beneficial for the admission and enrollment of whites and Asian Americans and had adverse effects on the representation of blacks and Hispanics. Unconditional on applicant characteristics, such as test scores, Asian Americans were the only group to increase their share of total admissions to UT after the repeal of affirmative action. Both whites and Asian Americans increased their total share of TAMU admittees and enrollees after affirmative action was judicially prohibited. In contrast, the total share of Hispanic and black admittees was highest during the affirmative action period, but both groups faced lower admission prospects compared with whites under the no-preference and uniform admission regimes.

Admission Policy and the College Pipeline: A Simulation

To estimate the gains and losses of students associated with changes in policy regimes, we simulate the number of admitted and enrolled students each group would have gained or lost had affirmative action not been repealed, or if the uniform admission policy did not alter the admittee and enrollee pools. Table 4 summarizes these results, which represent the policy impacts in student-units, or the "cost" in admissions (enrollment) to each group associated with change in their relative shares after the repeal of affirmative action. These simulations account for the carrying capacity of both UT and TAMU throughout the observation period, which is critically important under conditions of rising demand for slots at the public flagships.

The top panel of Table 4 indicates that if the group-specific share of students admitted to UT remained at affirmative action levels, an additional 393 Hispanics and 96 blacks would have gained admission to UT in 1997, when neither affirmative action nor the top 10 percent policy was in effect. As beneficiaries of the judicial ban on affirmative action, the gain in Asian and white shares admitted translates to 365 and 58 *additional* admittees relative to the number that would have been admitted had race-sensitive criteria not been prohibited. These gains came at the expense of blacks and Hispanics. The simulations for the top 10 percent regime show that Asians and "others" benefited from the admission guarantee, mostly at the expense of whites, who potentially lost 550 admits per year. The Top Ten Percent Law also cost UT 204 Hispanic and 14 black admittees annually, on average.

Parallel analyses for TAMU show that white students and "others," not Asians, benefited most from the repeal of affirmative action. TAMU admitted approximately 219 and an annual average of 506 additional white applicants during the no-policy period and top 10 percent regimes, respectively, relative to the numbers that would have been admitted had the judicial ban not altered the composition of the admittee pool. Asian Americans also benefited from the repeal of affirmative action at TAMU, but to a lesser degree than whites did. As occurred at UT, the repeal of affirmative action cost TAMU black and Hispanic admittees. If their admission shares had remained at affirmative action levels, TAMU would have gained 366 and an annual average of 493 additional Hispanic admits during the no-policy period and the top 10 percent regime, respectively. The comparable cost of black admittees is 173 and 253 per year, respectively, during the no-policy and top 10 percent regimes.

The bottom panel of Table 4 reports changes in yields—the measure of actual campus diversity resulting from the conditional probability of matriculating, conditional on applying and gaining admission. The baselines for these calculations are the enrollment group shares achieved under affirmative action. The relative costs are similar, except that absolute numbers are lower because students apply to multiple institutions but can ultimately enroll at only one. Whites and Asians gained 32 and 204 freshmen slots at UT when affirmative action was repealed, but under the top 10 percent regime, whites lost an average of 354 seats in the freshman class per year while Asians more than offset their gains. The repeal of affirmative action cost black and Hispanic admittees 160 and 83 slots in UT's freshman classes, respectively, but only 51 and 30 per year, on average, under the top 10 percent regime. Echoing the admission story, whites were the primary beneficiaries of the repeal of affirmative action at TAMU, netting 142 seats

TABLE 4
Estimated Changes in Admits and Enrollees under the Null Hypothesis of "No Change" Since Affirmative Action[a]

Change in Admits if Shares of Students Admitted Remained at Affirmative Action (AA) Levels

| | University of Texas at Austin | | | | | Texas A&M University | | | | |
| | | No Policy Regime | | Top 10 percent Regime | | | No Policy Regime | | Top 10 percent Regime | |
Group	AA Shares	%Δ in Shares	Cost in Admits	%Δ in Shares	Cost in Admits	AA Shares	%Δ in Shares	Cost in Admits	%Δ in Shares	Cost in Admits
Whites	.651	0.5	−58	−3.8	550	.730	1.9	−219	3.6	−506
Asians	.128	3.2	−365	4.3	−626	.052	0.8	−96	0.6	−83
Hispanics	.159	−3.5	393	−1.4	204	.144	−3.1	366	−3.5	493
Blacks	.040	−0.8	96	−0.1	14	.051	−1.5	173	−1.8	253
Other	.022	0.6	−66	1.0	−142	.023	1.9	−224	1.1	−157
Totals	1.000	0.0	0	0.0	0	1.000	0.0	0	0.0	0

Change in Enrollees if Shares of Admitted Students Who Enrolled Remained at AA Levels

| | University of Texas at Austin | | | | | Texas A&M University | | | | |
| | | No Policy Regime | | Top 10 percent Regime | | | No Policy Regime | | Top 10 percent Regime | |
Group	AA Shares	%Δ in Shares	Cost in Enrollees	%Δ in Shares	Cost in Enrollees	AA Shares	%Δ in Shares	Cost in Enrollees	%Δ in Shares	Cost in Enrollees
Whites	.664	0.5	−32	−4.1	354	.782	2.3	−142	4.0	−340
Asians	.134	2.9	−204	4.5	−389	.034	0.2	−13	0.1	−7
Hispanics	.150	−2.3	160	−0.6	51	.125	−2.7	171	−3.1	271
Blacks	.040	−1.2	83	−0.3	30	.041	−1.3	80	−1.4	120
Other	.012	0.1	−7	0.5	−46	.018	1.5	−96	0.4	−44
Totals	1.000	0.0	0	0.0	0	1.000	0.0	0.0	0	0

NOTE: Number of observations is 224,893 and 163,027 for UT-Austin and TAMU, respectively. Data for TAMU exclude 2003.

a. Cost in Admits = (Total Regime Admits × Group-Specific AA Share) − Groups' Actual Admits during Regime. Cost of admits is divided by 5 for UT-Austin and 4 for TAMU to obtain the yearly average during the top 10 percent regime. The previous formula is repeated using the analogous information for enrollment.

in 1997 and a whopping annual average of 340 seats under the uniform admission regime. Hispanic and black admittees to TAMU incurred high losses in freshman class seats, which averaged 271 and 120 per year once the Top Ten Percent Law was in place.

Explaining Group Differences in Admission and Enrollment Rates

Although informative, the findings discussed above do not account for group differences in characteristics associated with college admission prospects. In particular, the observed minority-white admission gaps likely reflect group differences in academic outcomes and high school quality, which is related to application behavior and college readiness (Niu and Tienda 2008; Koffman and Tienda 2008). Therefore, the final set of analyses examine how admission and enrollment outcomes change after accounting for variation in applicants' Scholastic Aptitude Test (SAT) and ACT college test scores, class rank, and high school attributes associated with college-going behavior, such as high school size, public-private status, and percentage of students who were ever economically disadvantaged (see Long and Tienda 2009, 2008). These findings are presented in Table 5.

The first model predicts the proportion of students admitted to both UT and TAMU, essentially replicating the findings reported in the top panel of Table 3 as proportions rather than percentages. These estimates serve as benchmarks for evaluating changes in the applicants' achievements on their admission outcomes. Both before and after affirmative action was rescinded, Asians' admission advantage at UT was largely due to their higher average test scores and class rank. Comparison of whites and Asians with equivalent test scores yielded similar admission rates under the top 10 percent regime, but whites had a 2 to 3 percent edge under affirmative action and the no-preferences year. These results are unaltered by taking into account differences in the types of high schools they attend.

Both blacks and Hispanics also enjoyed an admission advantage at UT under affirmative action; this is evident in the large positive coefficients (net deviations from the white rank) derived from model 2, which compares applicants with comparable test scores and class rank. Once race preferences were judicially banned, both Hispanics and blacks lost their admission advantage; black applicants were 17 percent less likely and Hispanics 13 percent less likely than comparably achieving whites to gain admission to UT. Under the top 10 percent regime, the admission prospects of blacks and Hispanics improved but remained below those of their white counterparts both because they are less likely to qualify for automatic admission in both integrated and segregated schools (Tienda and Niu 2006) and because they average lower test scores among those who do not qualify for the admission guarantee. Taking into account group differences in high school characteristics altered the main patterns only marginally.

TABLE 5
Estimates of Policy Effects on Admission and Enrollment at UT-Austin and TAMU

| | Admitted | | | | | | Enrolled[a] | | | | | |
| | UT-Austin | | | TAMU | | | UT-Austin | | | TAMU | | |
Independent Variables	(1)	(2)	(3)	(1)	(2)	(3)	(1)	(2)	(3)	(1)	(2)	(3)
Group (whites ref.)												
Asians	.026	-.028	-.028	-.007	-.036	-.024	.010	.025	.012	-.235	-.224	-.223
Hispanics	.032	.133	.121	.123	.179	.169	-.046	-.092	-.095	-.115	-.154	-.148
Blacks	-.077	.108	.104	.099	.205	.199	-.030	-.091	-.086	-.156	-.209	-.207
Policy by group												
No policy (NP)	.115	.123	.120	.059	.056	.044	.061	.062	.039	-.044	-.048	-.065
NP × Asians	-.014	-.020	-.020	-.067	-.066	-.067	-.014	-.015	-.019	-.017	-.008	-.010
NP × Hispanics	-.110	-.125	-.138	-.160	-.161	-.176	.019	.030	.018	.006	.013	.017
NP × blacks	-.175	-.170	-.168	-.253	-.244	-.247	-.115	-.105	-.113	-.007	.000	.001
Top 10 percent (TT)	-.003	-.004	-.030	.001	.003	-.004	.058	.067	-.014	.028	.025	.008
TT × Asians	.035	.033	.040	-.072	-.068	-.069	.011	.008	.023	-.046	-.036	-.037
TT × Hispanics	-.069	-.081	-.088	-.154	-.156	-.169	.026	.026	.043	-.015	-.011	-.007
TT × blacks	-.039	-.072	-.079	-.192	-.196	-.205	-.022	-.024	-.015	-.005	.001	.004
Academics												
SAT/ACT[b]	—	.010	.011	—	.008	.009	—	-.004	-.003	—	-.004	-.004
TT class rank	—	.282	.261	—	.309	.274	—	-.062	-.060	—	-.014	-.013
Constant	.717	-.575	-.679	.739	-.265	-.415	.536	1.057	.976	.618	1.107	1.120
R^2	.008	.305	.326	.009	.245	.259	.005	.027	.106	.024	.041	.045
Control vector	N	N	Y	N	N	Y	N	N	Y	N	N	Y
N	210,037			156,848			151,900			117,060		

NOTE: Control vector includes sex, class size, percentage of high school receiving free or reduced-price lunch, and public/private status of high school. Indicator variables for students with missing values on each covariate are also included in the regressions.

a. Data excludes students who enrolled but were not granted formal admission (e.g., waitlisted, deferred enrollment), which corresponds to 3 percent of the sample at UT.

b. SAT/ACT are composite scores divided by 10; ACT scores were converted to the SAT scale. Therefore, the estimates represent the average change in the outcome associated with every 10-point increase in test scores along the SAT scale.

Results for TAMU parallel those for UT with three notable differences. First, Asians did not enjoy an admission advantage under any of the policy regimes. That is, conditional on application to TAMU, Asian students were less likely to be admitted than whites with comparable test scores and class rank. Their lower admission chances, moreover, continued under the no-preference and top 10 percent regimes. Second, compared with UT applicants under affirmative action, black and Hispanic TAMU applicants enjoyed much larger admission advantages— on the order of 17 to 20 percent—relative to white applicants with comparable credentials. Furthermore, Hispanics' admission chances were lower than comparably achieving white applicants by almost as much—even more for African Americans—once race preferences were outlawed. Third, under the uniform admission law, the admission prospects of black and Hispanic TAMU applicants were not much better than under the no-preference regime, which is not the case at UT.

The right-hand panel of Table 5 estimates enrollment prospects conditional on admission after taking into account group differences in high school achievement and high school attributes that influence the likelihood of enrollment. Because the enrollment decision depends both on family financial resources as well as competing offers, neither of which we can observe, the statistical controls serve as crude proxies for group differences in resources and college climate of high schools.

Comparisons between institutions reveal sharp differences in enrollment behavior among minority groups. Under affirmative action, Asians admitted to UT were marginally more likely to enroll compared with similarly situated whites—on the order of 1 to 2 percent. At TAMU, however, Asians admitted prior to the judicial ban on affirmative action were about 23 percent less likely to enroll compared with equally achieving whites. These differences in enrollment behavior were moderated appreciably during the year that no preferences were in force. At both institutions, admitted Asian students were 1 to 2 percentage points less likely to enroll than their white counterparts. Under the uniform admission regime, Asian enrollment behavior differed by institution; they were more likely to enroll at UT, conditional on admission, but were less likely to do so at TAMU.

Hispanic admissions to both public flagships resulted in lower yields vis-à-vis whites under affirmative action. Once the race preferences were outlawed, however, the Hispanic yield rate was marginally higher than that of whites at both institutions. Most likely this reflects the higher socioeconomic selectivity of high-achieving Hispanics admitted post-*Hopwood*, but other unobservables, such as qualification for merit and means-tested financial aid, also contribute to this result. Mimicking Asian enrollment behavior under the uniform admission regime, Hispanics admitted to TAMU were less likely than whites to enroll. By contrast, at UT, admitted Hispanic students were 2.6 to 4.3 percent more likely to enroll than admitted white students with similar characteristics.

Throughout the period under consideration, African Americans admitted to the Texas public flagships were significantly less likely than their white counterparts to enroll at either institution. When race preferences were allowed, the black yield rate was about 8 percent below that of comparable whites at UT and nearly 21 percent below at TAMU. The ban on affirmative action lowered the yield of African Americans at UT, but there were only trivial differences at TAMU. This seemingly equal yield at TAMU is deceptive, however, because it largely reflects the tiny numbers admitted, as revealed by Table 3. The small black-white enrollment gap at TAMU under the uniform admission regime also reflects the low numbers of African American students who apply and are admitted to TAMU, where the share of blacks' enrollment has not rebounded to its pre-*Hopwood* level. By contrast, the black yield at UT is well above that observed under affirmative action, but it remains woefully low.

To summarize, the shift in admission regimes from affirmative action to no preferences resulted in lower admission rates to both flagships for Asian Americans, Hispanics, and blacks relative to whites, even when comparisons are standardized by students' academic achievements and high school characteristics. Furthermore, changes in admission rates to both flagships after affirmative action was rescinded and the top 10 percent regime implemented are negligible for statistically comparable minority groups. Inclusion of statistical controls for student achievements and high school characteristics does little to alter group differences in yield rates relative to those observed in Table 3.

Summary and Discussion

Our analyses show that changes in Texas college admission policies have been highly consequential for racial minority groups, the largest and fastest growing segment of the state's population. Using data from the TEA and from the administrative records of both flagships, we evaluate how white, Asian American, Hispanic, and African American students fared across three policy regimes: affirmative action, no-preference period, and the top 10 percent guarantee. Although it is commonplace to focus on admission and enrollment outcomes, our empirical analysis underscores that these outcomes are highly conditioned by the decision to apply (Long and Tienda 2009; Koffman and Tienda 2008). This conclusion echoes that reached by Brown and Hirschman (2006), who assessed the impact on minority representation in higher education after voters passed Initiative 200, a ballot measure that outlawed the use of race and ethnicity on college admissions in Washington State. They find that the largest impact was registered a the University of Washington, the state's public flagship; moreover, the drop in minority representation stemmed largely from the chilling effect of the ballot measure on application behavior and less from changes in admission rates.

The empirical analyses produce three major findings. First, Hispanic and black application rates to the Texas flagship universities fell after affirmative action was banned; moreover, owing to rapid growth in the number of high school graduates, their disadvantage in percentage of applicants relative to whites grew over time. Although the declines in application rates to both UT and TAMU averaged 1 percent or less, this implies an annual loss in Hispanic applications that range from 240 at UT to nearly 700 at TAMU. The estimated loss of black applicants ranges from more than 60 to UT to more than 300 to TAMU. Second, both Hispanics and blacks witnessed lower admission prospects at both UT and TAMU after the ban on affirmative action and reached their lowest point under the top 10 percent regime. This finding implies that the number of underrepresented minorities eligible for enrollment to Texas flagship universities is reduced even further—a compounding of application and admission disadvantages that translates to fewer potential enrollees. Third, even with the declines in admission rates for Hispanics and blacks since the repeal of affirmative action, our results suggest that these groups would gain substantial representation in Texas flagships if they had retained their share of admits during affirmative action.

This result has profound policy implications that transcend admission regimes because they redirect attention away from the seemingly irresolvable differences about race or class rank preferences to encouraging greater numbers of qualified applicants to apply for admission. Koffman and Tienda (2008) show that graduates from affluent schools are significantly more likely to seek admission at the public flagships compared with their cohorts who graduate from high schools that serve students of low to moderate socioeconomic status. Our simulations indicate that equalizing their application rates with those of white graduates would have yielded 2,604 and 4,683 additional Hispanic applications annually during the top 10 percent regime for UT and TAMU, respectively. Blacks would also have experienced an increase in applicants of more than 1,200 to UT and more than 2,000 to TAMU during this same period.

That the expansion of the postsecondary education system has failed to keep up with the growth of the college-eligible population represents a formidable policy challenge for the future for several reasons. First, competition for access to the state's public flagships will continue to intensify in Texas, at least through 2015 (Tienda 2006; WICHE 2008). Second, legal and statutory challenges to both race preferences and the percentage plan show no sign of abating (Haurwitz 2008; Schmidt 2008). Third, Texas invests less of its GDP on public education than several other states that have excellent public universities.[15] Over the long term, the postsecondary system will expand to accommodate slower growth of high school graduates, but the state faces enormous opportunity costs from continued underinvestment in the education of its fastest growing population. Texas Comptroller Strayhorn (2005) estimated a 500 percent return on every dollar invested in the state's higher education system. Educational underinvestment is seldom invoked as the culprit for the rising number of applicants denied admission to a four-year institution in the state, yet it is the ultimate cause of the college squeeze and a source of economic vulnerability for the state in the future.

In the short term, however, cultivating college-going cultures at underresourced high schools is a potentially high-impact, relatively low-cost strategy to raise college application rates for underrepresented minorities. The Longhorn and Century Scholars programs developed by UT and TAMU, respectively, enabled economically disadvantaged top 10 percent graduates to attend their institutions. As important, these programs were accompanied by an aggressive outreach program that promises to increase students' orientation to college. Domina (2007) shows that the Longhorn and Century programs were associated with lower absenteeism and higher completion of standardized tests required by selective postsecondary institutions. Finally, it warrants emphasizing that an admission guarantee cannot guarantee enrollment, particularly for students from limited economic means. That Hispanic and black students are disproportionately concentrated in low-resourced high schools requires strong financial aid programs to ensure that successful applicants actually enroll in and graduate from college.

Notes

1. *Hopwood v Texas*, 78 F.3d 932 (5th Cir. 1996), *cert. denied*, 518 U.S. 1033 (1996).

2. The University of Texas at Dallas and Texas Tech University also reported sharp declines in the number of minority first-time freshmen, as did their professional schools.

3. *Grutter v. Bollinger*, 539 U.S. 306, 328 (2003).

4. The 81st Legislature capped the share of students qualified for automatic admission at 75 percent, but only for UT, which was saturated with Top Ten Percent automatic admits. This provision does not go into effect until the 2010-2011 cohort; therefore, our analyses are unaffected. Because this revision is deemed minimalist by opponents, the admission guarantee based on a single metric remains highly controversial.

5. Because the *Hopwood* decision was delivered on March 18, 1996, and applications for the entering class of the fall of 1996 were mostly adjudicated, the *Hopwood* decision took effect for the class entering in fall 1997.

6. Although *Grutter* permits narrowly tailored consideration of race in college admissions, the Top Ten Percent Law explicitly required a full year's advance notice before announced changes in admission criteria could take effect. Therefore, no Texas universities could restore affirmative action until fall 2005 admissions.

7. Long, Saenz, and Tienda (2009 [this volume]) show that the number and geographic dispersion of high schools represented at UT did rise, but no similar change occurred at TAMU.

8. Our data do not span the post-*Grutter* period; therefore, we cannot evaluate changes under the fourth regime that permits affirmative action with the percent plan.

9. TEA reports higher graduation rates (circa 84 percent), but Swanson's Cumulative Promotion Index generates more accurate cohort estimates. Specifically, the 67 percent graduation rate indicates that only 67 of every 100 ninth-grade students will graduate four years later.

10. We used publicly available data from the National Center for Education Statistics (NCES) to determine which high schools to exclude from the analysis. Administrative data available to us for UT extend through 2003 and for TAMU through 2002.

11. The weight used is the product of two separate weights. The first weight accounts for the size of the graduating class by dividing the total number of graduates by 150, which is the average senior class size for the 942 high schools in the sample. Thus, a school with a graduating class size of 600 students will count double that of one with 300 graduates. The second weight accounts for the group specific share of the graduating class.

12. Administrative data were compiled by the Texas Higher Education Opportunity Project (THEOP). See http://www.texastop10.princeton.edu for further details.

13. WICHE (2003, appendix A, 137) reports 4,400 Asian and 45,519 Hispanic high school graduates in 1993, representing 2.7 and 28.3 percent of all public high school graduates. In 2003, the comparable numbers were 7,906 and 77,971, respectively.

14. The state of Texas does not reserve a fixed number of slots for non-Texas residents, but a 2001 internal report of the Texas Higher Education Coordinating board identifies economic and educational benefits from the presence of international students (THECB 2001).

15. In a June 2008 communication to alumni, UT President William Powers Jr. noted that in 2006, Texas spent 3.35 percent of GDP on public education, including postsecondary institutions, compared with 4.24 percent by California, 4.49 percent by Michigan, and 4.05 percent by North Carolina.

References

Alon, Sigal, and Marta Tienda. 2007. Diversity, opportunity and the shifting meritocracy in higher education. *American Sociological Review* 72 (4): 487-511.

Barr, Rita. 2002. Top 10 percent policy: Higher education diversity after *Hopwood*. *Interim News*, no. 77-9, Texas House of Representatives, House Research Organization, Austin, TX.

Bowen, William G., and Derek Bok. 1998. *The shape of the river: Long-term consequences of considering race in college and university admissions*. Princeton, NJ: Princeton University Press.

Brown, Susan K., and Charles Hirschman. 2006. The end of affirmative action in Washington State and its impact on the transition from high school to college. *Sociology of Education* 79 (2): 106-30.

Card, David, and Alan B. Krueger. 2005. Would the elimination of affirmative action affect highly qualified minority applicants? Evidence from California and Texas. *Industrial and Labor Relations Review* 58 (3): 416-34.

Domina, Thurston. 2007. Higher education policy as secondary school reform: Texas public high schools after Hopwood. *Educational Evaluation and Policy Analysis* 29 (3): 200-217.

Haurwitz, Ralph K. M. 2008. Judge considers legality of UT admissions policy: Lawsuit seeks to bar university's consideration of race, ethnicity. *Austin American-Statesman* (Texas), May 20.

Holley, Danielle, and Delia Spencer. 1999. The Texas ten percent plan. *Harvard Civil Rights-Civil Liberties Law Review* 34 (1): 245-78.

Koffman, Dawn, and Marta Tienda. 2008. Missing in application: The Texas top 10 percent law and campus socioeconomic diversity. Working Paper, Texas Higher Education Opportunity Project, Princeton University, Princeton, NJ. http://theop.princeton.edu/reports/wp/ApplicantSocialClass.pdf.

Long, Mark C. 2004. College applications and the effect of affirmative action. *Journal of Econometrics* 121 (1-2): 319-42.

Long, Mark C., Victor Saenz, and Marta Tienda. 2009. Policy transparency and college enrollment: Did the Texas top ten percent law broaden access to the public flagships? *The Annals of the American Academy of Political and Social Science* (This volume).

Long, Mark C., and Marta Tienda. 2008. Winners and losers: Changes in Texas university admissions post-Hopwood. *Education Evaluation and Policy Analysis* 30 (3): 255-80.

Long, Mark C., and Marta Tienda. 2009. Changes in Texas universities' applicant pools after the Hopwood decision. *Social Science Research*.

Montejano, David. 2001. Access to the University of Texas at Austin and the ten percent plan: A three-year assessment. Admissions Brief, Office of Admissions Research, University of Texas at Austin. http://www.utexas.edu/student/admissions/research/montejanopaper.html.

Niu, Sunny X., and Marta Tienda. 2008. Admissions regimes and minority student academic performance: Lessons from UT-Austin. Paper presented at annual meetings of the American Education Research Association, New York, April. http://theop.princeton.edu/reports/wp/MinorityAcademicPerformance062008.pdf.

Schmidt, Peter. 2008. New twists mark the debate over Texas' top 10-percent plan. *The Chronicle of Higher Education*, June 6.

Strayhorn, Carole Keeton. 2005. The impact of the state higher education system on the Texas economy. Report, Texas Comptroller of Public Accounts. http://www.window.state.tx.us/specialrpt/highered05.

Swanson, Christopher B. 2006. High school graduation in Texas. Report, Educational Projects in Education Research Center. http://www.edweek.org/media/texas_eperc.pdf.

Texas Higher Education Coordinating Board (THECB). 2001. Globalizing Texas higher education for the new century. http://www.thecb.state.tx.us/reports/doc/0318.doc.

Texas Higher Education Coordinating Board (THECB). 2005. Participation and success forecast, 2005-2015: Texas institutions of higher education. Report, Division of Planning and Information Resources, THECB, Austin, TX.

Tienda, Marta. 2006. Harnessing diversity in higher education: Lessons from Texas. In *Ford policy forum, 2006: Exploring the economics of higher education*, ed. Maureen Devlin, 7-14. Washington, DC: NACUBO and the Forum for the Future of Higher Education.

Tienda, Marta, and Sunny X. Niu. 2006. Capitalizing on segregation, pretending neutrality: College admissions and the Texas top 10 percent law. *American Law and Economics Review* 8 (2): 312-46.

Tienda, Marta, and Teresa A. Sullivan. 2009. The promise and peril of the Texas uniform admission law. In *The next twenty five years? Affirmative action and higher education in the United States and South Africa*, ed. Martin Hall, Marvin Krislov, and David L. Featherman. Ann Arbor: University of Michigan Press.

Western Interstate Commission for Higher Education (WICHE). 2003. *Knocking at the college door: Projections of high school graduates by state, income, and race/ethnicity, 1988 to 2018*. Boulder, CO: WICHE.

Western Interstate Commission for Higher Education (WICHE). 2008. *Knocking at the college door: Projections of high school graduates by state, income, and race/ethnicity, 1992 to 2022*. Boulder, CO: WICHE.

Wilgoren, Jodi. 1999. New law in Texas preserves racial mix in State's colleges. *New York Times*, November 19.

Policy Transparency and College Enrollment: Did the Texas Top Ten Percent Law Broaden Access to the Public Flagships?

By
MARK C. LONG,
VICTOR SAENZ,
and
MARTA TIENDA

By guaranteeing college admission to all students who graduate in the top 10 percent of their high school class, Texas H.B. 588 replaced an opaque *de facto* practice of admitting nearly all top 10 percent graduates with a transparent *de jure* policy that required public institutions to admit all applicants eligible for the guarantee. The new admission regime sent a clear message to students attending high schools that previously sent few students to the Texas flagships. Using 18 years of administrative data to examine sending patterns, we find a sizeable decrease in the concentration of flagship enrollees originating from select feeder schools and growing shares of enrollees originating from high schools located in rural areas, small towns, and midsize cities, as well as from schools with concentrations of poor and minority students. For new sending schools, we find substantial year-to-year persistence in sending behavior, which increased after the top 10 percent policy was implemented.

Keywords: higher education college enrollment; sending patterns; admission policy

In justifying Texas H.B. 588, the bill's chief architect, the late Irma Rangel, emphasized that public institutions should be available to all Texas residents, irrespective of socioeconomic circumstances, ethnic group membership, or geographic location (Giovanola 2005). Yet, with few exceptions (Montejano 2001; Saenz 2007; University of Texas, Office of Admission Research [UT-OAR] 2008), attention to the socioeconomic and geographic consequences of the law has been limited. Because the Top Ten Percent Law was implemented in response to the judicial ban on affirmative action, most evaluations of its impact have focused on its effectiveness in restoring campus ethno-racial diversity, particularly at the public flagships (see, e.g., Horn and Flores 2003; Kain and O'Brien 2003; Niu, Tienda, and Cortes 2006; Long and Tienda Forthcoming, 2008; Niu and Tienda 2008; Tienda and Niu 2006a).

Both because the law is allegedly race neutral (but see Forest 2002; Tienda and Niu 2006a)

DOI: 10.1177/0002716209348741

and because it grants college access by rewarding academic achievement (class rank), the top 10 percent admission regime was initially applauded as a viable alternative to affirmative action. However, bipartisan support for the law has eroded since its enactment (Hughes and Tresaugue 2007; Monastersky 2007; Tienda and Sullivan 2009). That students eligible for automatic admission were qualified on a *school-specific* basis is a key provision behind growing opposition to the law. Given large economic inequities and racial segregation of Texas public schools, this provision is the linchpin for broadening geographic, socioeconomic, and ethno-racial diversity as Rangel envisioned. Parents of lower-ranked students from high-performing schools perceive that high-achieving students from low-performing schools are gaining access to the public flagships at the expense of their children, and presume their children are being crowded out by less meritorious applicants (Niu and Tienda 2008; Tienda and Niu 2006b).[1] As growing numbers of students from affluent suburban districts that have historically been major feeders to the public flagships are denied admission, calls to repeal the law intensified and the 81st legislature imposed a 75 percent cap on the share of top 10 percent students that UT was required to admit (University of Texas 2008; Root 2009; Jaschik 2009). Because the cap does not go into effect until the 2010-2011 academic year, our analyses are unaffected.

Most academic research about the Top Ten Percent Law shows only modest increases in minority representation at the public flagships (Kain and O'Brien 2003; Forest 2002; Long and Tienda 2008), but there is emergent evidence that the policy changed students' application behavior in ways that depend both on

Mark C. Long is an associate professor of public affairs at the Daniel Evans School at the University of Washington. His research focuses on the effects of affirmative action and alternative college admissions policies on college entry; the effects of college financial aid on household savings; the effects of high school course-taking and school and college quality on test scores, educational attainment, labor market outcomes, family formation, and other behaviors; and the economics of nursing labor markets.

Victor Saenz is an assistant professor in the Department of Educational Administration at the University of Texas at Austin. Previously, Saenz served as research manager for the Cooperative Institutional Research Program (CIRP) at the UCLA Higher Education Research Institute. His research interests include the educational benefits of racial/ethnic diversity on college campuses and transition and retention issues for Hispanic, first-generation, and low-income college students.

Marta Tienda is the Maurice P. During '22 Professor in Demographic Studies and professor of sociology and public affairs at Princeton University. Her current research interests include equity and access to higher education and the causes and consequences of child migration and immigrant integration in new destinations. She is co–principal investigator of the Texas Higher Education Opportunity Project.

NOTE: This research was supported by grants from the Ford, Mellon, and Hewlett Foundations and the NSF (GRANT # SES-0350990). We gratefully acknowledge institutional support from Princeton University's Office of Population Research (NICHD Grant # R24 H0047879). We are grateful to Danielle Fumia for outstanding research assistance and to Dawn Koffman and Milagros Nores for helpful suggestions.

their class rank and type of high school attended (Long and Tienda Forthcoming; Koffman and Tienda 2008). The growth in applications to the University of Texas at Austin (UT) from students who graduated in the top 10 percent of their high school classes increased the shares of the freshman class automatically admitted from 41 to 81 percent between 1997 and 2008 (Schevitz 2008; University of Texas 2008). Concomitantly, high school sending patterns also appear to have changed. Between 1992 and 2002, the number of high schools that sent one or more applicants to UT rose from 678 to 798; at Texas A&M University (TAMU), the comparable increase was from 819 to 925 schools.[2]

These stylized facts provide some evidence that the uniform admission policy broadened geographic access to the two public flagships, a conclusion also consistent with Montejano's (2001) claim that the initial impact of the new admission regime was geographic. Three years after the top 10 percent policy was in place, Montejano observed an emergent sending pattern involving new high schools that previously had sent few if any students to UT. These students hailed from districts that largely served urban minority communities, such as inner-city Houston and poor white communities in northeast and west Texas. Montejano interpreted these incipient trends as evidence that the new admission regime supported one of Rangel's goals of reaching a broader geographic spectrum of the state's residents. More recent data indicate that the expansion of high school campuses that feed UT's enrollment has continued, even while the actual number of enrolled students has remained relatively stable.[3] In 2007, UT admitted students from over 900 different high schools across the state, up from 674 high schools in 1996, the year before the uniform admission regime was implemented (Saenz 2007).[4]

Although these changes seem to imply broadened access, it is also conceivable that the increases simply reflect growth in the total number of high schools in Texas. The state's school-age population has been growing much faster than the national average (Western Interstate Commission for Higher Education [WICHE] 2008), prompting the opening of new high schools. Therefore, claims about expanded access as a result of the Top Ten Percent Law must consider changes in the *shares* of high schools sending students to the public flagships.

Sending a single enrollee is a weak criterion for measuring a high school's "access" to the flagships. Whether growth in the number of high schools represented among UT and TAMU enrollees truly represents broadened access to "all Texas residents," as Rangel envisioned, also depends on the school's application and enrollment rates. Traditionally, the vast majority of high schools sent none or a handful of enrollees to the flagships, while a few high schools sent very large numbers of students. Tienda and Niu (2006b) distinguish between "sending" schools (those that send one or more applicants) and "feeder" schools (the top twenty high schools based on the number of students admitted to UT and to TAMU as of 2000). Because of substantial overlap in the college destinations of their graduates, feeder schools represented only 28 unique secondary campuses out of over 1,500 statewide. In 2000, the 28 feeder schools accounted for about 15 and 23 percent of freshman enrollment at TAMU and UT, respectively. Saenz (2007) reports a similar concentration of feeding patterns to UT. He shows that half of UT's 1996 freshman class came from 59 high schools, but by 2006, half of its enrollment came from 104 high schools. The top feeder schools use strategic resources, such as well-placed alumni networks, strong counseling offices, and well-educated parents, to maintain close relationships with the state's flagship institutions.

These shifts in sending patterns put into context the current controversy about the fairness of the uniform admission law. Specifically, legislators from sparsely settled rural districts allege that the provisions of the law guaranteeing admission to rank-eligible graduates "reserves" slots for them that would not be available otherwise; detractors emphasize that students from rural high schools represent less than 2 percent of total enrollment (see Hughes and Tresaugue 2007; Monastersky 2007). These legislative debates about whether the uniform admission law broadened geographic diversity at the public flagships by changing the sending patterns of applicant and enrollment pools show no signs of abating. UT, in particular, has been at the center of most controversy about the law because it has become saturated with top 10 percent admits, leaving little flexibility for administrators to shape the composition of freshman classes (Paredes 2006; Tienda and Sullivan 2009; University of Texas 2008).

Evaluating competing claims about increased geographic access based on changes in high school sending patterns is crucial for informed policy decisions (University of Texas 2008; Root 2009; Jaschik 2009).[5] Accordingly, we use administrative data from UT and TAMU, the two public flagship institutions, to investigate whether and in what ways the Top Ten Percent Law modified established high school feeder patterns. Specifically, we first ask whether the *share* of high schools sending applicants and enrollees has increased and whether the *concentration* of applicants and enrollees from particular high schools has decreased. Second, we ask to what extent applicant and enrollment sending patterns are (1) more expansive geographically, (2) more diverse along socioeconomic lines, and (3) from more diverse high schools under the top 10 percent admission regime compared with the pre-*Hopwood* period. Third, using a hazard model, we evaluate whether high school campuses continue sending students in subsequent years after becoming a sending school, and how this persistence has changed after the introduction of the Top Ten Percent Law. Our results have important policy implications beyond Texas, because other states (e.g., Michigan) have begun consideration of a percent plan (Fraser 2008) and because many states are seeking alternatives to diversify their student bodies along many dimensions, including geographic.

The first section of this article reviews prior studies about high school feeding patterns and college destinations. It is followed by a section that provides a brief description of the data used. Then, the methodology used to determine the nature and magnitudes of changes in feeding and sending patterns to UT and TAMU is presented followed by an examination of the hazard model results concerning the persistence of sending patterns. The conclusion discusses the policy implications of our empirical results, and stresses the importance of transparency as a key feature of the Top Ten Percent Law.

Background

A vast literature in sociology and economics shows a strong positive association between students' socioeconomic background and postsecondary outcomes, including enrollment persistence and completion. Comparatively fewer studies examine variation in high school characteristics and postsecondary outcomes, but several recent studies based on Texas are noteworthy exceptions. For example, Niu, Tienda, and Cortes (2006) demonstrate that graduates from affluent suburban high schools are more likely, and those from schools with large shares of economically disadvantaged students less likely, to seek admission to selective colleges compared with their statistical counterparts who graduate from typical Texas high schools. These differences in institutional preferences persist among students eligible for automatic admission to any Texas public university of choice. As a partial explanation, Niu, Sullivan, and Tienda (2008) explain that rank-eligible minority students are less likely to know about the provisions of the law than their nonminority counterparts, which results in a potential loss of talented applicants. Furthermore, high schools differ appreciably in their college-going traditions, which is an important context for cultivating postsecondary aspirations (Niu and Tienda 2008).

In addition to individual and family characteristics, claims that the attributes of schools also contribute independently to educational outcomes date back to the controversial 1966 *Coleman Report* (Coleman 1990), which documented huge inequities in the resources available in minority-dominated schools. Although Coleman argued that economically disadvantaged minority students benefited educationally from attending integrated schools and classrooms, he was criticized for minimizing the influence of schools on educational outcomes.[6] His subsequent work comparing students from public and private high schools showed that Catholic schools, although less generously funded than most private schools, fared better on a range of educational metrics than their counterparts who attended better endowed schools (Coleman and Hoffer 1987; Coleman, Hoffer, and Kilgore 1982).

Since Coleman's pioneering work, relatively few researchers have succeeded in detecting "school effects" on educational outcomes, despite formidable methodological and computational innovations. Two recent studies based on Texas are relevant exceptions. Frost (2007), who uses multilevel modeling to examine whether the socioeconomic and ethno-racial mix of Texas high schools is associated with students' expectations to graduate from a four-year college, finds that both school socioeconomic level and achievement composition influence students' college expectations. Niu and Tienda (2008) evaluate variation in college choice sets among a representative sample of Texas high school seniors. They too find that type of high school attended is far more decisive in shaping college choices than students' academic achievement. Both studies highlight the importance of evaluating whether the Top Ten Percent Law increased representation at the public flagships from schools populated by low-income and minority students.

The limited body of research about high school sending patterns indicates that well-developed social networks and access to academic resources are decisive in cultivating high post-secondary aspirations, including admission to the most competitive institutions (Frost 2007). Established alumni loyalties and parents' institutional affiliations further reinforce feeder patterns across generations by bolstering children's college choices based on their parents' legacy status. High school feeder patterns to colleges can embody long-standing regional and community loyalties that have lasting consequences for an institution's socioeconomic and geographic diversity because they can become self-perpetuating. Some scholars (Perna and Titus 2005) show that certain high schools are better at nurturing feeder legacies that can be leveraged effectively for the benefit of future cohorts of graduates, while other scholars (Wolniak and Engberg 2007) find that networks between high schools and colleges can strongly influence students' college aspirations, and hence application and enrollment decisions. Entrenched high school feeder patterns can thus "bound" or limit social influence on the college choice process (McDonough 1997; Niu and Tienda 2008).

Established high school feeder patterns also can privilege students from higher socioeconomic backgrounds in ways that simultaneously disadvantage students from lower socioeconomic and underrepresented populations. Martin, Karabel, and Jaquez (2005) examined admission patterns of high schools with long traditions of sending students to the University of California (UC) system. As appears to be the case in Texas, they find that a small group of high schools accounted for a disproportionate number of students at the premier UC campuses and that these feeder high schools largely enroll affluent white and Asian students. High schools that serve low-income or predominantly minority students send proportionately and numerically fewer applicants and enrollees to the UC campuses. Their findings are consistent with those of Wolniak and Engberg (2007), who argue that higher education institutions should seek to broaden sending networks from districts whose students are underrepresented on their campuses.

Social class barriers to college access, whether real or self-imposed due to poor understanding of entry requirements and financial aid opportunities, also restrict geographic and economic diversity at selective institutions (Bowen, Kurzweil, and Tobin 2005; Koffman and Tienda 2008; Niu, Sullivan, and Tienda 2008). For example, Astin and Oseguera (2004) find that students from the wealthiest families are overrepresented at selective institutions by a 2:1 margin relative to peers from the poorest families and that this socioeconomic enrollment gap has grown over time.

Given the entrenched nature of high school feeder patterns, meaningful changes are likely to evolve slowly. Yet, there is suggestive evidence that the Top Ten Percent Law altered the sending patterns to the public flagships not only by redistributing the applicant pool among public institutions, but also by explicitly allowing rank-eligible students to select their preferred campus (Long and Tienda Forthcoming). Because Texas students are qualified for the admission guarantee on a school-specific basis, eligibility is more transparent than in the UC system, where qualification is determined on a statewide basis using a multidimensional academic index. In Texas, students need only know their class rank, and school administrators and college counselors need to encourage their top performing students to submit applications—a requirement that often is conducted as part of senior English classes. Thus, the transparency of the admission guarantee for rank-eligible graduates potentially can weaken the social networks that perpetuate the entrenched feeder patterns and consequently broaden geographic, as well as socioeconomic diversity.[7] In the remainder of the article, we investigate whether and how high school sending patterns of applicants and enrollees to the public flagships changed in response to a more transparent admission policy.

Data

Administrative data from UT-Austin comes from two sources. One consists of individual-level applicant data for the years 1990 to 2003 that have been compiled by the Texas Higher Education Opportunity Project (THEOP; www.theop .princeton.edu). We have collapsed these data to the high school level and focus on the number of students attending regular Texas public high schools that apply to and enroll at UT during the observation period.[8] The second source is publicly available data from the UT Office of Admissions Research (OAR) for the years 1996 to 2007. These data contain high school–level information on the number of applicants and enrollees for Texas public high schools that sent one or more enrollees to UT. Because these data lack information on the universe of high schools that sent applications to UT, we use this dataset only to evaluate changes in enrollment. For the overlapping years 1996 to 2003, the THEOP and OAR data contain nearly identical numbers of enrollees per high school. Thus, we only use the OAR data for the years 2004 to 2007. The TAMU administrative data is individual-level applicant data for the years 1992 to 2002 compiled by THEOP.

These datasets have been merged with the U.S. Department of Education's Common Core of Data (CCD), which provides information about several high school attributes of interest on a time-varying basis, including location, enrollment, racial composition, and share of students receiving free or reduced-price lunch. The analysis sample excludes private and alternative high schools, as well as public high schools that lacked a senior class, which is the year college applications are submitted.[9] After exclusion restrictions, the analyses universe includes 1,846 unique secondary school campuses for the observation period.

The CCD identifies the "urbanicity" of high schools in eight categories.[10] We reduce this categorization into four types:

- "Urban" = Within the city limits of the principal city of a large urban area (Austin, Corpus Christi, Dallas-Fort Worth-Arlington, El Paso, Houston, or San Antonio).
- "Suburban" = Within the urban area of these large cities, but not within the city limits.
- "Rural" = Rural area outside of a Metropolitan or Micropolitan Statistical Area.
- "Town or Midsize City" = Any area not otherwise captured above, including midsize cities and towns.

FIGURE 1
Over/Underrepresentation among Enrollees to UT, by High School's Region

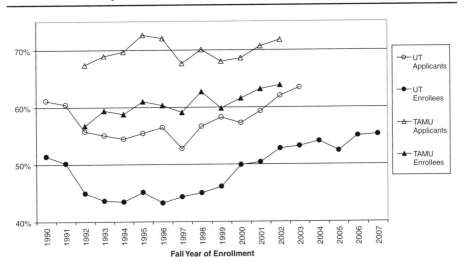

We further re-categorize any high school that lies within a 20-mile radius of the center of the large cities as "Suburban." Thus, "Rural" and "Town or Midsize City" only consists of areas outside those radii and outside of these large cities' Metropolitan Statistical Areas. Given its rapid population growth during the observation period, the "Town or Midsize City" category is of particular interest because it likely includes many new schools.

Findings: Have High Schools' Application and Enrollment Patterns Changed?

As presaged by Montejano's (2001) early assessment, Figure 1 shows that the share of public Texas high schools sending applicants and enrollees to UT increased over time. The share sending at least one applicant to UT remained stable between 1992 and 1996, a period when affirmative action was permitted, but plummeted in 1997, when the *Hopwood* decision banned consideration of race in college admissions. The chilling effect of the *Hopwood* decision on applications proved temporary, however. In 1998, the first year the Top Ten Percent Law was in force, the share of high schools sending applications rebounded and remained slightly above the pre-*Hopwood* level through 2001 and then steadily climbed higher through 2003. Enrollment trends followed suit, and the share of high schools sending enrollees continued to climb through 2007. The share of public high schools sending

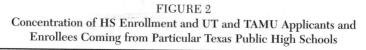

FIGURE 2
Concentration of HS Enrollment and UT and TAMU Applicants and
Enrollees Coming from Particular Texas Public High Schools

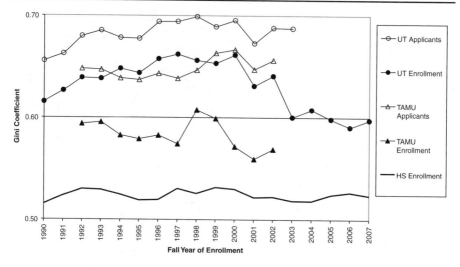

enrollees is 8 to 10 percentage points lower, on average, than the share sending applications, and the annual fluctuations are less pronounced.

While the number of sending schools remained higher at TAMU than at UT throughout the period, there is less evidence of *increased* access at TAMU resulting from the policy change. The share of high schools represented among TAMU applicants rose under affirmative action, sharply fell in 1997 when it was banned, and then modestly increased through 2002 while not returning to its pre-*Hopwood* peak. The share of high schools represented among TAMU enrollees increased gradually, with little evidence of any spike or change in trend after the uniform admission policy was implemented.

Gini indexes permit a more definitive assessment of whether the applicant and enrollee sending patterns became less concentrated.[11] Results shown in Figure 2 reveal clear evidence of a reduced concentration of enrollees at UT under the top 10 percent policy.[12] Between 1990 and 1997, application to and enrollment in UT became more concentrated at particular high schools, which squares with earlier claims that a handful of high schools sent disproportionately large numbers of graduates to UT (Montejano 2001; Tienda and Niu 2006b; Saenz 2007). After the Top Ten Percent Law was enacted, the trend toward increased concentration of applicants from a relatively few high schools halted, evident in the lower enroll-ment Gini ratio between 2000 and 2007. The steep fall in 2002 reflects the rescis-sion of a temporary increase in the size of the undergraduate class in 2000 that proved unsustainable because it exceeded the carrying capacity of the university (Tienda and Sullivan 2009).

For TAMU, which drew upon a larger number of sending high schools before the Top Ten Percent Law, there is no evidence of a reduced concentration of high school feeding patterns. Instead, the College Station campus witnessed an increased concentration of applications after 1997. Furthermore, the high school concentration of enrollment spiked sharply in 1998 and then fell steadily, converging to the 1997 level. Given the shorter observation period for TAMU, it is not clear whether the decline after 1998 is a reaction to the Top Ten Percent Law. The law's apparent disparate impact on high school feeder patterns to UT and TAMU reinforces the prevailing institutional cultures within each campus, namely, that TAMU has had more of a historical challenge in diversifying its student body. We consider this disparate impact further in the conclusion.

It is also worth noting that the Top Ten Percent Law has created a greater admission squeeze on UT than on TAMU (Tienda and Sullivan 2009). The share of admitted UT students who were in the top 10 percent of a Texas high school ranged from 41 percent to 54 percent between 1998 and 2002, surged to 70 percent in 2003, and reached 81 percent in 2008 (Schevitz 2008; University of Texas 2008). At TAMU, the share of admitted students who graduated in the top 10 percent of their Texas high school class rose from 42 percent to 47 percent between 1997 and 2002 (THEOP data) and has since receded back to 44 percent by 2007 (Texas Higher Education Coordinating Board [THECB] 2009). UT's growing enrollment saturation with top 10 percent students, coupled with less concentrated sending patterns, suggests that the characteristics of high schools sending enrollees to UT likely changed. Therefore, we consider whether the sending schools are more diverse in their geographic, ethno-racial composition, and socioeconomic characteristics. In the interest of parsimony, we focus on enrollees, but the patterns are quite similar for applicants.[13]

Findings: Have the Characteristics of Sending Schools Changed?

Representation by high school's urbanicity

Because of unsubstantiated claims that the Top Ten Percent Law has increased access to students from sparsely populated regions of the state, we first consider whether feeding patterns have changed by level of urbanization. To address this question, we compute the shares of UT's enrollees originating from urban, suburban, rural, and other midsize cities or towns as well as the shares of total twelfth-grade enrollment coming from each area. The ratio of each area's share of UT enrollees and its share of twelfth graders indicates over/underrepresentation by level of urbanicity. A ratio greater than one indicates overrepresentation for that category.

Figure 3 shows that both suburban and urban high school students have been overrepresented among enrollees in all years, with particularly high overrepresentation from suburban areas. The degree of suburban overrepresentation

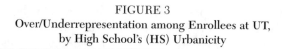

FIGURE 3
Over/Underrepresentation among Enrollees at UT,
by High School's (HS) Urbanicity

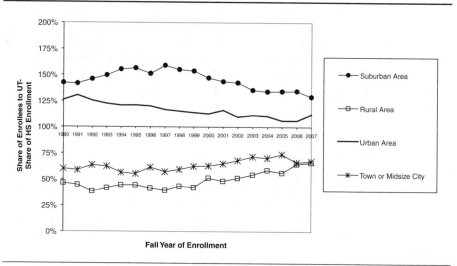

among enrollees increased steadily between 1990 and 1997 and then fell gradually but continuously over the next decade. By contrast, graduates from rural areas and small and midsized cities were severely underrepresented during the first half of the 1990s, and their underrepresentation modestly worsened by 1997. Under the top 10 percent regime, the underrepresentation of these students improved gradually, especially for graduates from rural high schools. By contrast, the *Hopwood* decision and the Top Ten Percent Law appear to have reduced access for students from urban high schools, whose relative overrepresentation declined steadily from 1991 to 2006. Thus, the Top Ten Percent Law appears to have shifted UT's enrollment representation away from suburban students toward those from rural and small and midsized cities, just as proponents (and critics) have suggested.

Representation by high school poverty

To address whether the deconcentration of sending to UT involved greater numbers of students who attended low-income schools with large minority populations, as envisioned by the architects of the Top Ten Percent Law, we replicate these analyses for several high school strata. We first divide high schools by percentage of their students receiving free or reduced-price lunch (FRPL), which serves as a proxy for student poverty. We then average the high school's percentage of FRPL students over the period 1990 to 2006 and classify them into four tiers: less than 20 percent, 20 to 40 percent, 40 to 60 percent, and greater than

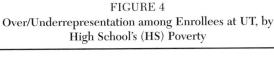

FIGURE 4
Over/Underrepresentation among Enrollees at UT, by
High School's (HS) Poverty

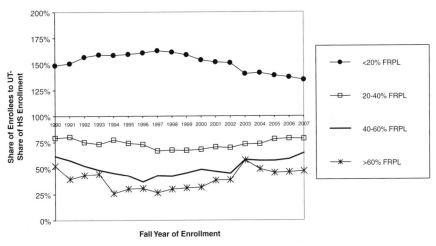

60 percent. We repeat this procedure using each high school's share of students who were black, Hispanic, or Native American.

Figure 4 reports trends in overrepresentation and underrepresentation of high schools according to their share of low-income students. Throughout the observation period, students from low-poverty high schools are overrepresented among UT enrollees and students from high schools where more than 20 percent of their students receive free or reduced-price lunch are underrepresented. Yet after 1998, the overrepresentation of students from low-poverty high schools began a downward trend, as the share of UT's enrollment from the highest-poverty schools inched upward. Most impressive is the growing representation of students from schools where 40 to 60 percent of students receive free or reduced-priced lunches.[14] These trends provide further evidence that the Top Ten Percent Law broadened access to students attending less affluent schools.

Representation by high school minority student share

As demonstrated by many studies, white students enjoyed disproportionate representation at the state's top public flagship. Figure 5 shows that high schools with less than 40 percent of their students from members of underrepresented minority groups (URMs) (i.e., black, Hispanic, or Native American) are overrepresented among enrollees at UT, while students from high schools with more than 60 percent of their student body consisting of URMs were underrepresented throughout the period. Between 1990 and 1997, the high schools with

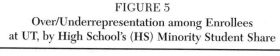

FIGURE 5
Over/Underrepresentation among Enrollees
at UT, by High School's (HS) Minority Student Share

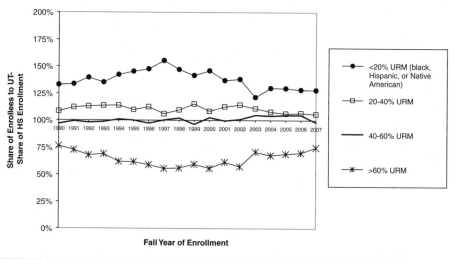

the lowest share of URMs increased their overrepresentation at UT, but this trend reversed after the introduction of the Top Ten Percent Law. By contrast, the highest-URM schools gained representation among freshman enrollees, particularly after 2002. The rapid convergence in representation between high- and low-URM schools in 2003 reflects the sudden contraction in total undergraduate enrollment following the rescission of the temporary expansion in class size between 2000 and 2002 (see Tienda and Sullivan 2009).

Representation by high school region

To further illustrate the geographic dimensions of less concentrated sending patterns, we examine changes in the regional composition of UT enrollment. It is conceivable that the Top Ten Percent Law might alter most of the application and enrollment behavior of students at high schools from regions of Texas that are distant from the capital because these schools likely had less consistent sending patterns to UT. To examine this proposition, we first classify high schools into the 13 regions defined by the Texas Comptroller, and then collapse the categories into five: Alamo (including San Antonio), Capital (including Austin), Gulf Coast (including Houston), Metroplex (including Dallas), and the remaining nine regions combined.[15] Figure 6 displays the degree of representation for these five regions. For simplicity of exposition, we use a different metric for comparisons—namely, the difference (rather than the ratio) between share of UT enrollment and share of twelfth-grade enrollment for each group of high schools.

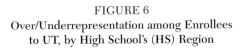

FIGURE 6
Over/Underrepresentation among Enrollees
to UT, by High School's (HS) Region

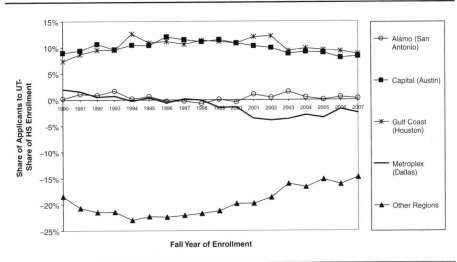

In 1990, the Capital and Gulf Coast regions were greatly overrepresented among UT enrollees, partly reflecting the historical feeding patterns facilitated by geographic proximity to the flagship institution. UT enrollment of students from the Alamo and Metroplex regions was comparable to their share of twelfth-grade enrollment, but the other nine regions were underrepresented at the Austin campus. By contrast, the share of UT enrollment coming from the Capital region in 1990 was three times larger than the region's share of twelfth-grade enrollment.

Overrepresentation of schools from the Capital and Gulf Coast regions rose through 1996, but has since fallen steadily. Representation of schools from the Metroplex region hovered around parity over the period, dipping slightly after 2000 but rebounding after 2003. Graduates from Alamo region schools maintained their UT enrollment share at par throughout the period. As the Capital and Gulf Coast region schools gained representation during the early 1990s, the relative shares of students from the other nine regions fell. Collectively, these regions contributed only 19 percent of UT enrollment in 1996 despite yielding 42 percent of Texas high school graduates that year. The tides turned in 1997 when students from these regions increased their representation on the UT campus.

Collectively, these results consistently show increased access to UT from high schools that traditionally have had low representation, namely those serving students from rural, midsize cities and from regions of the state that previously produced fewer enrollees. Students from schools that serve large numbers of URMs and low-income students also increased their UT enrollment shares after 1997. The widening of access appears to have accelerated in 2003, coincident with the contraction in total enrollment. For the most part, broadened geographic access aligns with the intent of the law and represents a reversal of trends underway before H.B. 588.

Change in share enrolling at UT as a function of high school characteristics

Because low-income and minority-dominated schools are disproportionately located in large urban districts, we evaluate the changes in a regression framework both to assess whether the observed trends are statistically significant and to determine which school characteristics are the most salient when considered jointly. The dependent variable for this analysis is the change in the share of a high school's graduates enrolling at UT between 1996 and 2007. We restrict the analysis to high schools in existence in both years. Given that the prior figures show pre-*Hopwood* trends favoring students from suburban, low-poverty, low-minority, and Capital and Gulf Coast region schools, the regression results are conservative estimates of the effect of the Top Ten Percent Law on high school representation. The results are shown in Table 1.

Column 1 reveals a significant decline in the share of students from urban high schools enrolling at UT (as reflected by the constant). Suburban schools' enrollment rate declined more than that of urban schools, but the difference is statistically trivial. Conversely, the enrollment rates of students from rural schools and schools in small to midsize cities significantly increased relative to urban schools. Column 2 shows a significant enrollment gain of students from high-poverty schools, but an enrollment share loss of students attending schools with larger shares of URMs, controlling for the high school's poverty. Column 3 reveals a significant loss in enrollment share at Capital and Gulf Coast region schools (relative to schools in the Alamo region, as reflected by the constant). UT enrollment rates of high schools in the other nine regions increased relative to the Alamo region, but the difference was not significant.

The final analysis (shown in column 4) combines geographic, socioeconomic, and population composition attributes to determine whether the bivariate associations capture co-variation among school attributes. Most bivariate relationships shown in columns 1 through 3 persist. Notably, controlling for other characteristics of the school, enrollment rates of students in suburban schools rose relative to urban schools. Once again, there is no evidence that schools in the "other" regions gained representation relative to schools in the Alamo, Gulf Coast, Metroplex, and Capital regions, controlling for the schools' different economic, demographic, and urbanicity attributes.

Findings: Persistence of Sending Schools

Given that the Top Ten Percent Law appears to have broadened access to UT for high schools that traditionally sent fewer students there, particularly

TABLE 1
1996 to 2007 Change in the Share of the High School's
Students Enrolling at UT-AUSTIN

	(1)	(2)	(3)	(4)
Urbanicity				
If in suburban area	−0.19%			0.66%*
	[0.37%]			[0.34%]
If in rural area	0.98%***			1.43%***
	[0.31%]			[0.33%]
If in town or midsized city	0.70%**			0.63%*
	[0.32%]			[0.33%]
Percent of students who were black, Hispanic, or Native American		−0.93%*		0.94%
		[0.49%]		[0.58%]
Percent of students receiving free or reduced-price lunch		5.46%***		2.70%***
		[0.95%]		[0.86%]
Region				
If in Capital region (Austin)			−3.37%***	−2.93%***
			[0.80%]	[0.75%]
If in Gulf Coast region (Houston)			−0.81%*	−0.47%
			[0.48%]	[0.42%]
If in Metroplex region (Dallas)			−0.20%	0.21%
			[0.41%]	[0.36%]
If in other region (excl. Alamo, Capital, Gulf Coast, Metroplex)			0.33%	−0.03%
			[0.37%]	[0.34%]
Constant	−0.87%***	−1.59%***	−0.27%	−2.11%***
	[0.28%]	[0.23%]	[0.36%]	[0.49%]
Observations	1,139	1,139	1,139	1,139
R-squared	3.6%	9.4%	12.2%	19.6%

NOTE: Standard errors in brackets.
*$p < 0.1$. **$p < 0.05$. ***$p < 0.01$.

high-poverty and rural schools, we next consider how long a high school remains a sender of enrollees, conditional on becoming a sender. For this analysis, we have constructed a dataset of "sending spells" where each "spell" represents the duration of the time that the school remains a sender of enrollees to UT. We then evaluate the factors that increase or decrease the "hazard" of the sending spell ending (i.e., the hazard that the high school sends zero enrollees to UT in a given year). The hazard analysis poses one major challenge: for a high school that sent enrollees to UT in 1990 (the first year of our data), we lack information about the number of "sending" years before 1990 (i.e., the data is "left-censored"). As a sensitivity analysis, we conduct the hazard analysis both including and excluding the spells that begin in 1990.

FIGURE 7
High Schools' Persistence in Sending Enrollees to UT

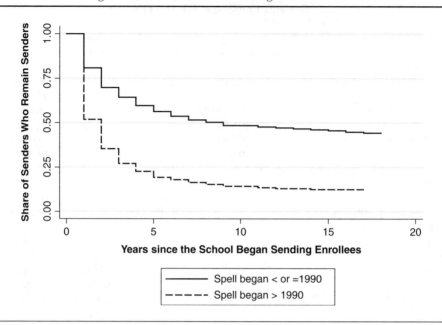

Figure 7, which plots the Kaplan-Meier survival functions, shows that nearly half of all high schools that sent enrollees to UT in 1990 sent enrollees continuously through 2007. The survival sending rate falls more quickly for sending spells that began after 1990, such that within four years less than one-quarter of these spells remain. The higher hazard rate for spells that begin after 1990 is as expected; by definition, these spells originate from high schools that have less attachment to UT as sender schools.

We next estimate the hazard rate as a function of school characteristics using a Weibull distribution.[16] Results reported in Table 2 present coefficients in exponentiated form, where those less than one indicate factors that lower the hazard that the high school's spell will end, and coefficients larger than one identify factors that raise the hazard rate. Columns 1 through 3 contain all spells, including those "beginning" in 1990. The first set of results show that spells end faster for schools with more poor students and schools in the Metroplex region; however, the hazard rate is lower for larger enrollment schools; those located in suburban areas; schools with more black, Hispanic, or Native American students; and those located in the Alamo, Capital, or Gulf Coast regions. Consistent with Figure 7, the hazard rate is lower for spells that "began" in 1990. Estimates in column 2 include a dummy variable for 1997 (the year that the *Hopwood* decision was effective) and another dummy variable that indexes the years after the *Hopwood* decision and the Top Ten Percent Law (H.B. 588) were in force (1998-2003 in

TABLE 2
Survival Analysis: Years that a High School
Remains a Sender of Enrollees to UT-AUSTIN

	All "Spells"			"Spells" Beginning after 1990		
	(1)	(2)	(3)	(4)	(5)	(6)
Number of enrollees in prior year				0.544***	0.544***	0.543***
				[0.015]	[0.015]	[0.015]
12th-grade enrollment	0.096***	0.117***	0.110***	0.183***	0.185***	0.167***
	[0.009]	[0.010]	[0.010]	[0.017]	[0.017]	[0.016]
Located in suburban area	0.549***	0.531***	0.314***	0.507***	0.475***	0.249***
	[0.089]	[0.083]	[0.062]	[0.084]	[0.080]	[0.055]
Located in rural area	0.914	0.935	0.578***	0.877	0.896	0.554***
	[0.152]	[0.149]	[0.114]	[0.147]	[0.153]	[0.121]
Located in town or midsized city	0.918	0.874	0.599***	0.807	0.779	0.516***
	[0.147]	[0.134]	[0.115]	[0.130]	[0.128]	[0.109]
Percent of students who were black, Hispanic, or Native American (URM)	0.797***	0.771***	0.969	0.811***	0.789***	0.938
	[0.061]	[0.056]	[0.091]	[0.061]	[0.060]	[0.094]
Percent of students receiving free- or reduced-price lunch (FRPL)	1.495***	1.519***	1.344***	1.405***	1.447***	1.329***
	[0.114]	[0.111]	[0.125]	[0.105]	[0.111]	[0.132]
Located in Alamo region (San Antonio)	0.666***	0.679***	0.823	0.743*	0.742*	0.883
	[0.103]	[0.100]	[0.150]	[0.114]	[0.116]	[0.172]
Located in Capital region (Austin)	0.213***	0.234***	0.273***	0.333***	0.322***	0.364***
	[0.041]	[0.044]	[0.065]	[0.066]	[0.066]	[0.096]
Located in Gulf Coast region (Houston)	0.702**	0.726**	0.942	0.703**	0.719**	1.024
	[0.101]	[0.100]	[0.163]	[0.101]	[0.105]	[0.190]
Located in Metroplex region (Dallas)	1.281**	1.285**	1.211	1.223*	1.253**	1.177
	[0.137]	[0.132]	[0.166]	[0.129]	[0.135]	[0.174]
Hopwood (1997)		0.824*	0.801**		0.969	0.958
		[0.085]	[0.082]		[0.101]	[0.100]
H.B. 588 Years (1998+)		0.450***	0.215***		0.582***	0.291***
		[0.025]	[0.048]		[0.032]	[0.069]
HB588 * Suburban			2.671***			3.127***
			[0.652]			[0.807]

(continued)

TABLE 2 (continued)

	All "Spells"			"Spells" Beginning after 1990		
	(1)	(2)	(3)	(4)	(5)	(6)
HB588 * Rural			2.389***			2.243***
			[0.563]			[0.555]
HB588 * Other Area			1.971***			2.024***
			[0.463]			[0.499]
HB588 * Percent URM			0.674***			0.745***
			[0.073]			[0.084]
HB588 * Percent FRPL			1.238**			1.150
			[0.133]			[0.129]
HB588 * Alamo			0.662*			0.677*
			[0.140]			[0.149]
HB588 * Capital			0.676			0.734
			[0.196]			[0.224]
HB588 * Gulf Coast			0.631**			0.540***
			[0.131]			[0.116]
HB588 * Metroplex			1.069			1.059
			[0.164]			[0.171]
Spell began in 1990	0.674***	0.387***	0.348***			
	[0.059]	[0.035]	[0.033]			
Constant	0.119***	0.202***	0.292***	0.195***	0.257***	0.363***
	[0.019]	[0.032]	[0.055]	[0.031]	[0.042]	[0.073]
Ln (p)	1.706***	1.777***	1.840***	2.084***	2.161***	2.225***
	[0.037]	[0.037]	[0.038]	[0.040]	[0.040]	[0.041]
Number of spells	2,690	2,690	2,690	2,588	2,588	2,588

NOTE: Standard errors in brackets.
*$p < 0.1$. **$p < 0.05$. ***$p < 0.01$.

our data).[17] These results indicate that the hazard of a sending spell's ending is significantly lower during the H.B. 588 period, which suggests that the Top Ten Percent Law may have strengthened persistence in sending rates. The interaction of the H.B. 588 period dummy with other control variables reveals that the higher persistence in sending patterns largely involves urban, high-minority, and Gulf Coast high schools.

To address left-censoring, columns 4 through 6 repeat these analysis using only spells that began after 1990. The results are virtually unchanged. One advantage of restricting the analysis in this way is that we can incorporate into the analysis the number of students who enrolled at UT from the prior year's graduates for each high school. Even controlling for the high school's twelfth-grade enrollment, the more students from the prior class are represented at UT, the lower the hazard that the high school will send no enrollees in the current year. This result confirms that high schools with a strong feeding history self-perpetuate UT representation by influencing the enrollment behavior of subsequent cohorts of students.

Combined with the finding that the Top Ten Percent Law has reduced the hazard rate (and thereby increased sending persistence), our results suggest that the law's impact on sending patterns could magnify over time as the high school accumulates a sending history. Thus, to some extent, the decreasing concentration of enrollment at UT from particular high schools, which gained momentum beginning in 2003 (five years after the beginning of the Top Ten Percent Law), could partly result from this dynamic cross-cohort relationship.

Conclusion

In this article, we sought to evaluate whether a state-level college admission policy that targets high schools and guarantees admission to a designated percentage of graduates can both weaken entrenched sending patterns and increase geographic and socioeconomic diversity. We find that the number and share of high schools represented among University of Texas applicants and enrollees rose in certain areas after the introduction of the Top Ten Percent Law, reversing a pre-policy trend toward more concentration. It is unclear whether the enrollment and sending patterns have been permanently changed, however. We find no evidence for similar effects at Texas A&M University, the state's first public university, but there are many reasons for this result. First, TAMU drew from a larger number of high schools than UT even before H.B. 588 went into effect. Second, TAMU's sending school patterns may be more entrenched, even if less concentrated, owing to the institution's long-standing presence in non-metropolitan communities (through its Agriculture Extension Service Offices across the state).[18] These long-standing institutional ties may have helped to forge feeder school legacies long ago, whereas UT is just now making inroads in these communities. Third, although situated within a triangle of Interstate highways that link three major cities—Houston, Dallas, and Austin—TAMU's non-metropolitan location (College Station) may be less appealing to students than metropolitan Austin.

Another major finding is that the new policy increased the representation at UT of students from high-poverty schools, those with greater shares of minority students, those located in rural areas as well as small and midsized cities, and schools located in regions that traditionally were underrepresented at UT. Further, we show that the number of consecutive years that high schools sent enrollees to UT increased after the introduction of the Top Ten Percent Law. Thus, schools that become new senders of enrollees to UT are likely to persist in sending enrollees for longer periods, potentially creating a historical legacy that will increase the likelihood of enrollment by future cohorts of students at these new sending schools. Our results suggest there is potential value in strengthening institutional linkages between new sending schools and public universities as a strategy to deepen college-going traditions in the new sending schools—actions that may become even more important in the future if the Top Ten Percent Law is rescinded.

To some extent, our finding that the number of high schools represented among UT's applicant and enrollee pools increased under the top 10 percent regime compared to the pre-*Hopwood* era is somewhat surprising because even before H.B. 588 became law, virtually all applicants who graduated in the top decile of their high school class were admitted to UT (Long and Tienda 2008). Presumably, many seniors who ranked highly in their class failed to apply because of the opaqueness of UT's admissions policy; as is the case at most institutions, students have no way of knowing whether they qualify for admission or the likelihood of being admitted. This opaqueness would be acute for students at high schools with low sending rates to UT—a student at such a high school would not have the experience of seeing their older peers' application results. Thus, the apparent increases in access may be due, in part, to the rendering of an opaque *de facto* policy that admitted nearly all top 10 percent students to a transparent *de jure* policy that clearly stipulated the criteria for automatic admission. Not only did this admission policy change influence the number of admitted and enrolled students to UT, but it also diversified their geographic and socioeconomic origins, which is consistent with Irma Rangel's vision when crafting the law.

The consistency of the law's provisions guaranteeing access to all public universities and the transparency of the uniform merit criterion applied to all Texas public school students differentiate it from the percent plans in California and Florida, which do not guarantee admission to all public universities in the state, as well from all the myriad variants of "full file review" currently used by public and private institutions that are not transparent.

Our results have broad implications for public policies where simplicity and transparency may matter for broadening access to government services or for spotlighting pervasive inequities in other public domains. For example, Currie's (2004) research shows that take-up rates of various programs, such as 401(k) retirement-savings plans and Medicare, rise when participants are automatically enrolled by their employer or through their participation in other social programs such as welfare. Additionally, program complexity and lack of information on the part of potential participants have been shown to lower participation in public programs such as welfare, Medicare, or the State Children's Health Insurance Program (Kleven and Kopczuk 2008; Aizer 2007; Bansak and Raphael 2007), further suggesting that policy transparency (and simplicity) may raise participation rates. Finally, the transparency provided by the No Child Left Behind Act, which requires schools and districts to report separate assessment results for demographic subgroups, has allowed researchers and advocates to document both progress and persistence of achievement gaps between these groups.

Notes

1. For anecdotal evidence, see Rebecca Leung, "Is the 'Top 10' Plan Unfair? Debate over Texas Law That Grants Preference to Certain Students," June 19, 2005, at www.cbsnews.com/stories/2005/06/17/60minutes/main702646.shtml.

2. These estimates are based on tabulations from the THEOP administrative files. Similar patterns obtain for admittee and enrollee pools, except that the absolute numbers are smaller. Over the same period, the number of Texas high schools represented among admittees increased from 635 to 773 at UT and from 787 to 900 at TAMU. Among enrollees at UT, 547 and 679 high schools were represented in 1992 and 2002, respectively. At TAMU, the enrollee pools in 1992 and 2002 represented 690 and 823 schools, respectively. Historically, TAMU has drawn from more rural populations compared with UT partly because of its land grant mission and partly because of its location outside of a major city.

3. A notable exception is the temporary increase in the size of the freshman classes in effect from 2000 to 2002, which was an attempt to offset the growing numbers of applicants eligible for automatic admission.

4. Forest (2002) examines the impact of using geographic criteria to diversify TAMU, but his data are only for 1998, the first year the law took effect, and rely only on Texas Education Agency data, which lack information about actual grades, class rank, or student test scores.

5. For the second consecutive legislative session, in 2007 the Texas Legislature considered and scuttled a bill to cap the number of students granted automatic admission at 50 percent, which is comparable to the share of top 10 percent graduates in 1996, in order to maintain institutional flexibility in shaping their freshmen classes. In 2009, the Texas Legislature voted to permit UT-Austin to cap the share of entering freshmen qualified for automatic admission to 75 percent of the incoming class.

6. Despite polarized scholarly debate about Coleman's research about school inequality, a more balanced interpretation of his findings is that, compared with family socioeconomic background, school attributes exert smaller influences on educational outcomes.

7. As several papers have demonstrated, an admission guarantee does not ensure enrollment for low-income students; hence, knowledge of and receipt of adequate financial aid packages is necessary as well (see Niu, Sullivan, and Tienda 2008).

8. We exclude alternative high schools and private high schools for different reasons. Alternative high schools have very low college sending programs, as many focus on behavioral problems and vocational programs. The CCD data lack information about private schools, therefore we cannot append comparable attributes for our comparisons. Only one private high school is included in the top 28 feeder schools identified by Tienda and Niu (2006b).

9. Not all public high schools include senior classes; some are separated according to class standing, with one notable large school that only includes seniors.

10. The CCD changed their location coding system for the 2006-2007 school year. We base the location code for high schools in this year based on the most recent data from prior years.

11. Gini indexes range from zero to one. A value of zero indicates perfect equality of high schools in terms of their enrollment (or admittees or enrollees). A value of one would indicate that all of the state's enrollment (or admittees or enrollees) are located in a single high school.

12. The UT-Applicant time-series only extends through 2003. Because the OAR data only includes high schools that sent at least one enrollee to UT, it cannot be used to compute Gini indexes for applicants after 2003. For all subsequent analysis beginning with Figure 2, high schools are weighted by their twelfth-grade enrollment.

13. These results are available from the lead author upon request. Because TAMU did not witness appreciable deconcentration in sending patterns or saturation with applicants whose admission was guaranteed, we do not included TAMU in these analyses.

14. We find a greater increase in representation of high poverty schools among enrollees than among applicants (through 2003). One plausible explanation is the efficacy of the Longhorn Opportunity Scholarships in permitting rank-eligible students from schools with historically low representation at UT to enroll. The Longhorn Opportunity program is targeted to urban public schools with high concentrations of low-income students and low college-going traditions (Domina 2007). The program involves targeted outreach to the designated schools, which simultaneously raises awareness of the admission guarantee and the prospects of a tuition subsidy. An additional interpretation is that the top 10 percent plan continued to crowd out students from affluent high schools who did not qualify for automatic admission (Niu and Tienda 2008).

15. http://www.window.state.tx.us/ecodata/regional/regions.html.

16. Because we may have multiple spells from single high schools, we incorporated high school–level shared frailty into the model. The incorporation of this shared frailty is analogous to incorporating a random effect in an analysis of panel data.

17. Although *Hopwood* was abrogated by the 2003 Supreme Court decision, H.B. 588 stipulated that any changes in admission policies could not be implemented for a full year following their becoming law. This means that race-sensitive criteria could not be used until the 2004-2005 admission season. Similarly, the 75 percent cap imposed on automatically admitted students to UT does not go into effect until 2010-2011.

18. The institution's original name was Agricultural and Mechanical College of Texas, which in 1963 was shortened to "Texas A&M," or TAMU. To what extent the "agricultural and mechanical" legacy is tied to its contemporary appeal has not been directly investigated, however.

References

Aizer, Anna. 2007. Public health insurance, program take-up, and child health. *Review of Economics and Statistics* 89 (3): 400-15.

Astin, Alexander W., and Leticia Oseguera. 2004. The declining "equity" of American higher education. *Review of Higher Education* 27 (3): 321-41.

Bansak, Cynthia, and Steven Raphael. 2007. The effects of state policy design features on take-up and crowd-out rates for the State Children's Health Insurance Program. *Journal of Policy Analysis and Management* 26 (1): 149-75.

Bowen, William G., Martin Kurzweil, and Eugene Tobin. 2005. *Equity and excellence in American higher education.* Charlottesville: University of Virginia Press.

Coleman, James S. 1990. A brief summary of the Coleman report. In *Equality and achievement in education,* ed. James S. Coleman, 69-74. Boulder, CO: Westview.

Coleman, James S., and Thomas Hoffer. 1987. *Public and private high schools: The impact of communities.* New York: Basic Books.

Coleman, James S., Thomas Hoffer, and Sally Kilgore. 1982. *High school achievement: Public, Catholic, and private schools compared.* New York: Basic Books.

Currie, Janet. 2004. The take up of social benefits. Working Paper 10488, National Bureau of Economic Research. http://www.nber.org/papers/w10488.pdf.

Domina, Thurston. 2007. Higher education policy as secondary school reform: Texas public high schools after Hopwood. *Educational Evaluation and Policy Analysis* 29:200-17.

Forest, Benjamin. 2002. Hidden segregation? The limits of geographically based affirmative action. *Political Geography* 21 (7): 855-80.

Fraser, Kelly. 2008. State lawmaker wants ten-percent rule: Automatic college admission policy has been implemented in Texas, California, and Florida. *Michigan Daily,* April 14.

Frost, Michelle B. 2007. Texas students' college expectations: Does high school racial composition matter? *Sociology of Education* 80 (1): 43-66.

Giovanola, Anouck. 2005. Irma Rangel. Women's Legal History Project. Palo Alto, CA: Stanford University. http://www.law.stanford.edu/library/womenslegalhistory/papers05/RangelI-Gio (accessed January 28, 2008).

Horn, Catherine L., and Stella M. Flores. 2003. Percent plans in college admissions: A comparative analysis of three states' experiences. The Civil Rights Project at Harvard University. http://www.civilrightsproject .harvard.edu/research/affirmativeaction/tristate.pdf.

Hughes, Polly R., and Matthew Tresaugue. 2007. Small-town GOP behind survival of top 10 percent rule; Republicans from rural cities say law essential for their students. *The Houston Chronicle,* May 30.

Jaschik, Scott. 2009. The 10 percent fight is back. *Inside Higher Education,* January 12.

Kain, John F., and Daniel M. O'Brien. 2003. Hopwood and the top 10 percent law: How they have effected college enrollment decisions of Texas high school graduates. Working Paper 26, Cecil and Ida Green Center for the Study of Science and Society, UT-Dallas. http://www.utdallas.edu/research/ tsp/pdfpapers/paper26.pdf.

Kleven, Henrik J., and Wojciech Kopczuk. 2008. Transfer program complexity and the take up of social benefits. Working Draft. Available from http://www2.warwick.ac.uk/fac/soc/economics/news/forums/ conferences/peuk/complexity2.pdf.

Koffman, Dawn, and Marta Tienda. 2008. Missing in application: The Texas top 10 percent law and campus socioeconomic diversity. Working Paper, Texas Higher Education Opportunity Project, Princeton University. http://theop.princeton.edu/reports/wp/ApplicantSocialClass.pdf.

Long, Mark C., and Marta Tienda. Forthcoming. Changes in Texas universities' applicant pools after the Hopwood decision. *Social Science Research.*

Long, Mark C., and Marta Tienda. 2008. Winners and losers: Changes in Texas university admissions post-Hopwood. *Educational Evaluation and Policy Analysis* 30:255-80.

Martin, Isaac, Jerome Karabel, and Sean W. Jaquez. 2005. High school segregation and access to the University of California. *Educational Policy* 19 (2): 308-30.

McDonough, Patricia M. 1997. *Choosing colleges: How social class and schools structure opportunity.* Albany: State University of New York Press.

Monastersky, Richard. 2007. Texas House rejects changes in top-10-percent plan for admissions. *Chronicle of Higher Education*, June 8.

Montejano, David. 2001. Access to the University of Texas at Austin and the ten percent plan: A three-year assessment. Admissions Brief, Office of Admissions Research, University of Texas at Austin. http://www.utexas.edu/student/admissions/research/montejanopaper.html.

Niu, Sunny X., Teresa A. Sullivan, and Marta Tienda. 2008. Minority talent loss and the Texas top 10 percent law. *Social Science Quarterly* 89 (4): 831-45.

Niu, Sunny X., and Marta Tienda. 2008. Minority student academic performance under the uniform admission law: Evidence from the University of Texas at Austin. Working Paper, Texas Higher Education Opportunity Project, Princeton University. http://theop.princeton.edu/reports/wp/MinorityAcademicPerformance062008.pdf.

Niu, Sunny X., Marta Tienda, and Kalena Cortes. 2006. College selectivity and the Texas top 10 percent law. *Economics of Education Review* 25 (3): 259-72.

Paredes, Raymund A. 2006. Testimony on the top ten percent law by Raymund A. Paredes, Commissioner on Higher Education. Hearing of the Texas State Senate Subcommittee on Higher Education. http://www.thecb.state.tx.us/commissioner/testimonytop10.pdf.

Perna, Laura, and Marvin Titus. 2005. The relationship between parental involvement as social capital and college enrollment: An examination of racial/ethnic group differences. *Journal of Higher Education* 76 (5): 485-518.

Root, Jay. 2009. UT pushes lawmakers to modify "Top 10 percent rule." *Houston Chronicle*, January 7.

Saenz, Victor. 2007. Democratization of access: How the top ten percent law has affected the geographic and socio-economic diversity of Texas high school feeders to UT-Austin. Paper presented at the Civil Rights Project Research Conference, Austin, TX, October.

Schevitz, Tanya. 2008. Texas Chancellor selected to lead UC. *San Francisco Chronicle*, March 21.

Texas Higher Education Coordinating Board (THECB). 2009. First-time undergraduate applicant, acceptance, and enrollment information for summer/fall 2007. Report, Texas Higher Education Coordinating Board. http://www.txhighereddata.org/interactive/AppAccEnr.cfm.

Tienda, Marta, and Sunny X. Niu. 2006a. Capitalizing on segregation, pretending neutrality: College admissions and the Texas top 10 percent law. *American Law and Economics Review* 8 (2): 312-46.

Tienda, Marta, and Sunny X. Niu. 2006b. Flagships, feeders, and the Texas top 10 percent law: a test of the "brain drain" hypothesis. *Journal of Higher Education* 77 (4): 712-39.

Tienda, Marta, and Teresa A. Sullivan. 2009. The promise and peril of the Texas uniform admission law. In *The next twenty five years? Affirmative action and higher education in the United States and South Africa*, ed. Martin Hall, Marvin Krislov, and David L. Featherman. Ann Arbor: University of Michigan Press.

University of Texas, Office of Admission Research (UT-OAR). 2008. An investigation into rural high school representation in entering freshman classes at the University of Texas at Austin, Summer/Fall Classes of 1996-2007. Report, Office of Admission Research, University of Texas. http://www.utexas.edu/student/admissions/research/RuralSchoolStudy-96-07.pdf.

University of Texas, Office of President. 2008. The top 10 percent law and its impact on the University of Texas at Austin. Report on the Top 10 percent Law, University of Texas.

Western Interstate Commission for Higher Education (WICHE). 2008. *Knocking at the college door: Projections of high school graduates by state, income, and race/ethnicity, 1992 to 2022.* Boulder, CO: WICHE.

Wolniak, Gregory C., and Mark E. Engberg. 2007. The effects of high school feeder networks on college enrollment. *Review of Higher Education* 31 (1): 27-53.

PART THREE

College Performance: Major Choices

Race and Gender Differences in College Major Choice

By
LISA DICKSON

College major choice varies substantially by gender, race, and ethnicity among college graduates. This study investigates whether these differences are present at the start of the college career and whether they can be explained by variation in academic preparation. It estimates a multinomial logit to evaluate whether students of similar academic backgrounds make similar college major choices at the start of their college career. The results demonstrate that significant differences by gender, race, and ethnicity persist in initial college major choice even after controlling for the Scholastic Aptitude Test (SAT) score of the student and the high school class rank of the student. Gender differences in major choice are much larger than racial and ethnic disparities. Furthermore, women are significantly more likely to switch away from an initial major in engineering than are white men.

Keywords: higher education; college majors; gender differences; minority students

Several studies have documented the relatively low representation of women, blacks, and Hispanics with degrees in the sciences and engineering (S&E).[1] Because choice of college major affects occupational choice, earnings, and the probability of pursuing advanced degrees, it is important to understand why it varies by race and gender.[2] This study uses administrative data from three Texas public

Lisa Dickson is an assistant professor of economics at the University of Maryland Baltimore County. Her research interests include labor economics and economics of education, with a specific focus on affirmative action policy and college accessibility. She has recently completed research about the effects of affirmative action policy on lowering the percentage of minority students applying to college and is currently investigating the economic returns to different college majors.

NOTE: The author thanks Marta Tienda for access to the Texas Higher Education Opportunity Project administrative dataset and for research support. The author also thanks Mark Long, Marta Tienda, Jason Fletcher, Brett Wendling, and an anonymous referee for helpful comments.

DOI: 10.1177/0002716209348747

universities to analyze the dynamics of college major choice and to determine why it varies by race and gender.

Students' college major choice is a dynamic process—it may change between their first semester of study and graduation. Previous economic studies on college major choice have focused on students' majors at the time of graduation.[3] Unlike previous studies, this study considers students' initial college major, the probability of switching majors, and the final major choice. An analysis of the dynamics of major choice is important to inform public policy as to where in the academic pipeline women, blacks, and Hispanics are deterred from pursuing majors in S&E.

College major choice varies by race and gender for at least four reasons. First, students may differ in their preparation for college work, and this may affect their initial major choice. For example, students may only choose to pursue a major in engineering if they have strong math skills. If females and nonwhites have lower math skills, they might be less likely to choose engineering as a major during their first semester. Second, students may differ in their propensity to switch majors during college. Women, blacks, and Hispanics who begin college intending to seek an engineering degree may be more likely to switch from these majors compared with whites. Third, the monetary reward for each major may vary by the characteristics of the student. Brown and Corcoran (1997) and Joy (2000) find unequal returns for the same major between men and women. Differences in returns could explain unequal investments in specific fields of study by race and gender. Finally, preferences may vary by gender, race, or ethnicity.

Accordingly, this study seeks to answer why college majors vary by gender, race, and ethnicity. Because academic preparation could potentially affect initial major choice, I estimate a multinomial logit regression to test whether race and gender affect college major choice after controlling for academic preparation. Differences in major choice observed at the end of the college career could also be due to differences in the probability of switching majors; therefore, I test whether women and nonwhites are more likely to switch majors. Finally, I estimate a multinomial logit model to ascertain whether final major choice varies by race and gender after controlling for initial major choice and academic background.

The dynamics of college major choice has implications for public and institution-specific policy. If the low number of graduates in S&E fields results because too few students proposed the major at the start of their college career, then perhaps public policies should be geared towards recruiting students to these majors at the K-12 level. If the paucity of students in S&E results because students change their major away from these fields during college, then universities may need to design programs to retain and mentor students who aspire to careers in these fields.

Data

I use administrative data from three public universities in Texas, which provide information on enrollees and their fields of study for up to ten years, depending on institution: the University of Texas at Austin (1991-2004); the University of Texas,

Pan American (1995-2005); and the University of Texas at San Antonio (1990-2004). The analysis sample is restricted to individuals who report a college major in both their first and last semesters. I also excluded observations with incomplete data on ethnicity, gender, an admissions test score, and a high school class rank. This study uses data for all of the available years for these three universities.

The administrative data identifies 17 different divisions, which were aggregated to 6 different major categories in this study, as summarized below.

Natural and physical sciences
   Agriculture, natural sciences, physical sciences, and health sciences
Business
Social science
Engineering and computer science
Humanities and other majors
   Architecture, education, fine arts, general studies, humanities, individualized/
      interdisciplinary, military sciences, other, social work, technical/
      vocational
Undecided

Empirical analyses are based on these six broad fields of study, which I call majors for parsimony of exposition.

Descriptive Statistics

Table 1 reports characteristics for all students enrolled at the three universities in their first semester. About 29 percent of students arrive on campus with no clear idea of their intended field of study. Of those reporting on major, the most popular major is the natural and physical sciences (18 percent); the least popular is humanities and other majors (12 percent). Students' characteristics differ appreciably according to intended major. Engineering and computer science majors report higher test scores and higher class ranks than students who choose other majors. Engineering and computer science majors average a Scholastic Aptitude Test (SAT) score of 1,194, and nearly half (48 percent) graduated in the top decile of their high school class. By contrast, only about one-quarter of students with an unspecified major graduated in the top decile of their high school class.

Table 1 also reports the fraction of students in each major category at the beginning of their college career who belong to each demographic group. White males make up 26 percent of the total sample but 42 percent of engineering and computer science majors. Hispanic females are underrepresented in these majors; they constitute 15 percent of the study population but only 5 percent of first-semester freshmen intending to pursue an engineering and computer science major.

Table 2 illustrates which demographic groups are more or less likely to choose particular majors. Approximately one in four male students choose a major in engineering or computer science, but only 6 percent of women do so. Instead,

TABLE 1

Summary Statistics for Students in their First Semester by Initial Major Choice (in Percentages)

Characteristics	Total Sample	Natural and Physical Sciences	Business	Social Sciences	Engineering and Computer Science	Humanities and Other Majors	Undecided
Demographic characteristics							
White male	26.2	17.0	28.3	20.8	42.1	19.1	27.2
Black male	1.7	1.2	1.7	1.2	2.6	0.8	2.0
Hispanic male	14.1	15.2	13.5	12.7	20.2	13.4	11.2
Asian male	6.2	6.4	5.0	2.0	14.2	2.6	5.0
Other male	0.7	0.7	0.7	0.5	1.2	0.6	0.5
White female	26.8	24.3	26.2	33.3	9.0	35.9	32.1
Black female	2.2	2.8	2.3	3.0	1.1	1.7	2.3
Hispanic female	15.4	23.3	14.6	21.2	5.1	19.8	12.3
Asian female	5.9	7.8	6.8	4.0	4.0	5.0	6.5
Other female	0.8	1.3	0.8	1.0	0.4	1.0	0.6
Academic preparation							
Test score (SAT/ACT)	1,108	1,066	1,115	1,090	1,194	1,113	1,087
Top decile in high school	36.8	37.4	49.8	34.2	48.4	38.5	24.5
Second decile in high school	21.9	22.2	19.0	22.9	22.8	20.9	22.3
University attended							
University of Texas (UT)–Austin	69.9	53.8	66.6	61.5	80.0	62.8	82.4
UT–Pan American	11.9	19.2	9.5	12.7	8.5	18.9	7.2
UT–San Antonio	18.1	27.0	23.8	25.8	11.5	18.3	10.4
Sample size (percentage)	100	17.8	12.9	12.7	16.2	11.7	28.7
Sample size (n)	127,330	22,698	16,374	16,209	20,591	14,953	36,505

NOTE: The admissions test score presented in this table is the average SAT score. For students who reported an ACT score, their score was converted to the SAT scale.

TABLE 2
Initial Major Choices by Demographic Group (in Percentages)

	Natural and Physical Sciences	Business	Social Sciences	Engineering and Computer Science	Humanities and Other Majors	Undecided	Sample Size
All students							
Male	14.8	13.0	9.7	26.6	8.8	27.1	62,201
Female	20.7	12.7	15.6	6.2	14.6	30.1	65,129
Male students							
White	11.6	14.0	10.1	26.0	8.6	29.8	33,311
Black	13.0	13.1	8.9	25.4	5.8	33.9	2,136
Hispanic	19.2	12.3	11.4	23.2	11.2	22.7	17,973
Asian	18.4	10.5	4.1	37.1	4.8	25.0	7,887
Other[a]	19.2	12.4	9.5	28.4	10.2	20.3	894
Female students							
White	16.2	12.6	15.8	5.5	15.7	34.3	34,134
Black	22.0	13.3	17.4	8.1	9.1	30.1	2,834
Hispanic	26.9	12.2	17.5	5.4	15.1	22.8	19,610
Asian	23.7	14.8	9.1	11.0	9.9	31.7	7,528
Other[a]	28.5	12.1	16.4	7.5	14.9	20.6	1,023

NOTE: The sample is for all individuals who are enrolled at the University of Texas (UT)–Austin, UT–San Antonio, or UT–Pan American. The data in this table come from students for their first semester enrolled.
a. Includes international students.

21 percent of women choose a major in the natural and physical sciences, compared with 15 percent of men. A higher proportion of women are concentrated in the lower-paying social sciences and humanities majors.[4]

Major choice also varies by race and ethnicity. White males are actually the least likely of all groups to choose a major in the natural and physical sciences. For engineering and computer science, slightly smaller shares of black and Hispanic males choose this field of study compared with white males. In their freshman year, Asian and other (including foreign students, American Indians, and unspecified ethnicities) males are much more likely than white males to identify a major in engineering and computer science. More than one-third (37 percent) of Asian males intend to major in engineering or computer science fields compared to 26 percent of white males. Among male students, African Americans are the most likely to be undecided at the start of their academic career.

Women's major preferences at college entry parallel those of men in many ways. Among female students, whites are the least likely to indicate their intention to major in the natural and physical sciences. However, Asian females, similar to their male counterparts, are more likely to choose a major in engineering and computer science than other women, with 11 percent opting for these fields. Black women are more likely to identify engineering or computer science as their first major than white, Hispanic, and other women. Finally, black and Hispanic women are more likely to declare a social science major than are white females, who, in turn, are more likely to be undecided than any other demographic group.

That students vary in their level of academic preparation may partly explain the observed differences in major choice. Several studies based on these data show that the average SAT score and the fractions of students who graduated in the top two deciles of their high school class vary by race, ethnicity, and gender (see Fletcher and Tienda 2009 [this volume]; Conger and Long 2009 [this volume]). For the three universities examined, the highest average SAT score corresponds to Asians (at 1,202 points), who also have the highest share of top-decile graduates (51 percent). In our study population, Hispanic students earn the lowest average SAT score (957) and the lowest proportion of top 10 percent graduates (27 percent). Black students report an average SAT score of 1,016, with one-third of enrollees graduating in the top decile of their high school class.

In general, males average higher test scores but a lower class rank for each race and ethnic category. The obverse holds for women, whose SAT test score averages 54 points below that of male students (1,135). Two in five women graduated in the top 10 percent of their high school class, but only one-third of all male students did so. For both males and females, Asians maintain the highest SAT score and the largest proportion of top-10-percent rank graduates. The largest gender performance gap corresponds to black students. Only 24 percent of black males graduated in the top 10 percent of their high school class, but 40 percent of black females did so.[5]

Because enrolled students who have not yet graduated can change their field of study, the analysis of switching majors focuses only on college graduates.

Limiting the analyses to college graduates reduces the total sample by 61 percent, which includes both dropouts and enrolled students (right censored). Specifically, the sample of graduates is whiter and more female than the population of freshmen enrollees. Hispanic males and females composed 14 and 15 percent of the enrollee population, respectively, but only 7 percent of graduates were Hispanic men and 9 percent Hispanic women. Furthermore, owing to higher attrition rates at the UT–San Antonio and UT–Pan American campuses, UT-Austin students comprise a higher share of the graduate population. Almost 70 percent of the enrollee sample attended UT-Austin, but they represented almost 92 percent of all graduates from these three universities.[6]

Table 3 presents the cross-classification of initial field of study and final major. For the entire sample of individuals, approximately 29 percent of graduates changed majors at least once, including students who switched their major from undecided to a specified major. The most popular final major for college graduates is the social sciences, with almost 31 percent of the population. Sorting the college graduate sample by the first major chosen permits analysis of switching propensities and the question of whether students from a particular major are more likely to change. Natural and physical sciences as well as engineering and computer science witnessed the highest attrition rates (other than undecided). More than 40 percent of students who intended to major in engineering and computer science left the field. This outflow compares with 38 percent of students from the natural and physical sciences and 19 percent from business majors.

As a result of switching fields of study, the gender and ethno-racial composition of the six major fields of study changes, but some initial patterns persist. Consistent with national trends, Asian males are overrepresented among graduates with degrees in science and engineering. Asian males comprise only 7 percent of college graduates at these three campuses but 20 percent of engineering and computer science graduates, and they receive 12 percent of natural and physical science degrees. White males are also overrepresented among engineering and computer science graduates, but white females are underrepresented relative to their share of all graduates. Black male college graduates appear to be rather evenly distributed across the different major categories. However, black females are overrepresented among the natural and physical science and the social science graduates relative to their share of all graduates, and they are underrepresented among business, engineering, and computer science majors.

Finally, Hispanic males are overrepresented in engineering and computer science and underrepresented in humanities and other majors, but the opposite obtains for Hispanic women graduates. Transitions into each major category reveal that very few students transition into engineering and computer science. More than 80 percent of students who graduated with these degrees began in the major. Almost half of the students who graduated with a degree in social science were originally undecided (43 percent). About one-quarter of natural and physical sciences graduates were undecided at the start of their college careers.

TABLE 3

Characteristics of College Graduates According to Initial Major Choice (Proportions)

		Initial Major Choice					
Variable	Total Sample	Natural and Physical Sciences	Business	Social Sciences	Engineering and Computer Science	Humanities and Other Majors	Undecided
Switched major	.289	.384	.194	.175	.421	.278	.904
Final major choice							
Natural and physical sciences	.169	**.616**	.021	.027	.173	.034	.187
Business	.200	.047	**.806**	.046	.048	.102	.072
Social sciences	.307	.184	.087	**.825**	.130	.128	.432
Engineering and computer science	.121	.034	.022	.004	**.579**	.014	.016
Humanities and other majors	.199	.118	.063	.097	.067	**.722**	.197
Undecided	.004	.002	.001	.001	.004	.001	**.096**
Sample size	49,159	9,548	9,259	12,254	9,028	8,634	375

NOTE: These statistics are for all students who graduated from one of the three universities. The admissions test score presented in this table is the average SAT score. For students who reported an ACT score, their score was converted to the SAT scale. The numbers in bold reflect the fraction of students who started with a major in a particular field and ended with a major in the same field. If all students remained in their initial field of study then the numbers on the diagonal in bold would be equal to one. The fact that the numbers are less than one suggest that there is attrition from the majors and that students who initially started with a major in a particular subject change their major while in college.

Empirical Methodology

Although large differences exist by gender and race in college major choice, there are also large differences across groups in test scores and academic preparation. The methodology employed in this study seeks to isolate the influence of race and gender in both initial field of study and in switching toward another field. Several studies have demonstrated that the choice of college major is related to students' aptitude scores in math. All but one (Arcidiacono 2004) of these studies relate the aptitude scores to the observed final choice of college major rather than the initial major students chose at the start of their academic career. I model for all enrollees the initial choice major; transitions out of the field; and, for graduates, the final field of study.

I first estimate the relationship between the students' major choice and their academic background using a multinomial logit (see Turner and Bowen 1999). The model of initial major choice is as follows:

$$\Pr(M_i = j) = \frac{e^{\beta'_j x_i}}{\sum_{k=0}^{5} e^{\beta'_k x_i}} \text{ for } j = 0, 1, 2, 3, 4, 5.$$

The M in the equation stands for the major choice of the student. The major can take on one of six values, which are $0 =$ natural and physical sciences, $1 =$ business, $2 =$ social sciences, $3 =$ engineering and computer science, $4 =$ humanities and other majors, and $5 =$ undecided. The initial choice of college major is specified as a function of matrix X, including the student's test scores, class rank, race, ethnicity, gender, as well as year and university identifiers. Students' test scores and class rank reflect ability and eagerness to learn. Race, ethnicity, and gender may influence college major choice independently of academic preparation. Because college major choice may change over time, year identifiers are included in the model. In addition, university fixed effects are included in the model because university-specific attributes may determine whether a student majors in a particular subject.

Upon arrival in college, students acquire new information about their ability and major options. This new information may lead to changes in intended field of study. To determine whether minorities and women are more likely to change their major than are white males, a logit is estimated for students who have graduated from college:

$$\Pr(Change = 1) = \Lambda(\beta'x),$$

where the dependent variable is equal to 1 when the student switches major. This model is estimated for each major separately. The X variables included in the model are gender, race, ethnicity, test scores, year indicators, and university identifiers. Because the logit is only estimated for college graduates, the results are conditional upon college graduation.

The final empirical model relates the graduation college major to students' academic background, using the following specification:

$$\Pr(M_i = j) = \frac{e^{\beta'_j x_i}}{\sum_{k=0}^{5} e^{\beta'_k x_i}} \text{ for } j = 0, 1, 2, 3, 4, 5,$$

where the X matrix includes test scores, class rank, race, ethnicity, gender, year identifiers, university fixed effects, and the initial choice of college major for the graduates.

Results

As expected, academic preparation, race, and gender are associated with initial choices of major. Table 4 shows the average marginal effects from estimating the multinomial logit regression on initial major choice.[7] The largest estimate is the 16 percentage point decrease in the probability of choosing engineering and computer science for white females. Similarly large estimates obtain for minority women. To appreciate the magnitude of these estimates, a standard deviation increase in test scores (200 points) increases the probability of choosing engineering and computer science by 6 percentage points. Thus, the gender effect is almost three times the size of a standard deviation increase in standardized test scores. Sample means revealed about a 20 percentage point gap between white women and white men in their tendencies to choose engineering and computer science as a major. Multivariate analysis allows comparisons of differences between white men and women after controlling for test scores, high school class rank, and fixed effects for university attended and year of first enrollment. Thereafter, a large portion of the gender gap in choice of engineering and computer science majors remains unexplained; a gap of 16 percentage points remains.[8]

All women are significantly more likely to major in the natural and physical sciences than are white males, even among those with similar test scores and class rank. The magnitude of the sex gap in these majors varies according to race and ethnicity, however. The effect is largest for Asian females, with a .069 higher probability, and smallest for white females, with a .017 higher probability of majoring in natural and physical sciences than their male counterparts. Hispanic, Asian, and other males are also more likely to choose the natural and physical sciences compared with white males. Specifically, Hispanic males are .013 more likely and Asian males .057 more likely to choose natural and physical sciences. Individuals with a higher test score and a higher class rank are more likely than less well-prepared students to choose a major in the natural and physical sciences.

TABLE 4
Determinants of College Major Choice in the First Semester

	Natural and Physical Sciences	Business	Engineering and Computer Science	Humanities and Other Majors	Undecided
White female	.017°°°	−.016°°°	−.163°°°	.052°°°	.063°°°
	(.002)	(.002)	(.003)	(.002)	(.004)
Black female	.063°°°	.001	−.106°°°	.034°°°	−.046°°°
	(.006)	(.005)	(.010)	(.004)	(.012)
Hispanic female	.050°°°	−.009°°°	−.141°°°	.049°°°	−.009
	(.003)	(.003)	(.005)	(.002)	(.006)
Asian female	.069°°°	−.001	−.140°°°	.017°°°	.068°°°
	(.004)	(.003)	(.005)	(.003)	(.007)
Other female	.058°°°	−.001	−.135°°°	.039°°°	−.011
	(.009)	(.009)	(.017)	(.006)	(.021)
Black male	.007	.000	.082°°°	−.007	−.076°°°
	(.005)	(.006)	(.008)	(.006)	(.013)
Hispanic male	.013°°°	−.014°°°	.062°°°	.013°°°	−.082°°°
	(.002)	(.003)	(.004)	(.002)	(.006)
Asian male	.057°°°	−.014°°°	.074°°°	−.026°°°	−.026°°°
	(.004)	(.003)	(.004)	(.003)	(.008)
Other male	.015°°	−.002	.078°°°	.001°°°	−.089°°°
	(.007)	(.009)	(.012)	(.007)	(.021)
Test score (SAT/ACT)	.004°°°	.0004	.030°°°	.020°°°	−.062°°°
divided by 100	(.001)	(.0006)	(.0007)	(.0006)	(.001)
Top decile	.036°°°	.118°°°	.123°°°	−.0002	−.268°°°
	(.002)	(.003)	(.004)	(.002)	(.003)
Second decile	.032°°°	.041°°°	.088°°°	.003°°	−.174°°°
	(.002)	(.003)	(.004)	(.002)	(.004)
University of Texas	.129°°°	.090°°°	.159°°°	.114°°°	−.544°°°
(UT)–Pan American	(.005)	(.003)	(.006)	(.002)	(.008)
UT–San Antonio	.131°°°	.139°°°	.089°°°	.068°°°	−.487°°°
	(.004)	(.003)	(.005)	(.002)	(.006)

NOTE: The numbers presented in the table are the average marginal effects for choosing each major relative to choosing a major in the social sciences at these universities after estimating a multinomial logit model. The average marginal effects are calculated using the margeff command in STATA. Year indicators are included in the regression.
°°Significant at 5 percent. °°°Significant at 1 percent.

Top-decile students are 3.6 percentage points more likely to choose the natural and physical sciences than the social sciences.

White females, both Hispanic men and women, and Asian males are significantly less likely to choose a business major than are white males. Although statistically significant, the point estimates are small in magnitude—implying approximately a 1 percentage point lower likelihood in choosing a business major. Class rank also influences pursuit of a major in business, with students ranked in the top decile approximately 12 percentage points more likely than lower-ranked students to choose a major in business than a major in the social sciences. Students ranked in the second decile are approximately 4 percentage points more likely to choose a major in business than a major in the social sciences relative to lower-ranked classmates.

Women are more likely to declare a major in the humanities and other majors relative to the social sciences at the beginning of their college career. White and Hispanic females are approximately .05 more likely and Asian females about .017 more likely to choose a humanities major than white males. Hispanic males also are slightly more likely to choose a major in the humanities compared with white males, but Asian males are slightly less likely to elect a humanities major than white males.

Students with higher test scores and higher class ranks are significantly less likely to be undecided at the start of their college careers compared with less well-prepared classmates. Black males, as well as black females and Hispanic, Asian, and other males are significantly less likely than white males to begin their college careers with no clear major preference. White and Asian females are significantly more likely than white men to be undecided at the beginning of their college career.

To investigate whether there are differences in the relative probabilities of switching majors, logit regressions are estimated separately for each major choice. Table 5 reports the average marginal effects of covariates on the probability of switching majors for college graduates by initial field of study. The likelihood of switching fields of study differs by demographic group, but these differences also depend on the major.

In accordance with descriptive results, the largest switching probabilities correspond to students who had originally proposed a major in engineering and computer science. White women are almost 19 percentage points more likely than white men to switch majors. Compared with white male grads, black women are 17 percentage points less likely to switch majors; Hispanic and Asian women are 19 and 15 percentage points, respectively, less likely to do so. Not only are equally qualified women less likely to declare a major in engineering and computer science (Table 4), but they are also significantly more likely to switch away from a major in that field (Table 5). Hispanic male graduates are significantly more likely to switch away from engineering and computer science than are white males, although the magnitude of the effect is much smaller than it is for women (.05). Asian male graduates are 3 percentage points less likely to switch out of engineering and computer science than are white males.

For the remaining majors, significant race and ethnic differences in the probability of switching majors exist, but the point estimates are smaller than for engineering and computer science majors. In the natural and physical sciences, white females (.03) and Hispanic females (.07) are significantly more likely to switch than white males. Black males are actually ten percentage points less likely to switch away from a major in the natural and physical sciences than are white males. Notably, white Hispanic graduates who begin college intending to major

TABLE 5
Determinants of Switching Majors: College Graduates

	Natural and Physical Sciences	Business	Social Sciences	Engineering and Computer Science	Humanities and Other Majors
White female	.030°°	.054°°°	.031°°°	.187°°°	−.049°°°
	(.015)	(.011)	(.008)	(.017)	(.011)
Black female	.025	.092°°°	.023	.172°°°	−.002
	(.035)	(.033)	(.021)	(.047)	(.040)
Hispanic female	.072°°°	.043°°°	.040°°°	.186°°°	−.074°°°
	(.021)	(.017)	(.013)	(.029)	(.018)
Asian female	−.015	−.030°°	.080°°°	.150°°°	.077°°°
	(.020)	(.013)	(.017)	(.023)	(.023)
Other female	.017	.025	.004	.130	−.044
	(.067)	(.057)	(.034)	(.103)	(.065)
Black male	−.101°	.053	.029	.049	−.036
	(.056)	(.042)	(.034)	(.040)	(.060)
Hispanic male	−.024	.008	.007	.047°°°	.025
	(.024)	(.016)	(.013)	(.019)	(.025)
Asian male	−.014	−.015	.066°°°	−.034°°	.137°°°
	(.021)	(.016)	(.023)	(.015)	(.034)
Other male	−.117	−.018	.101	−.036	.010
	(.098)	(.058)	(.066)	(.066)	(.097)
Test score (SAT/ACT) divided by 100	−.018°°°	−.003	.012°°°	−.018°°°	.030°°°
	(.004)	(.004)	(.004)	(.005)	(.006)
Top decile	−.122°°°	−.047°°°	.029°°°	−.051°°°	.043°°°
	(.013)	(.007)	(.008)	(.014)	(.015)
Second decile	−.055°°°	−.034°°°	.017°°	−.038°°	.018
	(.015)	(.009)	(.008)	(.016)	(.015)
University of Texas (UT)–Pan American	.211°°°	.350°°°	.443°°°	.136°°°	.297°°°
	(.027)	(.049)	(.040)	(.052)	(.035)
UT–San Antonio	.023	.151°°°	.083°°°	−.050	.098°°°
	(.022)	(.025)	(.020)	(.033)	(.029)

NOTE: The numbers presented in the table are the average marginal effects for switching away from each major after estimating a logit regression. The average marginal effects are calculated using the margeff command in STATA. Year indicators are included in the regression.
°Significant at 10 percent. °°Significant at 5 percent. °°°Significant at 1 percent.

in humanities are significantly less likely to switch away from this relatively low-paying field. Asian males and females are more likely to switch out of the humanities and other majors than are white males.

Graduates who were better prepared academically for college work are less likely to switch out of the natural and physical sciences and engineering and computer science. Average SAT score does not significantly affect whether students switch out of a business major, but a higher class rank reduces the likelihood that graduates changed their business major. Students with higher SAT scores and higher class ranks are actually more likely to switch out of the social sciences and the humanities.

Table 6 shows the average marginal effects of each variable for choosing the final major category from a multinomial logit specification. Results reveal that initial major choice significantly affects final major choice. For example, students who start college intending to major in the natural and physical sciences and engineering, as well as those who are undecided, are significantly more likely to major in natural and physical sciences. Students who initially select the natural and physical sciences or engineering and computer science fields are significantly less likely to major in business. Significant race and ethnic differences in graduation major exist after controlling for initial major choice, test score, and class rank. White, black, Hispanic, and Asian females are 2 to 7 percentage points more likely to major in the humanities and other majors than white males *conditional on initial major choice*.

Conclusion

The National Science Board and other policymakers have been concerned about the low representation of women, blacks, and Hispanics working in the S&E fields. Previous economic studies of college major choice have focused on the final major of college graduates, which presumes lack of interest in these fields. By analyzing major choice as a dynamic process, I show that both initial major choice and the probability of switching majors differ among race, ethnic, and gender groups.

Demographic variation in intended fields of study partly reflects group differences in academic preparedness. Men average higher test scores than women, who, in turn, achieve higher high school class rank than their male counterparts. Asians have higher test scores and class ranks than do students of other races. Because students in the natural and physical sciences and engineering and computer science average higher test scores and class ranks than students who select other majors, it is conceivable that these differences account for race, ethnic, and gender variation in major choice. Empirical results suggest that the differences in academic preparation explain only a small part of the variation in major choice by race and gender.

Race and ethnic variation in college major choice is small compared to gender differences. For example, women with SAT scores and class ranks equivalent to men are less likely to choose a major in engineering. Moreover, if women initially choose to major in engineering, they are more likely than men to switch away from this field. Although the gender differences in major choice are larger than the race differences, I still find that race and ethnicity affect major choice. Asian and other men are significantly more likely to choose a major in S&E than white males of equivalent academic preparation. Asian males are also significantly less likely to switch away from a major in engineering and computer science than are white males who begin in these fields. Despite claims that blacks and Hispanics

TABLE 6
Average Marginal Effects
for Final Major Choice: College Graduates

	Natural and Physical Sciences	Business	Engineering and Computer Science	Humanities and Other Majors
White female	−.002°°	−.013°°°	−.003°°°	.058°°°
	(.001)	(.002)	(.000)	(.004)
Black female	.002	−.025°°°	−.003°°°	.020°°
	(.002)	(.005)	(.001)	(.009)
Hispanic female	−.003°°°	−.018°°°	−.004°°°	.066°°°
	(.001)	(.003)	(.000)	(.006)
Asian female	.013°°°	.025°°°	−.001°	.036°°°
	(.002)	(.003)	(.000)	(.006)
Other female	−.002	−.022°°°	−.003°°	.024
	(.004)	(.011)	(.001)	(.017)
Black male	.008°°	−.005	.000	.022°
	(.004)	(.007)	(.001)	(.013)
Hispanic male	.003°°	−.007°°	.000	.008
	(.001)	(.003)	(.000)	(.006)
Asian male	.016°°°	.029°°°	.003°°°	−.018°°°
	(.002)	(.003)	(.000)	(.007)
Other male	.006	.010	.002	−.008
	(.007)	(.012)	(.001)	(.025)
Test score (SAT/ACT)	.007°°°	.004°°°	.007°°°	−.004°°°
divided by 100	(.001)	(.001)	(.001)	(.001)
Top decile	.025°°°	.038°°°	.003°°°	.010°°°
	(.002)	(.003)	(.000)	(.003)
Second decile	.006°°°	.016°°°	.001°°°	−.002
	(.001)	(.002)	(.000)	(.003)
Initially natural and	.416°°°	−.012°°°	.019°°°	−.010°
physical sciences	(.018)	(.004)	(.003)	(.006)
Initially business	−.004°°°	.504°°°	.001	−.052°°°
	(.002)	(.008)	(.002)	(.005)
Initially engineering and	.120°°°	−.052°°°	.756°°°	−.101°°°
computer science	(.013)	(.004)	(.026)	(.007)
Initially humanities and	.004	.047°°°	.006°°°	.372°°°
other majors	(.002)	(.004)	(.001)	(.007)
Initially undecided	.082°°°	.060°°°	.032°°°	.079°°°
	(.007)	(.005)	(.003)	(.006)
University of Texas	.011°°°	.051°°°	.004°°°	.081°°°
(UT)–Pan American	(.003)	(.005)	(.001)	(.009)
UT–San Antonio	.013°°°	.031°°°	.005°°°	.008
	(.002)	(.004)	(.000)	(.007)

NOTE: The numbers presented in the table are the average marginal effects for choosing each major relative to choosing a major in the social sciences at these universities after estimating a multinomial logit model. The average marginal effects are calculated using the margeff command in STATA. Year indicators are included in the regression.
°Significant at 10 percent. °°Significant at 5 percent. °°°Significant at 1 percent.

are underrepresented in S&E fields, I show that they appear to make major choices similar to white college graduates. Stated differently, the low levels of blacks and Hispanics with degrees in the S&E fields may be due to the low levels of blacks and Hispanics graduating from college.

Notes

1. The National Science Board (NSB; 2008) reports that while women represented 57.8 percent of the students who obtained a bachelor's degree in 2005, only 50.5 percent of bachelor's degrees in science and engineering (S&E) were awarded to women. According to the NSB, the low levels of black and Hispanic students with degrees in S&E are due to the low levels of blacks and Hispanics who graduate from college.

2. Several studies have found that the S&E fields are among the most highly rewarded in the labor market, including Black, Sanders, and Taylor (2003); Berger (1988); Dickson (2008); and Hamermesh and Donald (2008). Bedard and Herman (2008) and Black, Sanders and Taylor (2003) provide evidence that undergraduate major affects graduate school attendance.

3. Previous studies that used the final observed college major choice include Brown and Corcoran (1997), Daymont and Andrisani (1984), Gerhart (1990), Loury (1997), Polachek (1978), and Turner and Bowen (1999). Arcidiacono (2004) is the only study that investigates college major choice as a dynamic process.

4. Black, Sanders, and Taylor (2003); Berger (1988); Dickson (2008); and Hamermesh and Donald (2008) find that S&E majors are the most highly rewarded and that the social sciences and humanities are relatively lower-paying majors.

5. Detailed sample characteristics by demographic group and major are available from the author on request.

6. These tabulations are available from the author.

7. The test score used in this study is the total SAT score and not the separate SAT components. It is possible that differences in math scores may help to explain some more of the remaining difference in college major choice. The total SAT score was used as it was available for all three universities in the study.

8. An assumption maintained in the estimation of the multinomial logit is that the introduction of another alternative will not affect the relative probabilities of choosing a particular major. This is the independence of irrelevant alternatives assumption (IIA). For example, in this model, it means that the introduction of social sciences as a possible major choice should not affect the relative probability of choosing engineering and computer science over humanities. This assumption can be tested by comparing the estimated coefficients from the multinomial logit model with the estimated coefficients from the model with a subset of choices. This can be done using a Hausman test (see Hausman and McFadden 1984). I conducted the Hausman test by comparing the estimates from the model to the estimates obtained when the natural and physical sciences are excluded as an option. The results suggested that IIA is violated. I proceeded to estimate a multinomial probit regression of college major choice. I found that the results from the multinomial probit regression were similar to those obtained from the multinomial logit regression. Results from the multinomial probit regression are available upon request from the author.

References

Arcidiacono, Peter. 2004. Ability sorting and the returns to college major. *Journal of Econometrics* 121 (1-2): 343-75.

Bedard, Kelly, and Douglas Herman. 2008. Who goes on to graduate/professional school? The importance of economic fluctuations, undergraduate field, and ability. *Economics of Education Review* 27 (2): 197-210.

Berger, Mark C. 1988. Cohort size effects on earnings: Differences by college major. *Economics of Education Review* 7 (4): 375-83.

Black, Dan A., Seth Sanders, and Lowell Taylor. 2003. The economic reward for studying economics. *Economic Inquiry* 41 (3): 365-77.

Brown, Charles, and Mary Corcoran. 1997. Sex-based differences in school content and the male-female wage gap. *Journal of Labor Economics* 15 (3): 431-65.

Conger, Dylan, and Mark C. Long. 2009. Why are men falling behind? Gender gaps in college performance and persistence. *The Annals of the American Academy of Political and Social Science* (This Volume).

Daymont, Thomas M., and Paul J. Andrisani. 1984. Job preferences, college major, and the gender gap in earnings. *Journal of Human Resources* 19 (3): 408-28.

Dickson, Lisa. 2008. College major and the changing labor market. Unpublished manuscript.

Fletcher, Jason, and Marta Tienda. 2009. Race and ethnic differences in college achievement: Does high school attended matter? *The Annals of the American Academy of Political and Social Science* (This Volume).

Gerhart, Barry. 1990. Gender differences in current and starting salaries: The role of performance, college major and job title. *Industrial and Labor Relations Review* 43 (4): 418-33.

Hamermesh, Daniel S., and Stephen Donald. 2008. The effects of college curriculum on earnings: An affinity identifier for non-ignorable non-response bias. *Journal of Econometrics* 144 (2): 479-91.

Hausman, Jerry, and Daniel McFadden. 1984. Specification tests for the multinomiallogit model. *Econometrica* 52 (5): 1219-40.

Joy, Lois. 2000. Do colleges shortchange women? Gender differences in the transition from college to work. *American Economic Review* 90 (2): 471-74.

Loury, Linda Datcher. 1997. The gender earnings gap among college-educated workers. *Industrial and Labor Relations Review* 50 (4): 580-93.

National Science Board. 2008. *Science and engineering indicators 2008.* 2 vols (vol. 1, NSB 08-01; vol. 2, NSB 08-01A). Arlington, VA: National Science Foundation.

Polachek, Solomon W. 1978. Sex differences in college major. *Industrial and Labor Relations Review* 31 (4): 498-508.

Turner, Sarah E., and William G. Bowen. 1999. Choice of major: The changing (unchanging) gender gap. *Industrial and Labor Relations Review* 52 (2): 289-309.

Differences in College Major Choice by Citizenship Status

By
MILAGROS NORES

Studies about college majors largely ignore non-citizen or immigrant populations. Using the administrative data from two public universities in Texas, the author examine students' major choices by citizen status. In the context of legislation providing in-state tuition access for undocumented students (H.B. 1403, effective 2001), the author tests the effects of the policy on students' choices of major. Foreign-born populations have a higher propensity to select majors in Science, Engineering and Math (SEM) and a lower propensity to enroll in social sciences than citizens. Domestic students exhibit variable propensities to opt for SEMs, depending on their race. There is evidence of behavioral changes pre– to post–H.B. 1403, with foreign-born populations shifting away from high-return majors.

Keywords: college majors; citizenship; Texas; higher education; immigrants

The choice of major in postsecondary education has been studied for some time, with particular focus on gender gaps (see Staniec 2004; Leigh and Gill 2000; Turner and Bowen 1999; Ware and Lee 1988; and Polachek 1978, among others) and, more recently, racial gaps (Staniec 2004). No analysis exists on the major choices of non-citizens or immigrants (whether documented or undocumented).[1] Because students' choices of majors influence their labor market prospects and perpetuate class or gender

Milagros Nores specializes in the economics of education, poverty, early childhood, and international education. She has a PhD in education and economics from Columbia University and an EdM in educational administration and social policy from Harvard University and was a postdoctoral research associate at the Taubman Center in Public Policy, Brown University. She coauthored the Age 40 Perry Pre-school Cost-Effectiveness Study.

NOTE: The author is especially thankful to Marta Tienda and Mark Long and a blind reviewer for helpful comments and suggestions, as well as the participants of the Texas Higher Education Opportunity Project (THEOP) seminar at Princeton University, August 2008.

DOI: 10.1177/0002716209348748

differences in market outcomes (Eide 1994; Brown and Corcoran 1997; Leslie, McClure, and Oaxaca 1998; Porter and Umbach 2006), researchers have focused on the determinants of such choices and the extent to which these choices are related to educational inequities or differences in students' self-perceptions or self-concept (Daly 2005; Porter and Umbach 2006).

Models of students' major choices have traditionally been developed within the rational expectations model. According to this model, students choose majors on the basis of preferences and/or abilities, previous educational attainment, and expected labor market returns under the assumption of rational expectations (Berger 1998; Turner and Bowen 1999). For foreign-born populations, expected labor market returns might differ, as their expectations of postcollege work might be defined by a lower probability of being hired in the United States.[2] Likewise, for undocumented students, postcollege employment opportunities are limited because there is no pathway for legal work postgraduation. This circumstance implies even lower expected returns than the average college graduate in any respective field. Nevertheless, benefits to college education might include a higher within-group return, higher job stability and job satisfaction, as well as overall higher career opportunities and rewards (Porter and Umbach 2006). Similarly, a postsecondary degree might increase the probability of gaining residence or citizenship or applying for special employment visas. Therefore, policies that provide affordable access to postsecondary institutions might influence the postsecondary education choice of foreign-born students. This article attempts to measure the extent to which citizenship is associated with choice of major in college. I further examine how Texas House Bill (H.B.) 1403, which increased affordable access to higher education for undocumented populations, has altered major choices (for reasons discussed below).

An individual student's ability, self-concept, demographic attributes, family background, previous educational experience, and expected labor market returns influence choice of college major. Turner and Bowen (1999) find that Scholastic Aptitude Test (SAT) scores explain only part of the observed gender gap in choice of major and that large gender differences persist over time. Staniec (2004) finds significant race and gender differences in the choice of college major. She claims that gender gaps are explained by differences in expected labor market returns consistent with a rational expectations model, but this interpretation does not explain gender gaps in major choice among blacks. Policies that change students' perceptions of returns could alter their propensity to enroll in different majors, however.

Studies that examine the impact of background variables on the choice of college major produce mixed evidence. For men, Staniec (2004) finds no effect of socioeconomic variables (measured by parental education) on college major. Leppel, Williams, and Waldauer (2001) find that male and female students with parents in professional/executive professions are more likely to opt for majors in Science, Engineering and Math (SEM). Other studies emphasize previous educational experiences and major choice. Students' proficiency in math and science in high school also is related to college major. Staniec (2004) shows that students proficient in these subjects were more likely to choose related fields and that higher math scores decreased the likelihood of choosing humanities and fine arts (HFA) majors. Preferences, whether constructed through parental, societal, or individual expectations, also define such choices. Lackland and De Lisi (2001) argue that women prefer certain majors (education, nursing, etc.) because of their gender role orientation. Porter and Umbach (2006) find evidence that some choices reflect personality-environment fits. Finally, Altonji and Blank (1999) report that for the 1980s and early 1990s, about two-thirds of the observed race gap in male earnings was explained by educational attainment, experience, region, industry, and job characteristics. Leigh and Gill (2000) find that differences between two- and four-year college degrees and major field of study accounted for 8.5 to 11 percent of the gender wage gap in the early 1990s. Varied labor market returns by major choice also have been reported by Eide and Waehrer (1998), Thomas (2000), and Del Rossi and Hersch (2007).

No analyses exist on choices of major of foreign-born populations in postsecondary education (nor undocumented immigrants),[3] yet their college-enrollment behavior and patterns have been studied for quite some time. Foreign-born populations have different education profiles than their native-born counterparts, depending on their region of origin. By age 25, the foreign-born population is less likely to receive a BA (16.2 percent) than the U.S.-born population (26.7 percent). While individuals from Asia average higher BA attainment rates (28 percent) than U.S. natives, lower BA attainment levels are found in immigrants from Europe (18.7 percent) and Latin America and the Caribbean (13.5 percent) (Kaushal, Reimers, and Reimers 2007). Cross-generational analyses within racial groups have shown college enrollment rates of the foreign-born population to be higher than their first- or second-generation peers. Based on the High School and Beyond (HS&B) senior 1980 cohort, Ganderton and Santos (1995) show that foreign-born Hispanics were more likely to attend college than their native peers. Vernez and Abrahamse (1996) analyzed both the sophomore and senior HS&B cohorts and show that Hispanics and black immigrants are more likely to enroll in college than their native counterparts; however, this is not the case among whites or Asians. Using the National Educational Longitudinal Study of 1988 (NELS), Hagy and Staniec (2002) find that among foreign-born high school graduates, immigrants are more likely than natives to look to public institutions for access to higher education. Furthermore, Asian first-generation immigrants (foreign-born or one parent foreign-born) are more likely to enroll in four-year colleges (55 percent), while first-generation Hispanics are more likely to enroll in two-year colleges (35 percent) or not enroll at all (40 percent).

Until recently, foreign students without legal status were denied affordable access to higher education except at international tuition rates. In 2001, Texas passed H.B. 1403, which gave undocumented immigrants the opportunity of "qualifying for resident status for tuition purposes."[4] That is, after three years of continuous residence and a Texas high school diploma (or GED), undocumented youth are eligible to enroll in Texas's postsecondary system (all public junior, community, and senior colleges and universities; public health service centers; and technical institutes).[5] Texas therefore provides a unique opportunity to study nativity differences in higher education under the assumption that H.B. 1403 has increased access for foreign-born students to postsecondary institutions by reducing tuition. This law could potentially change expected returns in the labor market either by providing an additional pathway to obtain permanent residence, by signaling state support of immigration or less discrimination in Texas labor markets, or by providing access to foreign postsecondary labor markets. Additionally, over the long term the law may have made Texas more attractive to new waves of immigrants. The Texas Higher Education Coordinating Board (THECB) defines the requirements for residency classification for foreign-born students under H.B. 1403 as three years' high school attendance or having worked for a year in the state. To apply to a postsecondary education institution under H.B. 1403, individuals are required to submit a copy of a "Residency Affidavit."[6]

Using data from the Current Population Survey between 1997 and 2005,[7] Kaushal (2008) examined whether in-state tuition laws for undocumented students increased access for non-citizen Mexican youth. In a multistate panel analysis, Kaushal finds that the policy increased college enrollment for the population studied (31 percent increase in the base enrollment of 8 percent). Similarly, in a study that evaluates immigrant enrollment behavior among states with in-state tuition policies, Flores (forthcoming) finds that foreign-born non-citizen Latinos (of whom approximately one-third are estimated to be undocumented) were 1.54 times more likely to have enrolled in college after in-state tuition policies were implemented than similar students in other states without such policies (a 29 percent increase in the base enrollment of 1.8 percent).

For the United States, estimates of the total number of undocumented immigrants for 2008 were 11.9 million, with Texas estimated to be home to between 1.3 and 1.6 million (Passel and Cohn 2009). Before the Texas legislature passed H.B. 1403, an estimated 60,000 students per year could potentially have benefited from in-state tuition access. In 1998, there were approximately 1.2 million dropouts in the Texas system, partly due to lack of affordable access to higher education (Ruge and Iza 2005; National Conference of State Legislatures 2006). With increasing numbers of Texas youth with immigrant backgrounds (arising because of higher birthrates and increasing levels of immigration), it is a particularly opportune time to examine how the opportunities created by H.B. 1403 have altered the behavior of non-citizens.

The THECB tracks how many students have enrolled under H.B. 1403: 5,761 in fiscal year 2003, 8,512 in 2004, and 11,556 in 2005. In 2005, 71.8 percent attended community colleges and the remainder attended either four-year institutions or medical schools. In 2005, the University of Texas (UT) at Dallas received the largest number of H.B. 1403 students (715 students), followed by UT-Austin (513) and UT-Arlington (449).[8]

Based on previous models of higher education choices (Berger 1988; Hagy and Staniec 2002; Staniec 2004), I explore how choices of major may differ across international students versus domestic citizens and resident non-citizens by gender and race/ethnicity. Additionally, I examine the period before and after implementation of H.B. 1403 to observe whether legislation that produces different prices across cohorts of undocumented foreign-born students altered the major choices of foreign-born students. Building from prior models, I specify the choice of major as a function of preferences; previous educational achievements (preparation, such as taking advanced placement [AP] courses); and previous educational quality measured by students' high schools' percentage white, per pupil expenditures, pupil/teacher ratio, and percentage receiving free or reduced-price lunch. Finally, I compare differences in the determinants of the first college major choice at two public Texas institutions, UT-Austin and Texas Tech University.

Model

Empirical analyses build on prior studies that model the determinants of postsecondary major choices (Berger 1988; Turner and Bowen 1999; Staniec 2004; Porter and Umbach 2006). I assume that individuals arrive at college with a set of preexisting accumulated skills and differentiated resources (individual, family, and school) and maximize their utility choosing their first major from a set of six alternatives: SEM, social sciences, HFA, health, other, and undeclared. I focus on students' first major because changes in major are likely to be affected by information obtained subsequent to enrollment. Examples include changes in college composition of students (race/ethnic, gender, etc.), major composition (e.g., a woman might feel intimidated in a major with very few women), and by a student's own experience with the major (e.g., students learn how well matched are their capacities, interest, and abilities to the major). All individuals (i) maximize a utility function U, among a set of major choices (k):

$$U_i = \max(U_{1i}, U_{2i}, U_{3i}, U_{4i}, U_{5i}, U_{6i}),$$

where U_{ki} = utility for student i of majoring in k.

I define utility for person (i) in a major (k) (within a university) as a function of the characteristics of the major (Y) (that is, tuition costs, expected labor market returns, peer-group composition, legislation that might affect returns or prices, etc.), characteristics of the individual (X) that are not specifically related to the major (race, citizenship status, gender), characteristics of the individual (Z) that may be specifically related to the major (such as individual accumulated educational experience, previous education quality, and subject-related AP courses), and unobserved random components:

$$U_{ki} = \alpha_k Y_{ki} + \beta_k X_i + \delta_k Z_{ki} + \varepsilon_{ki}.$$

A student will choose major j if $U_{ji} > U_{ki}$ for any k different from j. Following Staniec (2004, 554), I use a maximum likelihood multinomial logit model to predict students' first choice of major:

$$\Pr(y_i = k) = \frac{\exp(\alpha_k Y_{ki} + \beta_k X_{ki} + \delta_k Z_{ki})}{1 + \sum\limits_k^K \exp(\alpha_k Y_{ki} + \beta_k X_{ki} + \delta_k Z_{ki})}.$$

The multinomial logit requires constraining one category of the dependent variable to be the reference category. The major category chosen as the reference category is "Health." For ease of interpretation, I report marginal effects for a discrete variable being present (e.g., being a non-citizen) on the probability of a specific major being chosen.

Similar to Turner and Bowen (1999), I take into account previous educational achievement as represented through high school percentile rank and aptitude tests (for UT-Austin only), given that prior achievement provides students with information about their capacities and relates to their motivation, abilities, and accumulated knowledge. High school experiences are represented through per pupil expenditures (thousands), pupil-to-teacher ratio, percentage of whites in the school, and percentage of students receiving free or reduced-price lunch. Given that minorities are more likely to attend lower-quality schools than the average white student and that school quality may be related to high school diploma attainment, college enrollment, and college major choice, controlling for these variables will reduce omitted variable bias on the variables of interest (i.e., origin, citizenship, race/ethnicity, and gender).

The administrative data permits pooling cohorts and tracking whether institutional differences exist by comparing outcomes across universities. Year fixed effects control for cohort variation in size, expected market returns, tuition increases, and other fluctuations. I pool data for college entrants from the years 1998 to 2003. Years 2001 to 2003 represent the period after the tuition legislation was introduced, and I estimate whether there is an "intent-to-treat" effect during these years by comparing major choices before and after the introduction of H.B. 1403.

I estimate three alternative variations of this model: (1) differentiating citizen groups, (2) interacting citizen status and gender, (3) interacting citizen status and race/ethnic groups; as well as (4) reproducing (1) separately for the 1998 to 2000 and 2001 to 2003 cohorts.

Data

I use administrative data from two Texas public universities: UT-Austin and Texas Tech—assembled by the THEOP as a part of a multiyear review of college behavior in Texas following the *Hopwood* decision, which banned affirmative action.[9] These two institutions are relevant in important ways. First, they serve geographically differentiated populations (central/southern versus west/north Texas, correspondingly), with UT-Austin being the second largest recipient of H.B. 1403 students. Consequently, I test whether choices of major depend on institutional variation for the population of interest. Second, they each have sufficient years of data for analysis of at least three "pretreatment" and three "posttreatment" years. Third, both institutions provided significant data about previous high school experiences to control for observables that would account for accumulated knowledge, secondary education quality, and selection into four-year postsecondary institutions.

UT-Austin is one of the top twenty-five producers of undergraduate degrees for minority students and considered a top college for Latinos based on enrollment.[10] In 2008, its tuition ranged between $4,045 and $4,677 ($4,045 for liberal arts, $4,465 for engineering, and $4,677 for business) for residents and $13,336 to $15,385 for nonresidents.[11] The 2008 freshman cohort of 6,718 students had an average SAT of 1,225.[12] Texas Tech tuition (30 credit hours) was $4,310 for in-state residents and residents of New Mexico and Oklahoma counties that share a border with West Texas, $5,210 for nonbordering counties of New Mexico and Oklahoma, and $12,650 for other nonresidents, with no differences across majors.[13] The 2008 freshman cohort of 4,407 students had an average SAT of 1,113.[14] *Barron's Profiles of American Colleges* (1996) classifies UT as "very competitive" and Texas Tech as "competitive" (as cited in Long and Tienda 2008).

These public universities differed in overall student composition. UT-Austin has a long history of serving Latinos and a total enrollment of more than 50,000, around 17 percent of whom were Hispanic and 4.5 percent of whom were black in 2004. (Hispanics account for around 35 percent of all Texans.[15]) Texas Tech self-describes as a university that retains the spirit of a small liberal arts institution. Its total enrollment is around 27,000, with 11 percent of its student body Hispanic and 3 percent black.[16]

Table 1 presents the distribution of major choice by race across six major fields: undeclared, SEM, social sciences, HFA, health, and other fields (including vocational).[17] These percentages provide a general picture of how choice of major differs by nativity and by racial/ethnic groups, but they do not control for differences across groups that are systematically associated with choice of major.

Among the combined group of students enrolled in either Texas Tech or UT-Austin, 26.9 percent were enrolled in SEMs, 37.5 percent in social sciences, and 9.6 percent in HFAs. Between 1998 and 2003, these two universities alone enrolled more than 25,000 foreign-born students. Domestic non-citizens were more concentrated in SEM (45.1 percent) and social science (27.5 percent) majors than were domestic citizens. One might expect Hispanics to be the most important domestic non-citizen group, but this was not the case. Two-thirds of non-citizens were Asian. These findings are in line with Hagy and Staniec's (2002) findings about first-generation Asian immigrants' higher propensity to enroll in four-year colleges and first-generation Hispanics' higher propensity to enroll in two-year colleges (or nonenrollment).

International students concentrated in SEM majors as well, but in much higher proportions, with 57.9 percent reporting an SEM major as their first choice and only 27.3 percent declaring social sciences as a first major. Also, there is a much lower incidence of undeclared majors among international students (4.8 percent) compared to domestic students (12 to 15 percent). Among citizens, Asians are more likely than all other racial/ethnic groups to opt for an SEM major (40.9 percent), with Hispanics also more likely than whites to choose SEM (30.5

TABLE 1
Distribution of Admitted Students across
Majors along Citizen and Race Characteristics

	N	Undeclared	Science, Engineering and Math (SEM)	Social Sciences	Humanities	Health	Other
			First Major Choice (percentage)				
Citizens							
Black, non-Hispanic	20,862	13.3	28.3	36.9	7.0	8.3	6.2
Hispanic	64,681	12.7	30.5	35.6	9.3	7.2	4.7
Asian	56,506	14.3	40.9	34.1	3.7	3.0	4.0
White, non-Hispanic	365,008	11.8	23.3	39.0	11.0	7.0	7.8
Total	507,057	12.3	26.4	38.0	9.8	6.6	6.9
Domestic non-citizens							
Black, non-Hispanic	702	22.2	40.3	16.8	1.9	11.7	7.1
Hispanic	2,897	12.4	32.0	37.4	9.7	4.2	4.3
Asian	11,998	16.5	48.5	25.5	4.1	2.9	2.4
White, non-Hispanic	3,012	11.7	45.0	28.3	7.4	2.9	4.7
Total	18,609	15.3	45.1	27.5	5.4	3.4	3.2
International							
Total	6,562	4.8	57.9	27.3	5.4	1.5	3.0
All students	1,057,894	12.3	27.2	37.5	9.6	6.5	6.8

SOURCE: University of Texas and Texas Tech administrative files, 1998-2003.

percent). Only 23.3 percent of white citizens opt for SEM majors. This relation-ship between race and major choice is quite unlike the pattern observed for domestic non-citizens, among which Hispanics (32 percent) are less likely than whites (45 percent) to select a SEM major.

At both universities, there are larger concentrations of non-citizens in SEM fields, with almost 15 percentage point differences relative to the enrollment of citizens in SEM majors (see Figure 1). Undeclared majors are more prevalent at UT-Austin, clearly an institutional curricular difference,[18] with up to 19 percent of U.S. citizens and 18 percent of domestic non-citizens reporting undeclared majors but less than 5 percent of international students with undeclared majors. Texas Tech shows a higher level of enrollment in health majors and, to a lesser degree, HFA majors. For domestic citizens, there is no apparent difference across institutions in students' propensity to enroll in the social sciences, but UT-Austin's citizen students are 12 percentage points more likely to choose an SEM major. Likewise, there is a 13 percentage point difference in SEM enrollment of non-citizens across institutions but no difference in social sciences. International

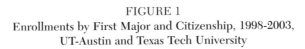

FIGURE 1
Enrollments by First Major and Citizenship, 1998-2003,
UT-Austin and Texas Tech University

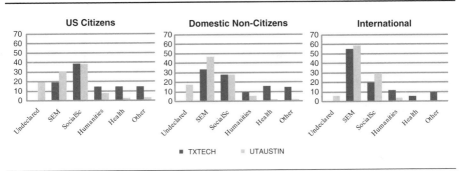

students show very little difference in SEM enrollments across institutions (4 percentage points), but there are larger institutional disparities in their social sciences enrollment (10 percentage points).

Observed differences in choice of first major by citizenship status may be attributed to other student characteristics that are systematically related to field of study. Therefore, I estimate a multinomial logit model predicting first major choice by citizenship status for each university. Table 2 presents estimated marginal effects and standard errors for non-citizens and permanent resident aliens (compared to citizens, the omitted group). Marginal effects allow for comparisons across models and among alternative choices.

Even with controls included, choice of major differs significantly by citizen status. Non-citizens are 6 to 9 percentage points more likely than citizens to enroll in SEMs at either institution. International students are 26.5 percentage points more likely to enroll in SEMs at UT-Austin and 33.6 percentage points more likely to do so at Texas Tech than citizens. However, the probability of enrolling in the social sciences was significantly lower for both domestic non-citizens and international students, relative to the citizen comparison group. International students are also less likely than citizens to choose humanities and fine arts majors at either institution (3 to 5 percentage points). There are institutional differences in the likelihood that domestic non-citizens will elect majors in HFA as well as the residual other fields (likely because of institutional differences in the prevalence of undeclared majors).

On balance, these results reveal differences in fields of study between domestic non-citizens and international students that could reflect different labor market references (international students might have their country of origin as the relevant labor market) or because of unobserved heterogeneity between domestic non-citizens and international students (in terms of educational quality, ability, motivation, or other unmeasured characteristics that might define selection into majors).

TABLE 2
Multinomial Estimations for UT-Austin and Texas Tech, 1998-2003,
Marginal Effects of First Major Choice across Citizen Status

	UT-Austin (N = 234,721)[a]				Texas Tech (N = 128,011)[b]			
	SEM	Social Sciences	HFA	Other	SEM	Social Sciences	HFA	Other
Non-citizen	.058°°°	−.082°°°	.014°°°	−.009°°°	.092°°°	−.089°°°	−.015	.022°°
	(.005)	(.005)	(.003)	(.001)	(.012)	(.014)	(.011)	(.011)
International	.265°°°	−.173°°°	−.026°°°	−.002	.336°°°	−.221°°°	−.048°°°	−.060°°°
	(.017)	(.015)	(.006)	(.004)	(.032)	(.023)	(.018)	(.015)

NOTE: Standard errors in parentheses. .
a. Controls: race/ethnic, gender, percentage of white students, per pupil expenditures (thousands), percentage free and reduced-price lunch, high school percentile rank, pupil:teacher ratio, year dummies, after legislation dummy.
b. Controls: race/ethnic, gender, advanced placement (AP) math, percentage of white students, per pupil expenditures (thousands), percentage free and reduced-price lunch, high school percentile rank, pupil/teacher ratio, year dummies, after legislation dummy.
°Significant at 10 percent. °°Significant at 5 percent. °°°Significant at 1 percent.

One question not addressed by Table 2 is whether gender disparities in major choice found in previous studies are also present among non-citizen and international students. Table 3 presents estimates of major choice with interactions of citizen status with gender. Male domestic citizens are the reference category for these specifications. At both institutions, male domestic non-citizens are more likely to be SEM majors than their male domestic citizen classmates, but female domestic citizens and non-citizens are less likely than their male counterparts to elect SEM majors. The gender gap in SEM majors is greater for domestic citizens than domestic non-citizens at Texas Tech.

Table 4 reports results for a specification that includes interactions of race/ethnicity with citizenship group, using white domestic citizens as a reference group. Note that race is not available for international students. At UT-Austin, white domestic citizens are less likely than all other groups to major in SEM fields and more likely to major in social science than every other group except domestic non-citizen Hispanics. The disparities in fields of study are largest between white domestic citizens and black domestic non-citizens (−24.3 and +30.7 percentage points for SEM and social sciences, respectively). At Texas Tech, likewise, white domestic citizens are more likely than every other group to major in social science. The largest ethno-racial gaps in choice of major among Tech students are between white domestic citizens and white and Asian domestic non-citizens (−24.2 and −21.8 percentage points for SEM majors, respectively, and +14.5 and +17.9 for social science, respectively). Finally, black non-citizens enrolled at Texas Tech are substantially less likely than white domestic citizens to

TABLE 3

Multinomial Estimations for UT-Austin and Texas Tech, 1998-2003,
Marginal Effects of First Major Choice by Citizen Status and Gender

	UT-Austin (N = 235,150)[a]				Texas Tech (N = 128,594)[b]			
	SEM	Social Sciences	HFA	Other	SEM	Social Sciences	HFA	Other
Citizen	−.220°°°	.085°°°	.034°°°	.007°°°	−.221°°°	.109°°°	.072°°°	−.042°°°
female	(.002)	(.002)	(.001)	(.001)	(.002)	(.003)	(.002)	(.002)
International								
Male	.228°°°	−.155°°°	−.027°°°	−.001	.360°°°	−.142°°°	−.083°°°	−.083°°°
	(.022)	(.019)	(.007)	(.006)	(.036)	(.028)	(.012)	(.017)
Female	−.034	−.046°°	.035°°	.010	.028	−.191°°°	.107°°°	−.066°°
	(.024)	(.023)	(.015)	(.007)	(.045)	(.031)	(.039)	(.028)
Non-citizen								
Male	.118°°°	−.104°°°	−.014°°°	−.007°°°	.128°°°	−.131°°°	−.007	−.005
	(.007)	(.006)	(.003)	(.001)	(.017)	(.013)	(.010)	(.012)
Female	−.124°°°	−.002	.028°°°	−.005°°°	−.044°°	−.012	−.021°	−.077°°°
	(.007)	(.007)	(.004)	(.001)	(.018)	(.020)	(.012)	(.012)

NOTE: Standard errors in parentheses.
a. Controls: race/ethnic, gender, percentage of white students, per pupil expenditures (thousands), percentage free and reduced-price lunch, high school percentile rank, pupil:teacher ratio, year dummies, after legislation dummy.
b. Controls: race/ethnic, gender, advanced placement (AP) math, percentage of white students, per pupil expenditures (thousands), percentage free and reduced-price lunch, high school percentile rank, pupil/teacher ratio, year dummies, after legislation dummy.
°Significant at 10 percent. °°Significant at 5 percent. °°°Significant at 1 percent.

major in social science or HFA, but they are more likely to major in a diverse range of other fields.

These results indicate that among those with the same citizen status, there are racial disparities in major choice that are not attributable to observable covariates. Most notable, while the comparison between Hispanic citizens and non-citizens does not show large disparities in major choices, this is not the case for black or for white students. Moreover, only modest differences across citizenship status in fields of study are observed for Asians. I cannot determine whether these differences in major choices within racial groups are due to variation in unobservable characteristics (e.g., motivation, unmeasured primary and secondary education quality, etc.) or to differences among groups in expected labor market returns to the fields of study.

Nevertheless, evidence of large and significant differences in major choice by citizenship status combined with ethno-racial variation in fields of study among domestic non-citizens suggests the plausible hypothesis that H.B. 1403 changed students' major choices. Accordingly, Table 5 presents separate estimations of

TABLE 4
Multinomial Estimations for UT-Austin and Texas Tech, 1998-2003,
Marginal Effects of First Major Choice across Citizen Status and Race

	UT-Austin (N = 234,721)[a]				Texas Tech (N = 128,011)[b]			
	SEM	Social Sciences	HFA	Other	SEM	Social Sciences	HFA	Other
Citizens								
Black	.097°°°	−.034°°°	−.031°°°	−.008°°°	.032°°°	−.017°°	−.062°°°	−.029°°°
	(.005)	(.005)	(.002)	(.001)	(.006)	(.008)	(.005)	(.005)
Hispanic	.088°°°	−.035°°°	−.018°°°	−.006°°°	.021°°°	−.040°°°	−.007°	−.038°°°
	(.003)	(.003)	(.002)	(.001)	(.004)	(.005)	(.004)	(.003)
Asian	.113°°°	−.040°°°	−.047°°°	−.003°°°	.092°°°	−.112°°°	−.068°°°	−.047°°°
	(.003)	(.003)	(.001)	(.001)	(.008)	(.009)	(.006)	(.006)
International	.259°°°	−.167°°°	−.030°°°	−.001	.334°°°	−.221°°°	−.048°°	−.061°°°
	(.018)	(.015)	(.008)	(.004)	(.032)	(.023)	(.019)	(.016)
Non-citizens								
White	.157°°°	−.111°°°	.009	−.009°°°	.242°°°	−.146°°°	−.012	−.045°°°
	(.013)	(.012)	(.008)	(.003)	(.028)	(.024)	(.019)	(.016)
Black	.243°°°	−.307°°°	−.076°°°	−.010°	.000	−.207°°°	−.126°°°	−.001
	(.027)	(.017)	(.005)	(.006)	(.032)	(.038)	(.016)	(.031)
Hispanic	.068°°°	−.009	.009	−.012°°°	.012	−.075°°°	−.001	.049°°
	(.012)	(.012)	(.007)	(.003)	(.019)	(.024)	(.019)	(.022)
Asian	.170°°°	−.131°°°	−.039°°°	−.012°°°	.218°°°	−.180°°°	−.094°°°	−.042°°°
	(.006)	(.006)	(.003)	(.001)	(.021)	(.017)	(.010)	(.012)

NOTE: Standard errors in parentheses.
a. Controls: race/ethnic, gender, percentage of white students, per pupil expenditures (thousands), percentage free and reduced-price lunch, high school percentile rank, pupil:teacher ratio, year dummies, after legislation dummy.
b. Controls: race/ethnic, gender, advanced placement (AP) math, percentage of white students, per pupil expenditures (thousands), percentage free and reduced-price lunch, high school percentile rank, pupil/teacher ratio, year dummies, after legislation dummy.
°Significant at 10 percent. °°Significant at 5 percent. °°°Significant at 1 percent.

major choice by citizen status for the pre– and post–H.B. 1403 cohorts. Because the legislation mainly affected the price for enrolling, and because it was limited to undocumented populations, one could imagine that the "treated" individuals were limited to those applicants qualified for instate tuition under H.B. 1403. To the extent that H.B. 1403 signals state-level openness to foreign-born populations, however, it might also affect perceptions about markets and induce behavioral changes in fields of study. This policy would operate counter to policies that signal "closed" or "discriminatory" markets.

Table 5 reveals large differences pre– and post–H.B. 1403 in choice of major by citizenship status at both universities. There were few differences in the major choices between domestic citizens and non-citizens in the postlegislation period

TABLE 5

Multinomial Estimations for UT-Austin and Texas Tech, 1998-2003,
Marginal Effects of First Major Choice across Citizen Status pre– and post–H.B. 1403

	UT-Austin[a]				Texas Tech[b]			
	SEM	Social Sciences	HFA	Other	SEM	Social Sciences	HFA	Other
Prelegislation (1998-2000)								
Non-citizen	.059°°°	−.087°°°	.015°°°	−.010°°°	.115°°°	−.089°°°	−.042°°°	.023°
	(.006)	(.006)	(.004)	(.001)	(.015)	(.017)	(.012)	(.013)
International	.254°°°	−.194°°°	−.029°°°	.030°°°	.382°°°	−.299°°°	−.054°°	−.028
	(.029)	(.024)	(.011)	(.011)	(.042)	(.026)	(.022)	(.021)
N	166,701				86,313			
Postlegislation (2001-2003)								
Non-citizen	.011°	.004	.008	−.072°°°	.042°°	.035°	.016	−.010
	(.003)	(.007)	(.010)	(.010)	(.018)	(.022)	(.020)	(.021)
International	−.171°°°	−.017°°°	−.039°°°	−.028°°°	−.039	−.095°°	.267°°°	−.116°°°
	(.003)	(.013)	(.003)	(.022)	(.029)	(.039)	(.036)	(.049)
N	68,020				41,698			

NOTE: Standard errors in parentheses.

a. Controls: race/ethnic, gender, percentage of white students, per pupil expenditures (thousands), percentage free and reduced-price lunch, high school percentile rank, pupil:teacher ratio, year dummies, after legislation dummy.

b. Controls: race/ethnic, gender, advanced placement (AP) math, percentage of white students, per pupil expenditures (thousands), percentage free and reduced-price lunch, high school percentile rank, pupil/teacher ratio, year dummies, after legislation dummy.

°Significant at 10 percent. °°Significant at 5 percent. °°°Significant at 1 percent.

at UT-Austin, which indicates a relative shift of non-citizens away from SEM and towards social science majors. International students, however, altered their major choices dramatically after in-state tuition was granted to qualifying students, significantly lowering their likelihood of pursuing SEM fields. At Texas Tech, the results were even more pronounced. For the prelegislation cohorts, non-citizens and international students were more likely than domestic citizens to major in SEM fields and less likely to major in social science, but these differences were eliminated or muted in the postlegislation period.

Discussion

This article examines the first choice of major by citizen status at two public four-year universities in Texas. I build on previous research about choices of major, expanding this work to foreign-born populations. Additionally, I evaluate how these choices vary across universities that differ in their location, their student body, and their curriculum. In the context of a state that is introducing proimmigrant policies in higher education, I test whether such policies have effects on students' behavior as measured in their choices of major.

I find a higher propensity to enroll in SEM fields for foreign-born populations and a lower propensity to enroll in social sciences compared to citizens. Domestic students differ in their propensity to choose SEMs over other majors depending on race. Among citizens, blacks, Hispanics, and especially Asians have particularly high representation in SEM majors. Among non-citizens, SEM majoring rates are lowest for Hispanics at UT-Austin and blacks and Hispanics at Texas Tech. Empirical analysis provides strong evidence that choices of major changed for domestic non-citizens after H.B. 1403 was implemented, such that differences between domestic citizens' and non-citizens' fields of study narrowed.

With the existing data, I cannot discern the causes for differences in choices of major across groups or over time because the reduced form model takes into account previous educational experiences but does not model them directly. Furthermore, I lack information about motivation and differences in quality of prior educational experiences, as well as the selection processes that sort students among an array of postsecondary options, including college enrollment (i.e., the processes of finishing high school, applying, being admitted, and enrolling), which likely differ among the groups compared.

These reservations notwithstanding, empirical results indicate that foreign-born populations enrolled at UT and Texas Tech between 1998 and 2003 opt for majors that have higher labor market returns. This generalization obtains regardless of ethnicity, international, or citizenship status. To the degree that some share of these individuals belong to recent immigration waves that average low education levels and poor labor market prospects (e.g., Hispanics), their proclivity to choose SEM majors could reduce wage gaps over the long run. Given Texas's projected high level of immigration in the near term, broadened access to higher education for qualified undocumented students will likely secure the economic future of second and third generations. Because there appears to be a shift away from SEM majors in the post–H.B. 1403 years, however, policymakers should monitor whether the shift persists and the actual labor market consequences.

Notes

1. American citizenship can be acquired in three primary ways: birth in the United States (the American tradition of *jus soli*); naturalization, which requires five years of resident status in the United States; and through descent from one or more American parents (*jus sanguinis*) (Schuck 2007).

2. Factors involved in lowering expectation of work after college include the price of sponsoring a working visa, expectations by some employers that the employee might eventually decide to go back to his or her home country, or biases to employing a foreign-born.

3. Undocumented individuals are defined as those either entering the United States legally and remaining beyond the expiration of their immigration status or entering the United States evading inspection at any port of entry.

4. Independent individuals aged eighteen years and older who are gainfully employed in Texas for twelve months before registration in a public institution of higher learning are entitled to resident status while maintaining legal Texas residence. Under Texas H.B. 1403 (effective 2001), addressing the issue of undocumented students qualifying for resident status for tuition purposes, international students who meet all of the following requirements and do not establish a residence outside Texas qualify for Texas residency regardless of their status with U.S. Citizenship and Immigration Services (CIS): (1) graduate from a Texas high school (public or private) or receive a GED after attending for three consecutive years; (2) live with a parent, legal guardian, or conservator during that time; (3) register as an entering student in a higher education institution not earlier than the fall 2001 semester; and (4) sign an affidavit stating that they meet the above qualifications and will apply for permanent residency at the earliest opportunity they are eligible to do so. An alien living in the United States under a visa permitting permanent residence or who is permitted by U.S. law to establish a domicile in this country has the same privileges of qualifying for resident status as a U.S. citizen (see College Board 2001).

5. Texas was among the first of several states including California, Illinois, Kansas, New Mexico, New York, Oklahoma, Utah, and Washington to pass such a law. Other states such as Rhode Island and North Carolina have rejected initiatives like this for years (Krueger 2006).

6. College Board (2001).

7. These data include citizenship status of foreign-born populations and country of origin and date of arrival. Self-reported data collected on citizenship status are likely to have a higher measurement error than other types of self-reported data (Kaushal 2008, 775-76).

8. See William Lutz (2006).

9. http://theop.princeton.edu/index.html.

10. http://www.hispaniconline.com/HispanicMag/2008_03/Feature-25Colleges.html; http://www.ir.ufl.edu/nat_rankings/media/hispanic_old.pdf; http://www.edexcelencia.org/pdf/publications/fact_sheets/Top25CollegesUniv-2008.pdf.

11. http://www.utexas.edu/tuition/costs.html.

12. http://bealonghorn.utexas.edu/whyut/profile/scores/index.html.

13. http://www.admissions.ttu.edu/fastfacts.pdf.

14. http://www.irim.ttu.edu/NEWFACTBOOK/FactSheets/FactSheet-Fall2008.pdf.

15. *Houston Chronicle* (2008).

16. Chang (2006).

17. Given the small number across groups, and the lack of observations across non-citizen categories, Native Americans and Others have been dropped from the ethnic and racial categorizations for these analyses.

18. The UT-Austin offers students the option of enrolling in the School of Undergraduate Studies (UGS), and students "enrolled in UGS obtain specialized advising designed to help them find the major that is right for them while taking courses that will apply toward any degree" (Office of Admissions 2008). There does not appear to a time limit to declaring a degree. On the other hand, at Texas Tech, a student can initially be admitted with an undeclared major "into a general major known as arts and sciences undeclared (ASUD) until they select the major degree program in which they intend to graduate. Students transferring from another institution with less than 60 hours (including coursework in progress) may choose Arts and Sciences Undeclared. Students who have completed 60 or more hours must declare a major to be considered for admission" (Office of Official Publications 2008).

References

Altonji, Joseph G., and Rebecca M. Blank. 1999. Gender and race in the labor market. *Handbook of Labor Economics* 3:3143–3259.

Berger, Mark C. 1988. Predicted future earnings and choice of college major. *Industrial and Labor Relations Review* 41 (3): 418-29.

Brown, Charles, and Mary Corcoran. 1997. Sex-Based Differences in School Content and the Male-Female Wage Gap. *Journal of Labor Economics*, 15(3), 431-465.

Chang, M. J. 2006. *Achieving institutional self-correction through diversity*. Texas Tech University. http://www.depts.ttu.edu/diversity/Diversity_Panel_PDF.

The College Board. 2001. Guide to state residency requirements: Policy and practice at U.S. public colleges and universities. http://www.collegeboard.com/about/association/international/pdf/sr_TX01.pdf.

Daly, Bonita A. 2005. Color and gender based differences in the sources of influence attributed to the choice of college major. *Critical Perspectives on Accounting* 16 (1): 27-45.

Del Rossi, Alison F., and Joni Hersch. 2008. Double your major, double your return? *Economics of Education Review.* 27 (4): 375-386.

Eide, Eric R. 1994. College major choice and changes in the gender wage gap. *Contemporary Economic Policy* 12 (2): 55-64.

Eide, Eric, and Geetha Waehrer. 1998. The role of the option value of college attendance in college major choice. *Economics of Education Review* 17 (1): 73-82.

Flores, Stella M. Forthcoming. State "dream acts": The effect of in-state resident tuition policies on the college enrollment of undocumented Latino students in the United States. *Review of Higher Education.*

Ganderton, Philip T., and Richard Santos. 1995. Hispanic college attendance and completion: Evidence from the high school and beyond surveys. *Economics of Education Review* 14 (1): 35-46.

Hagy, Alison P., and J. Farley O. Staniec. 2002. Immigrant status, race, and institutional choice in higher education. *Economics of Education Review* 21 (4): 381-92.

Houston Chronicle. 2008. White teen sues UT over admissions policy. Sugar Land student, in top of class, challenges racial preferences. April 8.

Kaushal, Neeraj. 2008. In-state tuition for the undocumented: Education effects on Mexican young adults. *Journal of Policy Analysis and Management* 27 (4): 771-92.

Kaushal, Neeraj, Cordelia W. Reimers, and David M. Reimers. 2007. Immigrants and the economy. In *The new Americans: A guide to immigration since 1965,* ed. Mary C. Waters and Reed Ueda with Helen B. Marrow, 176-88. Cambridge: University Press.

Krueger, Carl. 2006. In-state tuition for undocumented immigrants. Report, Education Commission of the States. Boulder, CO.

Lackland, Anne C., and Richard De Lisi. 2001. Students' choices of college majors that are gender traditional and nontraditional. *Journal of College Student Development* 42 (1): 39-48.

Leigh, Duane E., and Andrew M. Gill. 2000. Community college enrollment, college major, and the gender wage gap. *Industrial and Labor Relations Review* 54 (1): 163-81.

Leppel, Karen, Mary L. Williams, and Charles Waldauer. 2001. The impact of parental occupation and socioeconomic status on choice of college major. *Journal of Family and Economic Issues* 22 (4): 373-94.

Leslie, Larry L., Gregory T. McClure, and Ronald L. Oaxaca. 1998. Women and minorities in science and engineering: A life sequence analysis. *Journal of Higher Education* 69 (3): 239-76.

Long, Mark C., and Marta Tienda. 2008. Winners and losers: Changes in Texas university admissions post-Hopwood. *Education Evaluation and Policy Analysis* 30:255-80.

Lutz, William. 2006. Thousands of illegal immigrants get in-state tuition in Texas. February 20. http://dallasblog.nofloppies.com/index2.php?option=com_content&do_pdf=1&id=391238.

National Conference of State Legislatures. 2006. *College tuition and undocumented immigrants.* Washington, DC: National Conference of State Legislatures.

Office of Admissions. 2008. Selecting a major. University of Texas at Austin. http://bealonghorn.utexas.edu/freshmen/before/majors/index.html.

Office of Official Publications. 2008. Admission requirements for specific colleges. Texas Tech University. http://www.depts.ttu.edu/officialpublications/catalog/_AdmitSpecific.php.

Passel, Jeffrey S., and D'Vera Cohn. 2009. *A portrait of unauthorized immigrants in the United States.* Washington, DC: Pew Hispanic Center.

Polachek, Solomon W. 1978. Sex differences in college major. *Industrial and Labor Relations Review* 31 (4): 498-508.

Porter, Stephen R., and Paul D. Umbach. 2006. College major choice: An analysis of person–environment fit. *Research in Higher Education* 47 (4): 429-49.

Ruge, Thomas R., and Angela D. Iza. 2005. Higher education for undocumented students: The case for open admission and in-state tuition rates for students without lawful immigration status. *Indiana International and Comparative Law Review* 15:257-278.

Schuck, Peter H. 2007. Citizenship and nationality policy. In *The new Americans: A guide to immigration since 1965,* ed. Mary C. Waters and Reed Ueda with Helen B. Marrow, 43-55. Cambridge: University Press.

Staniec, J. Farley O. 2004. The effects of race, sex, and expected returns on the choice of college major. *Eastern Economic Journal* 30 (4): 549-69.

Thomas, Scott L. 2000. Deferred costs and economic returns to college major, quality, and performance. *Research in Higher Education* 41 (3): 281-313.

Turner, Sarah, and William G. Bowen. 1999. Choice of major: The changing (unchanging) gender gap. *Industrial and Labor Relations Review* 52 (2): 289-313.

Vernez, George, and Allan Abrahamse. 1996. *How immigrants fare in US education*. Santa Monica, CA: RAND.

Ware, Norma, and Valerie Lee. 1988. Sex differences in choice of college science majors. *American Educational Research Journal* 25 (4): 593-614.

PART FOUR

College Performance:
Academic Outcomes

Race and Ethnic Differences in College Achievement: Does High School Attended Matter?

By
JASON FLETCHER
and
MARTA TIENDA

Using ten years of enrollment data at four Texas public universities, the authors examine whether, to what extent, and in what ways high school attended contributes to racial and ethnic differences in college achievement. As with previous studies, the authors show that controlling for class rank and test scores shrinks, but does not eliminate, sizable racial differences in college achievement. Fixed-effects models that take into account differences across high schools that minority and nonminority youth attend largely eliminate, and often reverse, black-white and Hispanic-white gaps in several college outcomes. The results, which are quite robust across universities of varying selectivity, illustrate how high school quality foments race and ethnic inequality in college performance.

Keywords: minority students; college achievement; Texas higher education; high school quality

The No Child Left Behind Act of 2001 (NCLB) directed public attention to the low average academic achievement of black, Hispanic, and Native American students and promised to end the soft bigotry of low expectations. Declaring that our nation's schools have shortchanged millions of students, but minority and economically disadvantaged students in particular, the legislation imposed strict achievement standards that hold schools accountable for students' annual progress in core subjects. Claims about the success of NCLB reported by the White House and the Department of Education based on school-specific measures of annual progress are tempered by evidence from the National Assessment of Educational Progress (NAEP), which shows mixed results on achievement gains by grade and little, if any, narrowing of the gaps between minority and nonminority populations (Tough 2006; J. Lee 2006).

Despite voluminous social science literatures that document and evaluate the dimensions and evolution of academic achievement gaps, these gaps remain poorly understood (Kao and Thompson 2003; Tough 2006). Even

DOI: 10.1177/0002716209348749

as academic researchers seek to identify the causes of low achievement and persisting gaps, school administrators immersed in the day-to-day craft of teaching seek to raise student achievement using myriad testing and classification methods to comply with NCLB. Both contingents agree that the achievement gap is not inevitable, that it begins at very young ages, and that it widens as students progress in their educational careers (Fryer and Levitt 2006a, 2006b; Perna and Swail 2002). The growing consensus about the value of early intervention programs is well justified (Heckman 2006) but does little to address the reality of existing gaps between minority and nonminority youth or their consequences for postsecondary schooling and beyond.

Unlike K-12 schooling, postsecondary education is not compulsory and disproportionately draws from the upper half of the achievement distribution; therefore, one might expect smaller differences in academic performance at the collegiate level. Yet, there is ample evidence that racial gaps in academic achievement and graduation rates persist (Vars and Bowen 1998; Sacerdote 2001). Postsecondary achievement gaps are particularly thorny for selective institutions, where admission criteria are designed to identify applicants who are most likely to succeed. Affirmative action is often blamed for academic performance gaps between minority and nonminority students because race-sensitive admission policies downplay standardized test scores for the former group. To date, few studies have linked large racial/ethnic differences in high school achievement to academic performance in college. Tracing the determinants of racial/ethnic differences in postsecondary achievement promises new insights about the necessary and sufficient conditions to narrow performance and graduation gaps (Summers and Wolfe 1977).

As an initial foray to address this gap, we examine the determinants of racial/ethnic differences in college achievement using ten years of administrative data for enrollees at the two most selective Texas public universities—the University

Jason Fletcher is an assistant professor in the Yale University School of Public Health. His research focuses on examining social influences on adolescent education and health outcomes, long-term consequences of childhood mental illness, and child and adolescent mental health policy. Specific interests include autism, adolescent depression, child and adolescent obesity, attention deficit hyperactivity disorder (ADHD), and adolescent risky behavior choices. He is also examining the long-term health consequences of occupation choices and occupational stress.

Marta Tienda is the Maurice P. During '22 Professor in Demographic Studies and professor of sociology and public affairs at Princeton University. Her current research interests include equity and access to higher education and the causes and consequences of child migration and immigrant integration in new destinations. She is co–principal investigator of the Texas Higher Education Opportunity Project.

NOTE: This project was supported with a grant from the University of Kentucky Center for Poverty Research through the U.S. Department of Health and Human Services, Office of the Assistant Secretary for Planning and Evaluation, Grant no. 5 UO1 PE000002-05. Data collection was supported by the Ford, Mellon, Hewlett, and Spencer Foundations. We thank an anonymous reviewer, Thad Domina, Dawn Koffman, Mark Long, and participants at the American Education Research Association Annual Meeting for helpful comments and suggestions as well as Steven Brown for excellent research assistance. The usual disclaimers apply.

of Texas at Austin (UT) and Texas A&M University (TAMU)—as well as two less selective public universities—the University of Texas at San Antonio (UTSA) and Texas Tech University. As in previous research, we find substantial racial/ethnic differences in grade point average (GPA) and college persistence, which are somewhat attenuated after adjusting for observable student characteristics, including high school grades and standardized test scores. Using a fixed-effects modeling strategy, we demonstrate that taking into account the quality of high school attended largely eliminates and in some cases reverses college achievement gaps between minority and nonminority students. That students of different racial/ethnic groups who attended the same high school achieve similar college success across institutions of varying selectivity attests to the robustness of our findings and shows how precollegiate educational disadvantages persist through college.

The next section summarizes prior studies suggesting possible linkages between precollegiate experiences and postsecondary outcomes. The third section describes the administrative data analyzed and formulates an estimation strategy that builds on and extends studies of race differences in college attainment by considering whether variation in high school quality moderates the associations. Empirical results are discussed in the fourth section, and the conclusion considers the implications of our results in light of the school accountability standards imposed by NCLB.

Background

There is ample evidence that achievement gaps among racial and ethnic minorities widen over time (Schneider, Martinez, and Owens 2006; Kao and Thompson 2003). Despite negligible differences in measured cognitive ability between majority and minority toddlers through age two, large gaps in school readiness are already evident by the time children begin school (Fryer and Levitt 2004, 2006b). Moreover, the achievement gap expands rapidly in the early grades (Fryer and Levitt 2006a). Group differences in scholastic readiness at school entry are associated with a small number of family characteristics, but variation in school quality, another obvious candidate for the widening gap, does not appear to explain differences in early school achievement beyond second grade (Fryer and Levitt 2006a). NAEP assessments based on fourth-, eighth- and twelfth-grade performance measures show that gaps widen through elementary, middle, and high school (Perna and Swail 2002; National Center for Education Statistics [NCES] 2005; Schneider, Martinez, and Owens 2006). Heckman and LaFontaine (2007) identify unequal school experiences and incarceration rates as additional factors that maintain racial and ethnic differences in secondary school achievement and completion, but they do not link high school achievement to postsecondary educational outcomes.

Prior research has traced race and ethnic differences in college success to family background and early academic achievements, particularly high school grades (class rank), advanced placement (AP) course completion, and standardized test scores (see Rothstein 2004; Alon and Tienda 2007; Bowen and Bok 1998). Critics of affirmative action use race/ethnic gaps in standardized test scores to bolster claims that minority students are less well prepared than whites (Thernstrom and Thernstrom 1996). Even though minority students average lower scores on standardized tests, there is ample evidence establishing a positive association between college selectivity and success of minority students (Bowen and Bok 1998; Kane 1998; Rothstein 2004; Alon and Tienda 2005). A second explanation for race and ethnic disparities in college performance alleges that the benefits from distinct college environments are not uniform for minority and nonminority students. Evidence for both claims is mixed, depending on the outcome of interest, the selectivity of institutions in the study, and the time frame of the study.

For example, Vars and Bowen (1998) show that white students achieve higher college grades than black students across five Scholastic Aptitude Test (SAT) strata, even after controlling for high school grades and family socioeconomic background. Yet, Light and Strayer (2002) find that blacks and Hispanics are *more likely* to graduate from college (net of ability as measured by Armed Forces Qualification Test scores). Kane (1998) also finds that black students who attend more selective colleges have higher graduation rates compared with blacks who attended less selective colleges. Using a sample of 28 colleges and universities with selective to highly selective admissions, Bowen and Bok (1998) also find no evidence for the mismatch hypothesis.[1] Their sample of universities excluded less selective institutions and their analytic strategy did not consider the selection regime that matches students to institutions according to selectivity, however.

Alon and Tienda (2005) analyze two national datasets as well as the sample of selective institutions used by Bowen and Bok (1998), and they expand their comparisons to include Hispanics and Asians along with blacks and whites. By implementing a rigorous estimation strategy that jointly modeled enrollment in, and graduation from, competitive postsecondary institutions, they address criticisms wagered about the Bowen and Bok study on grounds that it was not representative of the full institutional selectivity range and disproportionately represented the most able students who were likely to graduate irrespective of college attended. Like Bowen and Bok, they refute the mismatch hypothesis and attribute part of the positive association between college selectivity and graduation to the stronger academic supports available at many highly selective institutions.

Nevertheless, many analysts agree that *within* selectivity tiers, minority students average lower grades and graduate at lower rates compared with nonminority students (Massey 2006; Bowen and Bok 1998; Alon and Tienda 2007). Yet, Dale and Krueger (2002) find that among students of comparable ability, those from low-income backgrounds benefit more from attending selective colleges compared with students from high-income families. That minority students benefit more than nonminority students from attending a selective institution is not inconsistent with the persistence of an achievement gap at both.[2]

Some college environments may be less conducive to academic success of black and Hispanic students, even those with academic qualifications similar to those of majority students, but there is little direct evidence about how college climate influences minority students' academic performance. Massey and Fischer (2005) find some evidence that college climate is associated with academic performance. They report that minority students enrolled at selective institutions who claim to have been stereotyped earn lower grades than their race counterparts who did not experience similar stereotyping. Whether their findings can be generalized to less selective institutions is unclear, however. Nor is it obvious what university attributes trigger stereotype threat or whether high school experiences with same and other race groups may be associated with campus outcomes.

Tienda and Niu (2006) report no differences in the reported salience of campus ethnic composition in college choices of freshmen enrolled at selective versus nonselective Texas public universities. Even students who graduated from predominantly minority high schools did not indicate that the racial makeup of the student body influenced their college-decision making. By contrast, cost, the availability of financial aid, and distance from home were important considerations in the college choices of high-achieving students who graduated from minority-dominated high schools. Although these authors do not relate high school attributes to college academic outcomes, there is growing evidence that quality of high school attended is a powerful determinant of students' college choice sets. McDonough (1997) notes that high school attended dictates whether selective postsecondary institutions are even envisioned as possible options. This claim is consistent with findings by Niu and associates (Niu and Tienda 2008; Niu, Tienda, and Cortes 2006) showing that minority students attending poor or highly segregated Texas public high schools are less likely than similarly situated whites to enroll at a selective postsecondary institution, even if they are guaranteed admission under the Top Ten Percent Law.

Recent scholarship suggests that racial and ethnic college achievement gaps may result from differences in the quality of high schools minority and nonminority students attend (Summers and Wolfe 1977; Massey 2006; Schneider, Martinez, and Owens 2006; Niu, Tienda, and Cortes 2006; Niu and Tienda 2008). For example, Massey (2006) demonstrates that minority students who attend selective universities hail disproportionately from high schools of lower quality on a variety of difficult-to-measure dimensions, such as levels of violence, and that these experiences carry over to their college experiences. That this potential determinant of postsecondary performance gaps has been understudied partly reflects the limited success of researchers to identify "school effects" on achievement outcomes beyond second grade and partly reflects the lack of adequate data to establish an association between high school quality and academic performance at the postsecondary level. Growing racial and ethnic segregation in public high schools, coupled with evidence that minority students are more likely than nonminority students to attend failing schools (according to NCLB criteria), underscores the importance of evaluating whether differences in quality of high schools minority students attend are responsible for observed collegiate performance gaps.

Accordingly, we analyze administrative data on the universe of enrollees at four Texas universities of varying selectivity. The empirical analysis provides compelling evidence that high school attended substantially reduces and in several instances reverses racial and ethnic disparities in several dimensions of college achievement. Other researchers have used similar empirical designs (Rothstein 2004; Pike and Saupe 2002), but we are unaware of any previous research that has considered racial/ethnic achievement disparities using this design, and none has examined these disparities across colleges of varying selectivity. Long, Iatarola, and Conger (2009) use middle school (and separately high school) fixed effects to predict racial/ethnic differences in math readiness during college but find little evidence that school attended is responsible for these differences. V. Lee and Bryk (1989) claim that high school attributes can promote an equitable distribution of achievement across diverse students but do not implement a fixed-effects research design to address this hypothesis. Finally, Pike and Saupe (2002) provide evidence that high school fixed effects are as accurate in predicting college achievement as hierarchical linear models that include high school characteristics.

Data and Empirical Methods

We examine three indicators of college performance to ascertain whether high school attended influences postsecondary academic outcomes: college GPA for both first- and sixth-semester cumulative average as well as fourth-year graduation for students who enroll at four public Texas universities: UT, TAMU, Texas Tech, and UTSA.[3] Two types of administrative records are available. The applicant files represent the universe of students who applied for admission at each target university from the early 1990s through 2003—nearly 200,000 individuals across the four institutions. Each applicant record includes key academic and demographic variables: SAT/American College Testing (ACT) scores, high school class rank, gender, ethnicity, and maternal education attainment, as well as admission decisions and, conditional on acceptance, enrollment outcomes.[4] Important for our purpose, the applicant files include codes for the high school attended and geographic identifiers. For matriculants, a transcript file tracks various measures of academic progress, including persistence, cumulative GPA, choice of major, and graduation status for each semester enrolled. Table 1 summarizes the available years for cohorts of first-time freshmen, campus characteristics, and the pooled numbers of student applicants for each institution.

The four universities examined differ by selectivity of their admissions as well as student demographic attributes. *Barron's Profiles of American Colleges* (Barron's 1996) classified UT as very competitive, TAMU as highly competitive, Texas Tech as competitive, and UTSA as noncompetitive. This classification corresponds with the precollegiate achievement of freshmen, indicated by SAT/ACT scores and high school class rank. Specifically, average standardized test scores earned by first-time freshmen at UT approached 1,200 during the observation

TABLE 1
Summary Statistics for Analysis Samples: Means or Proportions (Standard Deviation)

	University of Texas at Austin (1990-2003)	Texas A&M University (1992-2002)	Texas Tech (1991-2003)	University of Texas at San Antonio (1992-2004)
Composition[a]				
Hispanic	0.15	0.11	0.09	0.44
Black	0.04	0.03	0.03	0.05
White	0.64	0.81	0.86	0.46
Asian	0.17	0.04	0.02	0.05
Test score (M)	1,197.1	1,156.3	1,088.7	998.1
(SD)	(142.7)	(138.7)	(137.9)	(133.8)
Percentile class rank	85.7	86.1	72.3	66.9
(SD)	(13.5)	(12.4)	(19.6)	(21.6)
1st-semester GPA (M)	2.90	2.71	2.85	2.11
(SD)	(0.90)	(0.80)	(0.08)	(1.10)
6th-semester GPA (M)	3.01	2.95	2.99	2.52
(SD)	(0.60)	(0.50)	(0.50)	(0.70)
4-year graduation rate	.46	.31	.25	.15
4th-semester attrition	.15	.15	.29	.59
6th-semester attrition	.21	.19	.33	.65
N	77,219	61,546	31,157	21,287

SOURCE: THEOP data. Authors' compilation.
a. Other category comprises less than 1 percent of student body at all institutions except Texas A&M University. This category is not reported, but observations are retained in the analysis sample.

period, with TAMU's average slightly below at 1,156. At Texas Tech, freshmen scored just below 1,100 on their standardized tests, well above UTSA's average of 1,000. These disparities imply that the average student at TAMU scored approximately one standard deviation higher on her or his SAT/ACT test compared with the average student enrolled at UTSA. High school class rankings of enrollees at UT and TAMU are 86 percent on average, which indicates that only 14 percent of students ranked above the typical freshman at the two flagship campuses. At Texas Tech the average high school class rank of freshmen was 72 percent, compared with 67 percent at UTSA.

Partly owing to location and partly to their historical legacies, the four institutions also differ in the demographic composition of their student bodies: Hispanics constituted 9 percent of freshmen enrollment at Texas Tech, 11 percent at TAMU, and 15 percent at UT; but at UTSA, they made up 43 percent of the freshman class, on average. Black students represent 3 to 5 percent of freshmen at the four institutions, which is similar to the Asian average at all universities except UT, where they constitute 17 percent of first-time enrollees. UT, the most diverse campus of the four, is located in the capital city, which itself is highly varied ethnically, politically, and socially. TAMU, Texas's first public postsecondary institution, is situated within a triangle formed by three U.S. interstate highways linking the state's largest cities—Houston, Dallas, and Austin. A nonmetropolitan location combined with its original focus on agricultural fields historically attracted white applicants to TAMU. Texas Tech, likewise, is located in one of the world's largest cotton-growing regions, with the Lubbock area's population predominantly white. By contrast to the two public flagships and Texas Tech, whites make up less than half of first-time freshmen over the observation period at UTSA. Often described as a Hispanic-serving institution, UTSA is an urban campus that draws students from both its predominantly Hispanic local population and South Texas.[5]

The academic performance outcomes of interest also differ across institutions, but for first- and sixth-semester cumulative GPA the major divide is between institutions with selective admission criteria (i.e., the public flagships and Texas Tech) and UTSA, which is practically an open admission system for applicants who received high school diplomas. Fully appreciating the significance of the GPA disparities requires some attention to attrition because cumulative grades are based on the subset of students still enrolled, who are likely a selective subset of the initial cohort. Attrition varies inversely with institutional selectivity, with 80 percent of UT's freshmen persisting through their sixth semester compared with just more than one-third of UTSA freshmen.[6] Furthermore, less than half of the freshmen graduated within four years of matriculating at UT, but this is approximately three times higher than UTSA freshmen.[7]

In summary, the four public institutions represent considerable variation in college climate, defined by geography, demography, and selectivity of admissions. Existing studies indicate that the minority achievement gaps will be largest at the most selective institutions, but whether and how much variation in high school quality contributes to these differences is an empirical question.

Modeling Strategy

Our empirical models build on standard production functions, where educational outcomes are assumed to be the product of various inputs at the individual, family, and school levels. In particular, we specify the following linear relationship between college achievement outcomes and educational inputs:

$$outcome_{iut} = \beta X_{ist} + \alpha U + \tau_t + \varepsilon_{iut}, \tag{1}$$

where an educational outcome for student i at university u at time t is determined by the student's demographic and background characteristics (X), university characteristics (U), and an idiosyncratic error term. To control for secular trends in the freshman class, university grading standards, and so on, we also control for year fixed effects, τ_t. Analyzing results separately for each of the four universities obviates the need to control for institutional characteristics, U. For all specifications, the estimated β coefficients for student racial background represent institution-specific racial disparities in college achievement:

$$outcome_{iut} = \beta_u X_{ist} + \tau_t + \varepsilon_{iut}. \tag{2}$$

To evaluate whether high schools attended influence race and ethnic differences in college achievement, we estimate variants of (3),

$$outcome_{ist} = \beta X_{ist} + S_s + \tau_t + \varepsilon_{ist}. \tag{3}$$

This specification models all time-invariant characteristics about each student's high school (s) to control for school-specific differences ("fixed effects"). Results for equation (3) indicate whether racial disparities in college achievement exist for students who attended the same high school. That is, we use a within-high-school-of-origin estimator for racial gaps in college achievement, where our coefficient of interest is only identified by within-high-school disparities in college achievement between individuals of different race/ethnicity who attended the same high school.[8]

Results

Table 2 reports estimates of college achievement based on a variant of equations (2) and (3) for students enrolled in each of the four universities. The first specification, which includes students' gender and racial background as well as year fixed effects, reveals large performance differences among freshmen at all institutions. At UT, for example, black students earn a first-semester GPA 0.4 points below that of white students, and the average Hispanic-white GPA gap is 0.23 grade points. Similar gaps obtain for TAMU, Texas Tech, and UTSA, except that the magnitudes differ.

The second specification includes covariates known to influence freshman academic performance, namely, high school class rank and SAT/ACT score.[9] Adding these control variables reduces the UT black-white GPA gap by 75 percent, to 0.09 grade points, which represents a one-tenth standard deviation difference in first-semester GPA. The Hispanic-white GPA disparity at UT shrinks by more than 70 percent, to 0.04 grade points among students with comparable high

TABLE 2
Determinants of First-Semester Grade Point Average: Four Texas Public Universities

Specification	University of Texas at Austin (1992-2003)[a]			Texas A&M University (1992-2002)			Texas Tech (1996-2003)			University of Texas at San Antonio (1995-2003)		
	Basic	Extended	Fixed Effects	Basic	Extended	Fixed Effects	Basic	Extended	Fixed Effects	Basic	Extended	Fixed Effects
Male	-.150***	-.179***	-.118***	-.109***	-.110***	-.043***	-.222***	-.156***	-.097***	-.174***	-.157***	-.055***
	(.006)	(.006)	(.006)	(.006)	(.006)	(.006)	(.010)	(.010)	(.010)	(.016)	(.015)	(.015)
Black	-.406***	-.090***	.031**	-.386***	-.098***	.071***	-.314***	-.133***	.008	-.235***	-.026	.033
	(.016)	(.014)	(.015)	(.018)	(.016)	(.018)	(.031)	(.028)	(.030)	(.034)	(.032)	(.033)
Hispanic	-.228***	-.039***	.026***	-.331***	-.182***	-.094***	-.203***	-.132***	-.082***	-.197***	-.100***	.047***
	(.009)	(.008)	(.009)	(.010)	(.009)	(.011)	(.018)	(.017)	(.018)	(.017)	(.016)	(.018)
Asian	.152***	.096***	.014*	.072***	.017	.001	.053	.024	-.025	.184***	.186***	.059*
	(.008)	(.008)	(.008)	(.017)	(.015)	(.015)	(.038)	(.034)	(.035)	(.036)	(.033)	(.034)
Other	-.229***	-.149***	-.096**	-.118***	-.078***	-.044*	-.096	-.065	-.005	-.268**	-.179*	-.053
	(.049)	(.043)	(.042)	(.029)	(.026)	(.026)	(.075)	(.068)	(.069)	(.116)	(.106)	(.105)
Class rank		.020***	.029***		.017***	.026***		.014***	.021***		.013***	.022***
		(.000)	(.000)		(.000)	(.000)		(.000)	(.000)		(.000)	(.000)
Test score (SAT/ACT)		.184***	.114***		.170***	.109***		.113***	.059***		.199***	.104***
		(.002)	(.002)		(.002)	(.002)		(.004)	(.004)		(.006)	(.006)
Constant	2.807***	-1.004***	-.962***	2.741***	-.733***	-.849***	2.904***	.654***	.687***	2.090***	-.697***	-.491***
	(.008)	(.031)	(.031)	(.012)	(.030)	(.030)	(.018)	(.041)	(.042)	(.034)	(.061)	(.061)
Observations	77,219	77,218	77,130	61,546	61,542	61,542	24,936	24,936	24,300	18,771	18,771	18,771
R-squared	.06	.27	.29	.04	.22	.24	.03	.21	.24	.03	.19	.23
Number of high schools		2,117			1,864			1,154			1,049	

NOTE: All models include year fixed effects.

a. Extended and fixed effects models included mother's education, which is unavailable for other institutions.

*Significant at 10 percent. **Significant at 5 percent. ***Significant at 1 percent.

153

school grades and test scores. This model accounts for about a quarter of the variance in freshman GPA at UT, largely due to individual differences in high school achievement.

Inclusion of high school achievement measures also shrinks the black-white first-semester GPA gap at TAMU and Texas Tech, but somewhat less than at UT. The expanded specification reduces the black-white GPA gap at TAMU by 0.29 points (from –0.39 to –0.10) and the Hispanic-white gap by 0.15 points (from –0.33 to –0.18). The point estimates for Texas Tech students imply that black students earn 0.13 points below whites who arrived with similar high school class rank and SAT scores (versus –0.031 points), and the Hispanic-white GPA gap drops from –0.20 to –0.13 points among students with comparable precollegiate achievements. For UTSA, the least selective institution considered, controlling for students' SAT scores and class rank eliminates the black-white GPA gaps and reduces the Hispanic-white gap from –0.18 to –0.11 points. Probably due to lack of information about parental education for TAMU, Texas Tech, and UTSA students, the expanded model accounts for approximately 20 percent of the variance in first-semester GPA, with a slightly better fit at the selective institutions (where SAT scores are used for admissions).

The consistency of results across institutions that differ in the selectivity of their admissions implies that other factors are responsible for the college achievement gap. A contending explanation that has not been systematically examined is high school quality, which we model using a high school fixed effects specification (equation [3] above). Substantively, this approach captures those characteristics of high schools that are shared by graduates of the school, which could include similar curricula, teachers, college preparatory training, distance to college, and other measures of high school quality and access to college. However, any differences in experiences of individuals who attended the same high school (such as racial discrimination by teachers) would not be adequately captured with this method. Point estimates for the fixed-effects models changes the comparison groups from all whites, blacks, and Hispanics who were freshmen at one of the four institutions in a particular year to freshmen in a particular year who *attended the same high school*.

One caveat is in order before interpreting the results, namely, the coefficients are only identified based on high schools that send multiple students to a particular institution and where the students are of different racial or ethnic backgrounds. This occurs because the specification compares, for example, white and black students who attended the *same high school*. If a particular high school sends no black students to a university, an estimate of the black-white gap in college success cannot be generated for this high school. Consequently, the analysis samples for the fixed-effects specification change because some schools lack race variation in their enrollees at a university in a given year.[10] Given the pervasive segregation of Texas high schools (Tienda and Niu 2006), we reestimated the analysis restricting the sample to high schools that send students from multiple race groups and show that the basic results are robust (see Appendix A).[11]

The fixed-effects results reveal substantial changes in the black-white and Hispanic-white performance gaps, indicating that differences in college preparedness associated with high school quality carry over to college careers, although the impacts appear to depend on institutional selectivity. For example, at UT, the black-white and Hispanic-white first-semester performance gaps change from deficits of 0.09 and 0.04 points, respectively, to a 0.03 point advantage for both groups. The Asian GPA advantage, evident across all estimates, shrinks once Asian students are compared with their same-high-school classmates.

The racial gap in first-semester GPA also is reversed at TAMU in the fixed-effects specification, indicating that black students who attended the same high school outperformed their white counterparts. Hispanic students attending TAMU do not outperform their white high school classmates, but the achievement gap is only half as large as the institution-wide average for all white and Hispanic students. The different outcomes for blacks and Hispanics at TAMU reflect several circumstances. First, over the observation period, black students made up only 3 percent of TAMU students compared with 11 percent for Hispanics (see Table 1), which suggests less heterogeneity among blacks. Second, TAMU has a more difficult time attracting minority students compared with UT, partly because of its location (more than an hour's travel from a large metropolitan area) and partly because of its reputation as being less hospitable to minority students (Tienda and Sullivan 2009).

At Texas Tech, the school fixed effects specification eliminated the black-white first-semester GPA gap, but not that for Hispanics. Still, when Hispanic freshmen are compared with white classmates from the same high school, the GPA gap is roughly 40 percent smaller relative to the specification that only considers precollegiate academic achievements. On average, black students constitute only 3 percent of freshmen cohorts at Tech, compared with 9 percent for Hispanics, suggesting greater heterogeneity among the latter. Yet, at UTSA, where Hispanics make up more than two-fifths of the freshman cohorts and blacks constitute an additional 5 percent, the fixed-effects model indicates that both minority groups outperform their white counterparts who attended the same high school (although the black coefficient is imprecisely estimated).

The first year of college serves as a sifting and sorting period as students acclimate to the demands of higher education. Those unable to handle the academic load, either for personal or academic reasons, withdraw along the way. By the end of the third year, however, the more successful students remain.[12] Appendix B, which reports sixth-semester attrition probabilities for each institution, confirms that students with higher GPAs were more likely to persist (and therefore be in the sixth-semester GPA analysis). Nevertheless, attrition differs by demographic group, institution, and semester.[13]

Success begets success; therefore, it is conceivable that the performance gap between minority and nonminority students has narrowed because the cohort "survivors" will exclude students who withdrew or were dropped for academic reasons. Table 3 considers this proposition by examining whether the racial and

TABLE 3

Determinants of Sixth-Semester Cumulative GPA: Four Texas Public Universities

Specification	University of Texas at Austin (1992-2001)[a]			Texas A&M University (1992-2002)			Texas Tech (1996-2001)			University of Texas at San Antonio (1995-2001)		
	Basic	Extended	Fixed Effects	Basic	Extended	Fixed Effects	Basic	Extended	Fixed Effects	Basic	Extended	Fixed Effects
Male	-.151*** (.005)	-.179*** (.004)	-.144*** (.004)	-.147*** (.005)	-.150*** (.004)	-.114*** (.004)	-.227*** (.010)	-.187*** (.009)	-.158*** (.009)	-.172*** (.018)	-.160*** (.016)	-.108*** (.018)
Black	-.386*** (.013)	-.192*** (.012)	-.125*** (.012)	-.352*** (.014)	-.160*** (.012)	-.067*** (.013)	-.362*** (.029)	-.183*** (.025)	-.103*** (.029)	-.213*** (.039)	-.110*** (.036)	-.066* (.040)
Hispanic	-.214*** (.007)	-.101*** (.007)	-.044*** (.007)	-.236*** (.008)	-.141*** (.007)	-.085*** (.008)	-.159*** (.018)	-.087*** (.016)	-.065*** (.017)	-.145*** (.019)	-.097*** (.018)	-.020 (.021)
Asian	.024*** (.007)	-.011* (.006)	-.048*** (.006)	.017 (.013)	-.023* (.011)	-.030*** (.011)	-.083** (.037)	-.072** (.032)	-.058* (.033)	-.046 (.042)	-.033 (.038)	-.048 (.040)
Other	-.065 (.041)	-.022 (.036)	-.004 (.035)	-.082*** (.022)	-.070*** (.019)	-.051*** (.019)	.051 (.077)	.096 (.067)	.109 (.070)	-.095 (.161)	-.116 (.146)	.007 (.147)
Class Rank		.012*** (.000)	.019*** (.000)		.013*** (.000)	.019*** (.000)		.010*** (.000)	.014*** (.000)		.009*** (.000)	.014*** (.001)
Test score (SAT/ACT)		.123*** (.000)	.080*** (.000)		.121*** (.000)	.085*** (.000)		.099*** (.000)	.067*** (.000)		.112*** (.000)	.068*** (.000)
		(.002)	(.002)		(.002)	(.002)		(.003)	(.004)		(.006)	(.007)
Constant	3.004*** (.006)	.408*** (.024)	.397*** (.025)	2.996*** (.009)	.474*** (.022)	.333*** (.022)	3.079*** (.014)	1.255*** (.036)	1.259*** (.037)	2.678*** (.034)	.934*** (.068)	.963*** (.071)
Observations	52,025	52,025	51,976	50,260	50,259	50,259	11,573	11,573	11,334	5,419	5,419	5,419
R-squared	.07	.28	.31	.06	.27	.29	.07	.31	.33	.03	.20	.22
Number of high schools		1,728			1,713			925			590	

NOTE: All models include year fixed effects.

a. Extended and fixed effects models included mother's education, which is unavailable for other institutions.

*Significant at 10 percent. **Significant at 5 percent. ***Significant at 1 percent.

ethnic differences in college performance persist through students' college careers using sixth-semester cumulative GPA as the performance outcome.

Results parallel those observed for first-semester academic achievement in that the average black-white and Hispanic-white gaps in sixth-semester GPA are reduced by approximately 50 percent when controls for test scores, class rank, and maternal education (UT only) are modeled. The expanded model explains more than one-quarter of the variance in sixth-semester GPA for UT and TAMU matriculants, nearly one-third among Texas Tech students, but only about 20 percent at UTSA. These differences reflect the low dispersion of test scores at UTSA compared with selective institutions that use this criterion for admissions (see Table 1).

Sixth-semester grade disparities between minority and nonminority students are sizable, often in excess of one-fifth of a standard deviation after high school performance indicators are considered. At UT, for example, the black-white and Hispanic-white gaps for cumulative sixth-semester GPA are 0.39 and 0.21 points, respectively, which is relatively similar to those based on first-semester GPA. Thus, selective attrition does not appear to attenuate UT minority achievement gaps. At TAMU, the unadjusted Hispanic-white GPA gap increases over time; but at Texas Tech the drop in performance gap, based on sixth-semester cumulative GPA, is smaller than the first-semester GPA (0.16 as compared to 0.20 points).

Results from the fixed-effects specification were less powerful for sixth-semester GPA differentials in that controls for high school attended did not reverse any of the point estimates and reduced only one to zero (black-white differential at UTSA). That all the sixth-semester GPA point estimates reported in Table 3 shrink when school-specific differences are modeled, by 50 percent or more in many instances, suggests that quality differences in the high schools minority and white students attend impact not only early collegiate achievement but also continue through postsecondary careers.[14] Despite the reduction in the GPA gaps based on the fixed-effect specification, significant differences remain. At UT, for instance, black students earn a sixth-semester GPA 0.12 points below their white counterparts when compared with white students who attended the same high school, versus a 0.19 differential when compared with all white students who completed six semesters of coursework. Average GPA for Hispanic juniors was only 0.04 points below that of white juniors who attended the same high school, however.

There are several potential explanations for the persistence of these achievement differences, including racial and ethnic variation in choice of majors, course selection, peer influences, employment status while enrolled, or other unmeasured factors (such as whether students live on or off campus). The administrative data allow us to examine only the first explanation, namely, whether variation in choice of major is a possible mechanism maintaining achievement differences after six semesters. By this point in their postsecondary training, most students have declared their academic major.

TABLE 4

Determinants of Sixth-Semester Cumulative GPA with High School
Fixed Effects and Choice of Major: Four Texas Public Universities

Fixed Effects	University of Texas at Austin (1992-2001)[a]		Texas A&M University (1992-2002)		Texas Tech (1996-2001)		University of Texas at San Antonio (1995-2001)	
	High School (HS)	Major/HS	HS	Major/HS	HS	Major/HS	HS	Major/HS
Male	-.144***	-.110***	-.114***	-.073***	-.160***	-.087***	-.119***	-.052**
	(.004)	(.005)	(.004)	(.004)	(.010)	(.011)	(.021)	(.021)
Black	-.124***	-.118***	-.067***	-.058***	-.118***	-.090***	-.075	-.043
	(.012)	(.012)	(.013)	(.013)	(.033)	(.032)	(.049)	(.046)
Hispanic	-.044***	-.047***	-.085***	-.086***	-.060***	-.039**	-.048**	-.031
	(.007)	(.007)	(.008)	(.008)	(.020)	(.019)	(.025)	(.023)
Asian	-.048***	-.025***	-.030***	-.034***	-.082**	-.071*	-.136***	-.127***
	(.006)	(.006)	(.011)	(.011)	(.038)	(.037)	(.051)	(.048)
Other	-.004	-.004	-.051***	-.048***	.118	.085	.011	-.032
	(.035)	(.034)	(.019)	(.018)	(.077)	(.074)	(.161)	(.147)
Class rank	.019***	.017***	.019***	.017***	.014***	.014***	.013***	.012***
	(.000)	(.000)	(.000)	(.000)	(.000)	(.000)	(.001)	(.001)
Test score (SAT/ACT)	.080***	.074***	.085***	.084***	.071***	.074***	.066***	.064***
	(.002)	(.002)	(.002)	(.002)	(.004)	(.004)	(.008)	(.008)
Constant	.412***	.506***	.333***	.354*	1.199***	1.394***	1.118***	1.013***
	(.024)	(.152)	(.022)	(.192)	(.041)	(.202)	(.082)	(.384)
Observations	51,968	51,968	50,259	50,259	9,161	9,161	4,027	3,747
R-squared	.31	.37	.29	.35	.34	.39	.21	.3
Number of high schools	1,725	1,725	1,713	1,713	864	864	500	490

NOTE: All models include year fixed effects.

a. Extended and fixed effects models included mother's education, which is unavailable for other institutions.

*Significant at 10 percent. **Significant at 5 percent. ***Significant at 1 percent.

Results reported in Table 4 include controls for choice of major in predicting sixth-semester cumulative GPA. Here, the data for academic major are characterized by the academic department (e.g., Finance, Psychology) containing the major reported by each student by the sixth semester of college. For the two most selective institutions, UT and TAMU, we find little evidence that black and Hispanic students are sorting into majors that are systematically related to cumulative GPAs. For less selective universities (Texas Tech and UTSA), there is slightly more evidence that choice of major is one potential channel through which racial GPA differences are generated. Furthermore, the direction of the coefficients suggests that minority students are *more* likely to choose "more difficult" majors or courses (as measured by GPA) compared with similarly situated white students.

Analyses of four-year graduation parallel the GPA results inasmuch as the fixed effect specifications narrow the ethnic gaps (see Table 5). In our baseline specifications, we find large racial/ethnic differences in four-year graduation rates for three of the more selective universities; UTSA is an exception. Black students have lower rates of graduation than white students at UT (18 percentage points), TAMU (13 points), and Texas Tech (15 points). The extended control variables reduce these disparities by 20 to 50 percent. Likewise, Hispanic students have lower rates of graduation than white students at the three selective institutions: UT (12 points), TAMU (11 points), and Texas Tech (11 points). Similar to the results for black students, the extended control variables reduce these disparities by 10 to 40 percent. Finally, we narrow our comparisons to examine students who attended the same high school by modeling high school fixed effects. The school-level controls shrink the black-white disparities in graduation rates by 40 to 50 percent. As with the results for black students, introducing school-level controls also shrinks the Hispanic-white disparities in graduation rates around 40 to 50 percent. Similar to the estimates for blacks, the fixed-effects specification fails to eliminate the Hispanic-white disparities in four-year graduation rates. These results are consistent with our findings for sixth-semester cumulative GPA and warrant additional research to explain why racial/ethnic academic performance gaps widen during college.

That the empirical estimates are highly consistent across institutions that differ in the selectivity of admissions, from very selective to open admissions based on the Barron's (1996) classification, attests to their robustness. Overall, our empirical analysis provides strong evidence that high school attended has long-lasting effects on human capital accumulation, as measured by college success, even for the select group of students who attend selective public institutions.

Conclusion

Our examination of the college achievement gap between white and underrepresented minority students sought to establish a link between precollegiate

TABLE 5

Determinants of Four-Year Graduation with High School Fixed Effects: Four Texas Public Universities

Specification	University of Texas at Austin (1992–2003)[a]			Texas A&M University (1992–2002)			Texas Tech (1996–2003)			University of Texas at San Antonio (1995–2003)		
	Basic	Extended	High School Fixed Effect (HS FE)	Basic	Extended	HS FE	Basic	Extended	HS FE	Basic	Extended	HS FE
Male	−.140*** (.004)	−.143*** (.004)	−.124*** (.004)	−.223*** (.004)	−.220*** (.004)	−.205*** (.004)	−.144*** (.007)	−.124*** (.007)	−.111*** (.008)	−.029*** (.004)	−.026*** (.004)	−.022*** (.005)
Black	−.177*** (.009)	−.107*** (.009)	−.066*** (.010)	−.134*** (.011)	−.075*** (.011)	−.030** (.013)	−.148*** (.020)	−.117*** (.020)	−.078*** (.024)	−.012 (.009)	.001 (.009)	.003 (.010)
Hispanic	−.115*** (.005)	−.068*** (.005)	−.030*** (.006)	−.106*** (.006)	−.077*** (.006)	−.041*** (.008)	−.114*** (.013)	−.100*** (.013)	−.057*** (.014)	−.012*** (.004)	−.007 (.005)	−.004 (.005)
Asian	−.003 (.005)	−.009* (.005)	−.036*** (.006)	.015 (.011)	.004 (.011)	−.001 (.011)	−.099*** (.028)	−.107*** (.028)	−.107*** (.029)	.010 (.012)	.010 (.011)	.009 (.012)
Other	−.080*** (.029)	−.060** (.029)	−.044 (.029)	−.052*** (.018)	−.043** (.017)	−.026 (.018)	.092 (.061)	.097 (.060)	.103 (.063)	.010 (.033)	.014 (.033)	.025 (.035)
Class rank		.004*** (.000)	.007*** (.000)		.004*** (.000)	.006*** (.000)		.003*** (.000)	.005*** (.000)		.001*** (.000)	.001*** (.000)
Test score (SAT/ACT)		.038*** (.001)	.014*** (.002)		.031*** (.002)	.017*** (.000)		.013*** (.000)	−.001		.011*** (.000)	.006*** (.000)
Constant	.361*** (.007)	−.507*** (.020)	−.447*** (.020)	.388*** (.007)	−.331*** (.021)	−.372*** (.021)	.307*** (.009)	−.072** (.029)	−.048 (.031)	.059*** (.005)	−.107*** (.016)	−.088*** (.017)
Observations	62,062	62,061	61,997	49,690	49,686	49,686	13,793	13,793	13,499	10,900	10,900	10,900
R-squared	.05	.09	.09	.07	.10	.10	.04	.07	.07	.01	.03	.03
Number of high schools			1,969			1,754			986			839

NOTE: All models include year fixed effects.

a. Extended and fixed effects models included mother's education, which is unavailable for other institutions.

*Significant at 10 percent. **Significant at 5 percent. ***Significant at 1 percent.

and postcollegiate outcomes using a unique administrative dataset for the universe of enrollees at four Texas public universities over a ten-year period. We consider three academic outcomes—first- and sixth-semester GPA and fourth-year graduation. Empirical results confirm prior studies that narrow collegiate achievement gaps by controlling for observable precollege achievements (e.g., test scores, class rank based on high school GPA). Yet, substantial gaps persist.

Our main hypothesis—that differences in the quality of high schools attended by minority versus majority students contribute to the collegiate achievement gaps—finds considerable support. Using fixed-effects specifications to model differences in the quality of schools attended by entering freshmen, we show that the racial and ethnic disparities reverse, suggesting that black and Hispanic students perform better than their white high school classmates. This inference is particularly strong for first-semester GPA. Empirical estimates are also quite robust across institutions that differ in the selectivity of their admissions. For later college achievement, our fixed-effects specifications explain some, but not all, of the gaps in sixth-semester GPA, even after taking into account differences in choice of major.

On balance, our analyses reveal the dynamic human capital consequences stemming from differences in high school quality across racial groups and also suggest the need for future research to examine mechanisms that sustain moderate racial and ethnic differences in later college achievement. This consideration highlights the importance of NCLB in holding schools accountable for student academic performance. Many studies have concluded that high school quality does not explain group differences in postcollegiate achievement, partly because postsecondary enrollment is a voluntary decision that selects from the most accomplished students and partly because analysts have not clearly specified which high school inputs carry over to college. Our findings suggest a pressing need to further specify the mechanisms that maintain race and ethnic differences in collegiate achievement as an adjunct to designing policy interventions that can eliminate disparities.

Narrowing output differences across high schools, even within a single state like Texas, is a long-term undertaking. Whether NCLB has narrowed achievement differences among Texas high schools is highly uncertain, but our findings suggest that narrowing achievement gains across schools is an important accountability metric for underperforming campuses in addition to the goals explicitly required by the original legislation. Unless the achievement gaps are narrowed across high schools, particularly those highly segregated by race and ethnicity, it is unlikely that differentials in college performance will be closed. In the short run, however, the testing requirements of NCLB might be used to identify weaknesses in students' mastery of core academic subjects as a way of targeting the substantive areas that need improvement. Whether remediation programs are best administered by universities or community colleges is unclear, but bolstering academic deficiencies before students enroll at a university could result in significant cost savings and even reduce attrition due to failure.

Appendix A
Comparison of Full Sample versus Heterogeneous School Sample: Results for First-Semester GPA

Specification	University of Texas at Austin (1992-2003)[a]		Texas A&M University (1992-2002)		Texas Tech (1996-2003)		University of Texas at San Antonio (1996-2004)	
	Extended	Mixed Schools	Extended	Mixed Schools	Extended	Mixed Schools	Extended	Mixed Schools
Male	-.179***	-.171***	-.110***	-.104***	-.156***	-.133***	-.165***	-.190***
	(.006)	(.007)	(.006)	(.009)	(.010)	(.017)	(.015)	(.021)
Black	-.090***	-.079***	-.098***	-.077***	-.133***	-.120***	.007	-.032
	(.014)	(.016)	(.016)	(.020)	(.028)	(.042)	(.034)	(.041)
Hispanic	-.039***	-.034***	-.182***	-.183***	-.132***	-.155***	-.107***	-.099***
	(.008)	(.011)	(.009)	(.015)	(.017)	(.029)	(.017)	(.023)
Asian	.096***	.063***	.017	.020	.024	.037	.197***	.165***
	(.008)	(.008)	(.015)	(.019)	(.034)	(.053)	(.035)	(.043)
Other	-.149***	-.180***	-.078***	-.096***	-.065	-.008	-.198**	-.244
	(.043)	(.051)	(.026)	(.039)	(.068)	(.110)	(.115)	(.176)
Class rank	.020***	.020***	.017***	.019***	.014***	.014***	.014***	.014***
	(.000)	(.000)	(.000)	(.000)	(.000)	(.000)	(.000)	(.000)
Test score (SAT/ACT)	.184***	.174***	.170***	.155***	.113***	.114***	.211***	.201***
	(.002)	(.003)	(.002)	(.003)	(.004)	(.006)	(.006)	(.008)
Constant	-1.004***	-.903***	-.733***	-.618***	.654***	.717***	-.838***	-.726***
	(.031)	(.036)	(.030)	(.045)	(.041)	(.069)	(.067)	(.091)
Observations	77,218	53,529	61,542	26,085	24,936	8,882	16,916	8,936
R-squared	.27	.28	.22	.24	.21	.21	.18	.19

NOTE: All models include year fixed effects. "Mixed schools" refers to schools that send at least one black and Hispanic student to the university.

a. Extended and fixed effects models included mother's education, which is unavailable for other institutions.

*Significant at 10 percent. **Significant at 5 percent. ***Significant at 1 percent.

Appendix B
Predictors of Sixth-Semester Attrition: Extended and Fixed Effects Models

Specification	University of Texas at Austin (1992-2003)[a]		Texas A&M University (1992-2002)		Texas Tech (1996-2003)		University of Texas at San Antonio (1996-2004)	
	Extended	Fixed Effects	Extended	Fixed Effects	Extended	Fixed Effects	Extended	Fixed Effects
First-semester grade point average (GPA)	-.193***	-.181***	-.195***	-.185***	-.197***	-.190***	-.193***	-.193***
	(.002)	(.002)	(.002)	(.002)	(.005)	(.005)	(.004)	(.004)
Male	.013***	.008**	.007**	-.002	-.023***	-.030***	-.018**	-.016*
	(.003)	(.003)	(.003)	(.003)	(.007)	(.007)	(.008)	(.009)
Black	-.009	-.034***	.027***	-.003	-.000	-.034	-.045**	-.046**
	(.008)	(.008)	(.009)	(.010)	(.020)	(.023)	(.018)	(.020)
Hispanic	.030***	.006	.045***	.028***	.050***	.037***	-.049***	-.043***
	(.004)	(.005)	(.005)	(.006)	(.012)	(.013)	(.009)	(.011)
Asian	-.032***	-.022***	.044***	.048***	.001	.002	-.070***	-.084***
	(.004)	(.004)	(.008)	(.009)	(.025)	(.026)	(.021)	(.022)
Other race	.039*	.027	.044***	.031**	-.039	-.053	.003	-.044
	(.023)	(.024)	(.014)	(.014)	(.055)	(.058)	(.064)	(.067)
High school rank	.001***	-.001***	-.000***	-.002***	-.001***	-.002***	-.001***	-.002***
	(.000)	(.000)	(.000)	(.000)	(.000)	(.000)	(.000)	(.000)
SAT/ACT	.013***	.021***	.018***	.026***	.023***	.029***	.009***	.014***
	(.001)	(.001)	(.001)	(.001)	(.003)	(.003)	(.003)	(.004)
Constant	.556***	.560***	.538***	.553***	.702***	.697***	1.021***	.994***
	(.015)	(.015)	(.016)	(.017)	(.028)	(.030)	(.032)	(.034)
Observations	64916	64854	55397	55397	16869	16494	12271	12271
R-squared	.17	.16	.15	.15	.12	.12	.19	.20
Number of high schools		2,008		1,809		1,036		884

NOTE: All models include year fixed effects.

a. Extended and fixed effects models included mother's education, which is unavailable for other institutions.

*Significant at 10 percent. **Significant at 5 percent. ***Significant at 1 percent.

Notes

1. The mismatch hypothesis was originally dubbed the "fit" hypothesis (see, e.g., Bowen and Bok 1998), but in fact the claim is that minority students admitted under affirmative action policies are not a proper "fit" at selective institutions. Rather than use the term "misfit," Alon and Tienda (2005) coined the term "mismatch" hypothesis, which is now more widely used.

2. This finding is not inconsistent with the mismatch hypothesis, which requires comparisons between comparable minority students who attended more versus less selective institutions.

3. These data were collected under the auspices of the THEOP. THEOP is a longitudinal study of postsecondary behavior among two cohorts of Texas high school students that is designed to understand the consequences of changing admissions regimes after 1996. The description of this project is available at www.THEOP.Princeton.edu.

4. Only the UT includes information on maternal education.

5. More than 60 percent of San Antonio's population is Hispanic, which is more than four times the national average (American Community Survey 2005-07, http://www.census.gov/acs/www/).

6. It is important to note, though, that our measure of attrition includes transfers to other universities, which are much higher at the University of Texas at San Antonio compared with the other universities in our sample.

7. To minimize the extent of right censoring, we examine four-year graduation rates rather than the more customary six-year rates.

8. A complementary approach to the method of using high school fixed effects would be to measure and examine the predictors of school specific race gaps (Stiefel, Schwartz, and Ellen 2007). This is a promising direction for future research using these data.

9. For UT, we also control for maternal education, but this information is not available for other institutions.

10. The modest change in R-squared is an artifact of STATA's calculation of the partial R-squared, which does not include the school fixed effects in the "xtreg" program.

11. Results for sixth-semester GPA and fourth-year graduation are available upon request.

12. Because sixth-semester GPA outcomes are censored, some students (namely those who enrolled after 2001 or those who left college before the sixth semester) were eliminated from the analysis. We also estimated our earlier models dropping the censored observations. These results (available from authors) show that our estimates for first-semester GPA are similar if censored observations are dropped. Texas A&M University has no students who are right censored.

13. At UT, for example, blacks were no more likely to attrite than whites with comparable achievement, but they were more likely than their white classmates from the same high school to remain enrolled by the sixth semester. Hispanics were less likely than whites to remain enrolled, but these average differences disappear when restricted to students who attended the same high school.

14. In results reported in Appendix B, we predict attrition between first and sixth semesters. We find some evidence that black students are less likely to attrite, which may imply that part of the black-white gap in sixth-semester GPA could be the result of less able black students remaining in college.

References

Alon, Sigal, and Marta Tienda. 2005. Assesing the "mismatch" hypothesis: Differentials in college graduation rates by institutional selectivity. *Sociology of Education* 78 (4): 294-315.

Alon, Sigal, and Marta Tienda. 2007. Diversity, opportunity and the shifting meritocracy in higher education. *American Sociological Review* 72 (4): 487-511.

Barron's. 1996. *Barron's profiles of American colleges*. 21st ed. Hauppauge, NY: Barron's Educational Series, Inc.

Bowen, William G., and Derek Bok. 1998. *The shape of the river: Long-term consequences of considering race in college and university admissions*. Princeton, NJ: Princeton University Press.

Dale, Stacy B., and Alan B. Krueger. 2002. Estimating the payoff to attending a more selective college: An application of selection on observables and unobservables. *Quarterly Journal of Economics* 117 (4): 1491-1527.

Fryer, Roland G., and Steven D. Levitt. 2004. Understanding the black-white test score gap in the first two years of school. *Review of Economics and Statistics* 86 (2): 447-64.

Fryer, Roland G., and Steven D. Levitt. 2006a. The black-white test score gap through third grade. *American Law and Economics Review* 8 (2): 249-81.

Fryer, Roland G., and Steven D. Levitt. 2006b. Testing for racial differences in the mental ability of young children. Working Paper 12066, National Bureau of Economic Research, Cambridge, MA. http://www .nber.org/papers/w12066.pdf.

Heckman, James J. 2006. Skill formation and the economics of investing in disadvantaged children. *Science* 312:1900-1902.

Heckman, James J., and Paul A. LaFontaine. 2007. The American high school graduate rate trends and levels. Working Paper 13670, National Bureau of Economic Research, Cambridge, MA. http://www.nber.org/ papers/w13670.pdf.

Kane, Thomas. 1998. Racial and ethnic preferences in college admissions. In *The black-white test score gap*, ed. Christopher Jencks and Meredith Phillips, 431-56. Washington, DC: Brookings Institution.

Kao, Grace, and Jennifer S. Thompson. 2003. Racial and ethnic stratification in educational achievement and attainment. *Annual Review of Sociology* 29:417-42.

Lee, Jaekyung. 2006. Tracking achievement gaps and assessing the impact of NCLB on the gaps: An in-depth look into national and state reading and math outcome trends. Report, Civil Rights Project at Harvard University, Cambridge, MA.

Lee, Valerie E., and Anthony S. Bryk. 1989. A multilevel model of the social distribution of high school achievement. *Sociology of Education* 62 (3): 172-92.

Light, Audrey, and Wayne Strayer. 2002. From Bakke to Hopwood: Does race affect college attendance and completion? *Review of Economics and Statistics* 84 (1): 34-44.

Long, Mark C., Patrice Iatarola, and Dylan Conger. 2009. Explaining gaps in readiness for college-level math: The role of high school courses. *Education Finance and Policy* 41 (1): 1-33.

Massey, Douglas S. 2006. Social background and academic performance differentials: White and minority students at selective colleges. *American Law and Economic Review* 8 (2): 390-409.

Massey, Douglas S., and Mary J. Fischer. 2005. Stereotype threat and academic performance: New findings from a racially diverse sample of college freshmen. *Du Bois Review: Social Science Research on Race* 2 (1): 45-67.

McDonough, Patricia M. 1997. *Choosing colleges: How social class and schools structure opportunity.* Albany: State University of New York Press.

National Center for Education Statistics (NCES). 2005. Postsecondary participation rates by sex and race/ ethnicity: 1974-2003. Issue Brief. NCES 2005-028, National Center for Education Statistics, Washington, DC. http://www.nces.ed.gov/pubs2005/2005028.pdf.

Niu, Sunny X., and Marta Tienda. 2008. Choosing colleges: Identifying and modeling choice sets. *Social Science Research* 37 (2): 413-33.

Niu, Sunny X., Marta Tienda, and Kalena Cortes. 2006. College selectivity and the Texas top 10% law. *Economics of Education Review* 25 (3): 259-72.

Perna, Laura, and Watson S. Swail. 2002. Pre-college outreach and early intervention programs. In *Condition of access: Higher education for lower income students*, ed. Donald Heller, 97-112. Westport, CT: American Council on Education/Praeger.

Pike, Gary R., and Joseph L. Saupe. 2002. Does high school matter? An analysis of three methods of predicting first-year grades. *Research in Higher Education* 43 (2): 187-207.

Rothstein, Jesse M. 2004. College performance predictions and the SAT. *Journal of Econometrics* 121 (1-2): 297-317.

Sacerdote, Bruce. 2001. Peer effects with random assignment: Results for Dartmouth roommates. *Quarterly Journal of Economics* 116 (2): 681-704.

Schneider, Barbara, Sylvia Martinez, and Ann Owens. 2006. Barriers to educational opportunities for Hispanics in the United States. In *Hispanics and the future of America*, ed. Marta Tienda and Faith Mitchell, 179-227. Washington, DC: National Academics Press.

Stiefel, Leanna, Amy Ellen Schwartz, and Ingrid Gould Ellen. 2007. Disentangling the racial test score gap: Probing the evidence in a large urban school district. *Journal of Policy Analysis and Management* 26 (1): 7-30.

Summers, Anita, and Barbara Wolfe. 1977. Do schools make a difference? *American Economic Review* 67 (4): 639-52.

Thernstrom, Abigail, and Stephan Thernstrom. 1996. Reflections on the shape of the river. *UCLA Law Review* 46 (5): 1583-1632.

Tienda, Marta, and Sunny X. Niu. 2006. Capitalizing on segregation, pretending neutrality: College admissions and the Texas top 10% law. *American Law and Economics Review* 8 (2): 312-46.

Tienda, Marta, and Teresa A. Sullivan. 2009. The promise and peril of the Texas Uniform Admission Law. In *The next twenty five years? Affirmative action and higher education in the United States and South Africa*, ed. Martin Hall, Marvin Krislov, and David L. Featherman. Ann Arbor: University of Michigan Press.

Tough, Paul. 2006. What it takes to make a student. *New York Times Magazine*, November 26.

Vars, Frederick E., and William G. Bowen. 1998. Scholastic aptitude test scores, race, and academic performance in selective colleges and universities. In *The black-white test score gap*, ed. Christopher Jencks and Meredith Phillips, 457-79. Washington, DC: Brookings Institution.

In this article, the author estimates the causal effect of attending a selective college on a student's academic performance. The results differ from previous studies because the author estimates a local effect, identified only for students who enroll in a selective college but would not have been able to do so without the guaranteed admissions granted to them by Texas's Top Ten Percent Law. Differing from many previous studies, the author finds significant negative effects of attending a selective college on the following measures: first- and sixth-semester grade point average, probability of completing the sixth semester, and graduation probability.

Keywords: higher education; admission policy; college performance; human capital

Academic Outcomes and Texas's Top Ten Percent Law

By
ERIC FURSTENBERG

Following the 1996 *Hopwood*[1] decision ending affirmative action admissions programs in Texas, minority student enrollments fell precipitously at the state's flagship public universities. As an alternative to affirmative action, in 1997 the Texas legislature passed H.B. 588, the Top Ten Percent Law, which guarantees to students graduating in the top decile of their high school class admission to any public college or university. The policy is designed to compensate for the prohibition of affirmative action and increase minority access to the flagship institutions by taking advantage of moderately segregated public high schools and granting

Eric Furstenberg is an assistant professor of economics at the University of Virginia. His primary research interests include the economics of discrimination and economics of education. He is currently working on a project that studies racial differences in youth gang participation. He is also interested in political economy, particularly voting behavior and racial differences in voting behavior.

NOTE: I thank Mark Long, John Pepper, Marta Tienda, Sarah Turner, and an anonymous referee for helpful comments and suggestions. In addition, Dawn Koffman graciously answered all my questions about the Texas Higher Education Opportunity Project (THEOP) dataset. All errors are my own.

DOI: 10.1177/0002716209348750

admissions to 10 percent of the students in each high school. Even though many top-decile high school students would earn admission to Texas's selective institutions without the Top Ten Percent Law, that law does open access to these institutions for many other students. A natural question to ask is how these students have performed academically while attending an institution more selective than they would have been able to attend had the law not been enacted.

The goal of this article is to estimate the effect of attending a more selective institution, examining a variety of measures of collegiate academic performance for the students whose admissions outcomes (and enrollment decisions) were affected by the Top Ten Percent Law. To identify this effect, I rely on a two-stage least squares (2SLS) estimation of a local average treatment effect (LATE). The counterfactual evaluated in this article considers a student who ranks in the top decile of her or his class and enrolls at a selective school—the University of Texas-Austin (UT), for example. It further supposes she would not have been admitted without the Top Ten Percent Law. The LATE framework estimates the effect of attending UT on her collegiate academic performance relative to her academic performance if admission to UT had not been available to her via the 1997 law.

Many studies have shown that the Top Ten Percent Law altered application and enrollment patterns of Texas's college-bound high school students.[2] While the goal of this article is not to detail the effects of the Top Ten Percent Law on application and enrollment decisions, it is important to note that the law did have a significant impact in those areas. Raw enrollments at UT in 1995 were 55, 350, 434, and 1,501 for blacks, Hispanics, Asians, and whites, respectively, graduating in the top decile of their high school class. In 1999, the second year in which top-decile students were eligible for admission under the law, the corresponding numbers were 161, 513, 610, and 1,632. There are corresponding declines for students graduating in the third decile of their high school class.[3] In addition to increasing top-decile minority enrollments at UT, the Top Ten Percent Law also dramatically increased top-decile nonminority enrollments. This article evaluates the academic performance of all of these students.

Others have studied the effects of attending a more selective college, with most authors focusing on labor market returns to selectivity,[4] or on the effects of attending a selective college on academic outcomes. The goal for much of these papers has been to study effects of affirmative action programs and specifically to assess the "mismatch hypothesis." In the context of race-based admissions preferences, the mismatch hypothesis states that the beneficiaries of the policy are in fact harmed because they are allowed entry to schools where they are underqualified academically. The majority of authors have found minimal, if any, evidence in support of the mismatch hypothesis.[5] This article does not provide a direct assessment of the mismatch hypothesis, although by estimating the effects of attending a selective college, it furthers our understanding of the costs or benefits of attending a selective institution.

In an approach most similar to that adopted by this article, Cortes (2008) used a two-pronged strategy to analyze the mismatch hypothesis in the context of the shift between the admissions regimes defined by affirmative action and the Top Ten Percent Law. First, in a 2SLS model, she shows that attending a more selective college has a significant positive effect on college graduation probability for both minority and nonminority students. However, this is a global effect, not a local average effect specific to the individuals whose behavior is affected by the policy. Second, she uses differences-in-differences to show that the change from affirmative action to the Top Ten Percent Law reduced the graduation probability of second-decile students when compared to first-decile students and that this effect is larger for nonminority students than minority students.

I find strong *negative* selectivity effects on first-semester and sixth-semester grade point average (GPA) for students admitted under the Top Ten Percent Law. Additionally, I find significant negative selectivity effects on completion of the sixth semester and on graduation probability. These results are robust to a number of alternative specifications and are strongest for white and Hispanic students. In general, my estimates are opposite the sign of Cortes's (2008) estimates. However, as I discuss in the third section, our methods, while similar, differ in crucial ways.

Data

The data used in this article are part of the Texas Higher Education Opportunity Project (THEOP) Administrative Dataset.[6] The THEOP data contain applicant data for more than 500,000 applicants to nine Texas colleges and universities from 1992 to 2005. The main dataset includes a wide variety of applicant information. Among the variables common to all of the reporting institutions are gender, race and ethnicity, citizenship, Texas residency, Scholastic Aptitude Test (SAT) and American College Testing (ACT) scores, high school class rank, geographic identifiers, and high school identifiers. The dataset also includes student records for all students who enrolled at each institution. The student records include information about each enrolled student's performance for each semester. These data include semester GPA, cumulative GPA, credit hours completed, total credit hours completed, and choice of major. Table 1 lists the main variables (and their descriptions).

Test Score is constructed as a composite test score, based on either or both SAT and ACT scores, depending on which test each student takes. This allows me to use a single variable to represent each student's standardized test performance and avoids issues of nonrandom selection into the groups of students taking the SAT or ACT. The composite variable is based on recentered SAT scores.[7]

To study the performance of students affected by the Top Ten Percent Law, it is necessary to identify high school class rank. In some cases, the institutions report class rank as a percentile, and in other cases, it must be calculated as the ratio of numeric class rank to class size. The class rank information is contained in the *HS Rank* variable. Lower values correspond to higher class rank. For

TABLE 1
Variables and Descriptions

Variable	Description
Test Score	Composite test score (constructed)
HS Rank	High school class rank, percentile (constructed)
topten	1 = top decile of HS class rank & year ≥ 1998
rank_1	= *topten* × (*HS Rank*)
rank_r	= (1 – *topten*) × (*HS Rank*)
gender	1 = male
year	Time trend
black	1 = black
hispanic	1 = Hispanic
nat_am	1 = Native American
asian	1 = Asian
other	Base category (does not include white)
sel	median of *Test Score* of enrolled school / 100

NOTE: Variables denoted "constructed" are constructed by THEOP staff.

example, the valedictorian has *HS Rank* = 1, and the lowest-ranked student has *HS Rank* = 100.[8]

Three variables are derived from *HS Rank*, and ultimately *HS Rank* is not used in the analysis. The variable *topten* is an indicator variable, equal to one if a high school student graduated in the top decile of her or his class and the Top Ten Percent Law was in place (years 1998 and forward). The variable *rank_1* is equal to an interaction of *topten* and *HS Rank*, and *rank_r* is equal to an interaction of 1-*topten* and *HS Rank*. The terms *rank_1* and *rank_r* allow the marginal effect of high school rank on postsecondary GPA to have different slopes on either side of the discontinuity at *HS Rank* = 10.

Identifying the admissions selectivity of the colleges and universities is important for this article. My conclusions are based on four alternative definitions of selectivity. First, I use the median value of *Test Score*, divided by 100, at the institution attended by each individual as a continuous measure of selectivity. Higher values of the variable *sel* denote a more selective school. Second, I use a binary variable to indicate whether a student attends a selective postsecondary school. UT or Texas A&M University (TAMU) are the two schools defined as selective. The nonselective schools are Texas Tech, TAMU-Kingsville, and UT–San Antonio.[9] Third, I use a binary variable for selectivity, for which only UT is defined as selective. Fourth, I use a categorical variable with five different selectivity categories, as defined by *Barron's Profiles of American Colleges*. With a few minor exceptions, all of my results are robust to these specification changes. Therefore, I report only the results using the first selectivity variable described above.[10] Table 2 reports the median values of *sel* for the five schools included in the analysis.

TABLE 2
Median Values of *SEL*

School	*Sel* × 100
UT	1,210
TAMU	1,160
Texas Tech	1,090
UT–San Antonio	870
TAMU-Kingsville	950

NOTE: Based on author's calculations from THEOP Administrative Dataset.

TABLE 3
Summary Statistics

Variable	Mean	Standard Error
cgpa	2.87	0.88
HS Rank	17.31	16.74
Test Score	1153.87	162.15
gender	0.48	0.49
black	0.032	0.17
hispanic	0.14	0.35
asian	0.089	0.28

Descriptive Analysis

Table 3 shows summary statistics for selected variables. Each of the sample means fall well within the range of acceptable values.

Table 4 shows the enrollments at UT-Austin for 1995 to 2003, by race and decile of high school class rank. Soon after the implementation of the Top Ten Percent Law, UT enrollments of students from the top decile of their high school class increased dramatically, while the enrollments of students from outside the top decile of their high school class shrank. Additionally, Table 4 shows that in addition to increasing minority enrollments at UT, the Top Ten Percent Law also dramatically increased nonminority enrollments.

It is important to note the relationship between high school class rank and the selectivity of the college attended. Similar to Niu and Tienda (2007), Figure 1, based on data from 1998 forward, plots the average value of *sel*°*100* as a function of high school class rank.

The effect of the Top Ten Percent Law is clear, as evidenced by the sharp discontinuity at class rank equal to 10. Students in the top decile of their graduating class are significantly more likely to attend a selective postsecondary institution.[11]

TABLE 4
UT Enrollments by Race and Decile of High School Class Rank, 1995–2003

	Top Decile				Second Decile				Third Decile			
	Black	Hispanic	Asian	White	Black	Hispanic	Asian	White	Black	Hispanic	Asian	White
1995	74	375	351	1,425	54	206	171	903	85	200	144	1,023
1996	94	409	402	1,412	65	205	166	832	94	254	172	1,040
1997	76	319	444	1,446	65	206	212	861	100	269	192	1,130
1998	62	360	476	1,556	41	208	193	916	103	272	179	1,084
1999	55	350	434	1,501	45	216	222	994	95	284	247	1,177
2000	48	338	501	1,406	51	212	246	1,006	79	259	292	1,467
2001	60	392	509	1,503	47	214	258	956	78	222	276	1,261
2002	161	513	610	1,632	40	214	249	978	80	237	301	1,258

NOTE: Based on author's calculations from THEOP Administrative Dataset.

FIGURE 1
Average Selectivity and High School (HS) Class Rank

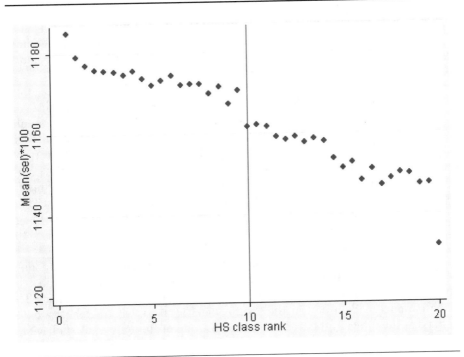

Empirical Methodology

The basic empirical model used is a simple linear model of a student's academic outcome as a function of the selectivity of the college attended and a set of control variables:

$$Y_i = \beta_0 + \beta_{1,i} sel_i + \gamma Z_i + e_i. \tag{1}$$

The coefficient of interest is $\beta_{1,i}$, the effect of attending a more selective institution on Y_i, the student's academic outcome.[12] The matrix Z_i is a matrix of control variables containing test score, high school class rank, gender, race dummy variables, and a time trend. The error term, e_i, is assumed to be mean zero. Therefore, if larger values of Y_i indicate better academic performance, then positive values of $\beta_{1,i}$ indicate positive effects of attending a more selective school on Y_i: attending a more selective school improves academic performance.

When the treatment variable is uncorrelated with unobservable variables that affect the outcome, then equation (1) can be estimated with ordinary least squares (OLS) and $\beta_{1,i}$ is identified as the average treatment effect (ATE).[13] In this case, the treatment is attending a more selective postsecondary institution. Clearly, the ATE estimates are biased if students select into the treatment group based on unobservable characteristics that are related to academic performance.[14] Endogeneity problems with the OLS estimation immediately suggest use of 2SLS estimation of the selectivity effects. Before proceeding, additional discussion is necessary to clarify the interpretation of the parameters in the 2SLS models.

When the response to the treatment varies within the treated population, then different instruments identify the effect of the treatment for different subsets of the population. If the treatment effect is homogeneous throughout the population, then the choice of instruments does not matter for the estimation: any valid instrument will give a consistent estimate of the average treatment effect. If this were the case, then LATE and ATE are equivalent. Imbens and Angrist (1994) show that when the treatment effect is heterogeneous, then the choice of instruments in the 2SLS model is critical for the interpretation of the estimates. Then, the slope parameter is interpreted as the treatment effect for the group of eligible individuals who accept the treatment, where the instrument defines the subpopulation who is eligible for the treatment. This is the LATE.

In documenting the effects of the Top Ten Percent Law on Texas students' academic outcomes, the population of particular interest is those students who attend more selective schools than they would have in the absence of the law. The slope parameter identified in the 2SLS model is the LATE parameter and is defined as the effect of the treatment on the group of students whose behavior is affected by a change of the instrument. The instrument I use is the indicator variable *topten*. As described in Table 1, *topten* is equal to one if the individual graduated in the top decile of his or her high school class and the year is 1998 or later (zero otherwise). Students matriculating in fall 1998 are the first students affected by the Top Ten Percent Law; therefore, *topten* defines the population of students affected by the law. In this context of the 2SLS model, the slope parameter in equation (1) is the effect of attending a more selective school on the outcome of interest for the individuals who attend a more selective school than they would have in the absence of the law.

In the 2SLS model, identification of the treatment effect ($\beta_{1,i}$) is generated from this discontinuity in the relationship between attending a selective institution and high school class rank. The discontinuity in Figure 1 can also be estimated by the first-stage regression in the 2SLS model (see Table 5). The effect of the Top Ten Percent Law is clear in Figure 1, and this effect is statistically significant in the first-stage regression.

The LATE or 2SLS method is related to the fuzzy regression design (FRD) framework.[15] While the two methods have similar interpretation, they have important differences. The FRD can be interpreted in the same manner as the LATE, except that the estimate is valid for individuals whose *HS Rank* is in a vanishingly small neighborhood of ten. That is, the FRD is valid only for students at the threshold of the Top Ten Percent Law. Therefore, the FRD approach

TABLE 5
Effect of Selectivity on First-Semester Grade Point Average (GPA)

	OLS	LATE	First Stage	Reduced Form
sel	−.043° (.005)	−.649° (.064)		
topten	−.088° (.008)		.146° (.007)	−.094° (.008)
Test Score	.002° (.000)	.002° (.000)	.001° (.000)	.002° (.000)
rank_1	−.042° (.001)	−.041° (.001)	.002°° (.001)	−.042° (.001)
rank_r	−.031° (.001)	−.031° (.001)	−.001°° (.000)	−.031° (.001)
gender	−.147° (.004)	−.164° (.005)	−.027° (.003)	−.146° (.004)
year	.025° (.001)	.007° (.002)	−.029° (.001)	.026° (.001)
black	−.169° (.013)	−.057° (.019)	.186° (.008)	−.177° (.013)
hispanic	−.124° (.007)	−.161° (.009)	−.060° (.007)	−.122° (.007)
nat_am	−.189° (.038)	−.156° (.041)	.055°° (.023)	−.191° (.038)
asian	.085° (.007)	.241° (.018)	.258° (.003)	.074° (.007)
other	.088° (.025)	.119° (.027)	.051° (.014)	.086° (.025)
Constant	−48.536° (1.608)	−6.591° (3.940)	69.434° (1.170)	−51.478° (1.592)
n	121,411	121,411	121,562	121,411

NOTE: Based on author's calculations from THEOP Administrative Dataset. Standard errors in parentheses. The first-stage model uses *sel* as the dependent variable, and the reduced form uses *GPA* as the dependent variable.
°Significant at 10 percent. °°Significant at 5 percent. °Significant at 1 percent.

would be warranted if one wished to estimate the effect of marginal changes of the threshold of the law, because the FRD method gives an estimate of the causal effect for the marginal student affected by the law. The goal of this article is not to estimate this marginal effect but to estimate the effect of the law on all the students who attended more selective schools because of it. Therefore, the LATE method is appropriate.

As noted above, Cortes (2008) uses a 2SLS framework to study the effect of attending a selective college on graduation probability.[16] However, Cortes's analysis is based on a constructed instrumental variable. The first step of the construction is to estimate a probit model of attending a selective college on the X variables from the model of interest. This probit model is estimated using data from the time period covered by neither the Top Ten Percent Law nor affirmative action. The instrumental variable is then constructed by predicting the probability of attending a selective college, using the coefficients estimated with the "out-of-sample" probit model. Because the instrumental variable is based on coefficients estimated using data outside the period of time covered by the Top Ten Percent Law, the instrumental variable is unable to identify any of the effects of the Law. Therefore, it is inappropriate to interpret the results of Cortes's 2SLS estimation as a local effect of the Top Ten Percent Law.[17]

Results

The first set of results uses first-semester GPA on a 4-point scale as the dependent variable. Throughout the analysis, I limit the sample to include students who graduated in the first or second decile of their high school class. The LATE methodology relies on comparing the academic outcomes of a student in the top decile of her or his high school class and an otherwise equivalent student outside the top decile so that students outside the second decile are not relevant to the analysis.[18]

Table 5 displays the estimates of four regressions. The first column shows a baseline OLS model, the second shows the LATE estimates, and the third and fourth show the estimated first-stage and reduced-form models corresponding to the 2SLS interpretation of the LATE design. The reference racial group is whites.

Table 5 shows a negative and statistically significant effect of attending a selective college. Consider a 100-point increase in the median SAT of the school attended.[19] According to the OLS model, one's expected first-semester GPA would decrease by 0.043 points. This corresponds to a one-third of a letter-grade decrease in one of eight courses, or a one-sixth letter-grade decrease in one of four courses (a typical course load in a semester). According to the LATE design, such a change in selectivity would lead to a decrease of first-semester GPA of 0.65 points. This is approximately two-thirds of a letter-grade change of the first-semester GPA. Note that the OLS estimates should be interpreted as a population-level treatment effect, and the estimates from the LATE design should be interpreted as the causal effect of attending a more selective school on GPA for the students who accepted the treatment.[20] All of the other coefficients have the predicted sign.

Based on the first-stage model, the estimated discontinuity in the relationship between *sel* and class rank at class rank equal to 10 is statistically significant and equal to .146. This estimate corresponds to the discontinuity shown in Figures 1. Similarly, the reduced form shows a statistically significant discontinuity in the relationship between GPA and class rank equal to −.094.

Using alternative definitions of selectivity yields similar results. Based on *Barron's* definition of selectivity, *sel* is equal to 5, 4, 3, 2, and 1 for the schools UT, TAMU, Texas Tech, TAMU-Kingsville, and UT–San Antonio, respectively. Using *Barron's* definition of selectivity, the LATE estimate is −.432, with a standard error of .042. Additionally, I used two binary definitions of *sel*. The first uses only UT-Austin as the selective school. The LATE estimate is −.790, with a standard error of .081. The second uses UT and TAMU as the selective schools. The LATE estimate is −1.33, with a standard error of .134. All of these estimates are statistically significant and are similar in magnitude to the LATE estimate in Table 5.

LATE estimates by year and by race

Next, I repeated the LATE regressions for each year covered by the THEOP data. As suggested by Table 4, the main "action" of the Top Ten Percent Law

TABLE 6
LATE Selectivity Effects by Year

	1996	1997	1998	1999	2000	2001	2002
sel	0.268	1.305	2.163	0.094	−0.415	−1.284°°	−0.606°°
	(1.14)	(2.23)	(1.96)	(1.98)	(0.57)	(0.59)	(0.28)
n	9,513	9,629	9,972	10,179	11,143	11,249	12,029

NOTE: Based on author's calculations from Texas Higher Education Opportunity Project (THEOP) Administrative Dataset. Standard errors in parentheses. The full regression results are available upon request.

TABLE 7
LATE Selectivity Effects by Race

	Black	Hispanic	Asian	White
sel	−.208	−.337°	−.67	−.902°
	(.20)	(.08)	(.47)	(.10)
n	3,722	16,519	12,298	87,607

NOTE: Based on author's calculations from THEOP Administrative Dataset. Standard errors in parentheses. The full regression results are available upon request.
°Significant at 10 percent.

appears to take place after 1998. Table 6 shows the LATE estimates by year for the years 1996 to 2002.

The LATE estimates by year follow a predictable pattern. As shown in Table 6, the LATE selectivity effects do not surface in the data until the fall 2001 semester. The estimates from the years 1996 to 2000 are not statistically significant. As discussed previously and illustrated in Table 4, the enrollment of top-decile high school students at the selective schools grew consistently in the years following 1998, the first year the Top Ten Percent Law was in place. The results above suggest that in each successive year, the additional students taking advantage of the law performed worse academically. Perhaps these students are the ones who, despite their top decile rankings, are the least prepared for the challenging academic environment of a selective institution.[21]

To check if the LATE effects are consistent across races, I ran the regressions separately for the four major ethnic groups (white, black, Hispanic, Asian). Table 7 shows the results.

Only the coefficients for Hispanics and whites are significant. The estimates are negative and large in magnitude for both groups. The estimates show that

TABLE 8
Effect of Selectivity on Sixth-Semester GPA and Graduation

	Local Average Treatment Effect (LATE)	LATE Probit	
	Dep. Var. = Sixth-Semester GPA	Dep. Var. = Completion of Sixth Semester	Dep. Var. = Graduation
sel	−.839°	−.173°°	−.47°°
	(.11)	(.08)	(.02)
n	34,937	85,206	70,006

NOTE: Based on author's calculations from THEOP Administrative Dataset. Standard errors in parentheses. The estimates reported for the LATE Probit models are marginal effects. The full regression results are available upon request.
°Significant at 10 percent. °°Significant at 5 percent.

Hispanics' first-semester GPA decreases by about one-third of a letter grade and whites' first-semester GPA decreases by almost a full letter grade for every 100-point increase of selectivity. The estimates for blacks and Asians are not statistically significant. For both groups, the estimates are negative and large, but imprecisely estimated. The likely explanations for the lack of precision are small sample size for blacks and the small number of Asians attending schools in the lower-selectivity categories.

Selectivity effects on sixth-semester GPA, completion of sixth semester, and graduation probability

It is possible that the selectivity effects on first-semester GPA are temporary and that the lasting and more appropriate measures of academic performance occur later in students' academic career. Therefore, I repeated the LATE design using sixth-semester GPA and graduation as the dependent variables. Table 8 displays the relevant estimates from the models using sixth-semester GPA (conditional on completion of the sixth semester), completion of the sixth semester, and graduation (completion of 100 credit hours) as the dependent variables.

As a word of caution, note that the number of students eligible for admission via the Top Ten Percent Law is very small for these regressions. Students who are eligible for admission under the law began enrolling in fall 1998. At the earliest, these students would have completed their sixth semester in spring 2001 and would have graduated in spring 2002. For most institutions, the THEOP data do not contain complete administrative records for years later than 2002. Therefore, the estimates for the sixth-semester models are based on two years of Top Ten Percent–eligible students, and the graduation models are based on only one year.

The first column of Table 8 shows the LATE estimates of the effect of attending a selective college on sixth-semester GPA. The second and third columns show the marginal effects from the LATE probit estimates of the selectivity effect on completion of the sixth semester and graduation. The marginal effects are calculated at the mean values of the regressors. All of the estimates are negative and statistically significant. In fact, the effect of attending a more selective institution (as measured by a 100-point increase of *Test Score*) is a 0.8-point decrease of sixth-semester GPA. This is more than two-thirds of a letter grade. Furthermore, the LATE probit regressions show a decrease of the probability of completing the sixth semester of 17 percentage points and a decrease in the probability of graduation of 47 percentage points. These results show the potential for significant and long-lasting effects for underqualified students who attend a selective institution, especially when we consider the effect on graduation versus the effect on GPA.

Finally, I split the sample by ethnicity to determine if the long-term effects of attending a selective school vary across ethnic groups. The effects of attending a selective institution on sixth-semester GPA are large and significant for whites (–1.321) but statistically insignificant for blacks and Hispanics. The LATE probit regressions are less revealing. Similar to the GPA regressions, the regressions using completion of the sixth semester as the dependent variable yield a significant result only for whites (the marginal effect is –32 percentage points). The regressions using graduation as the dependent variable yield no statistically significant results. This is primarily due to small sample size and subsequently large standard errors.

Robustness checks

As described above, I estimated all of the regressions using three alternative definitions of selectivity. In addition, I tested the following alternative specifications. First, because GPA is not directly comparable across universities, I estimated the models using rank of college GPA as the dependent variable. Second, I estimated the models using high school fixed effects and choice of major fixed effects. Third, I estimated a number of alternative models using quadratic and cubic terms. Fourth, in the graduation equations, I used completion of 120 credit hours instead of completion of 100 credit hours as the dependent variable. Finally, I estimated the main regressions using quadratic forms of the variables *rank_1*, *rank_r*, and *Test Score*.

Few of the results are substantively different from those presented above. The most notable difference is that some of the specifications using the alternative definitions of selectivity fail to produce statistically significant results for the sixth-semester GPA and graduation regressions. The complete results of the alternative specifications are available upon request.

Conclusion

In this article, I use a 2SLS method to estimate the LATE of attending a selective college. The population of interest is the group of students who enroll in a selective college but would not have been able to without the guaranteed admissions granted to them by Texas's Top Ten Percent Law. Thus, I estimate the causal effect of attending a more selective college, although the results only apply to a subset of the college-going population.

I find significant negative effects for those students of attending a selective college on the following outcomes: first- and sixth-semester GPA, probability of completing the sixth semester, and probability of graduation. These negative effects should not be surprising. Constraining universities' admissions decisions in the manner dictated by the Top Ten Percent Law must have the results of selecting less qualified students. The results are strongest starting a few years after the implementation of the law and coincide with the large increases in the number of top-decile students attending Texas's most selective institutions. Whites and Hispanics appear to be affected more than blacks.

It is important to note that Texas's flagship institutions (UT and TAMU) both increased their efforts to recruit underrepresented students during the time period studied in this article. It is unclear how such efforts affect my analysis, because it is impossible to identify which students enrolled as a result of the increased recruitment programs. The recruitment programs may have attracted top-decile students from weak high schools, in which case my results overstate the true selectivity effect. Alternatively, the recruitment programs may have attracted second-decile students from weak high schools, in which case my results understate the true selectivity effect.

My results are important given the scale of the Top Ten Percent Law. At UT, roughly 40 percent of incoming students graduated in the top decile of their high school class in 1997, the last year before the law was in effect. In 2002, almost 75 percent of UT students graduated in the top decile of their high school class. While I do not consider the benefit of attending a selective institution such as UT or conduct a full cost-benefit analysis of the Top Ten Percent Law, my results suggest that many students suffer adverse academic outcomes as a result of the law.

To the extent that administrators at selective institutions want to maintain their academic standards, policymakers should reconsider policies that use a single metric to gauge academic merit, as does the Top Ten Percent Law. Admissions policies without guarantees and admissions decisions based on individual evaluation of the applicants' qualifications are likely to avoid this problem. Alternatively, policymakers might consider a guaranteed admissions law with higher standards: for example, a policy under which only the top 5 percent of students from each high school are guaranteed admission might reduce the number of adverse academic outcomes associated with the Top Ten Percent Law.

Appendix

The SAT recentering procedure is as follows. Note that UT and TAMU data contain SAT quantitative (SATQ) and SAT verbal (SATV) scores. Based on conversion tables available from the College Board, THEOP staff were able to convert pre-1996 SAT scores to the same scale as the post-1996 recentered SAT scores. Data from other institutions do not contain SATQ and SATV scores, so the conversion described above was not possible. As an alternative, I performed the following procedure:[a]

1. Using Data UT and TAMU for the pre-1996 period, the recentered SATQ and SATV scores contained in the THEOP data were converted back to the original un-recentered scale.
2. Both the un-recentered and recentered SATQ and SATV scores were summed to derive an un-recentered and a recentered total SAT score.
3. The recentered total SAT score was regressed on a fourth-order polynomial of the un-recentered SAT score.

I predicted the recentered total SAT score based on the un-recentered SAT scores for the institutions and years for which the recentered scores were not previously available.

a. I thank Mark Long for suggesting this procedure.

Notes

1. *Hopwood v. Texas*, U.S. Fifth Circuit of Appeals (1996).

2. Niu and Tienda (2007) show that the Top Ten Percent Law does boost enrollment at Texas's flagship public universities for eligible students at predominantly minority high schools. However, Niu, Sullivan, and Tienda (2008) show that lack of information about the law mitigates its effect on bringing more minority students to the flagship institutions. Niu, Tienda, and Cortes (2006) study students' preferences over college selectivity levels. Bucks (2002) concludes that the law was unsuccessful at restoring minority enrollment levels at the flagship institutions to pre-*Hopwood* levels. Long and Tienda (2008) show that average standardized test scores rose at less selective schools following the implementation of the law and that at UT, the trend of increasing standardized test scores halted.

3. Source: Author's calculations using the THEOP Administrative data files. See Table 4.

4. Brewer, Eide, and Ehrenberg (1999) and Dale and Krueger (2002), for example.

5. E.g., Bowen and Bok (1998), Alon and Tienda (2005), and Rothstein and Yoon (2007).

6. See www.texastop10.princeton.edu/admin_overview.html for further information.

7. Because the SAT was recentered in 1996, the SAT scores before and after 1996 are not directly comparable. Comparison tables exist for SAT and ACT scores after 1996, but the pre-1996 SAT scores would need to be recentered to be compared to the ACT scores. To include data from these years in the analysis, I estimated a recentered SAT score for students taking the SAT in the years prior to 1996. The details of this procedure are discussed in the appendix. Because the LATE method does not rely on before/after analysis, inclusion of these observations from these years is not critical to the empirical identification strategy. All of the results discussed are robust to exclusion of these observations.

8. Note that before 1997 and for certain high schools, UT reports class rank as 8 for all top-decile students, 18 for all second-decile students, and so on. This is not a major issue for this article because it only involves data from a few high schools, from the pre-1997 period. All of my analysis is based on data from 1996 and forward, so therefore there are few observations that are subject to this discretization.

9. The THEOP data contain information for four other institutions: Rice, Southern Methodist University (SMU), UT-Arlington, and UT–Pan American. Rice and SMU are omitted because they are private and not subject to the Top Ten Percent Law. The data from UT-Arlington do not contain class rank

information and are therefore unusable for this study. Hispanic students account for approximately 90 percent of UT–Pan American's student body (almost 60 percent of the student body are Hispanic students in the third decile of their high school class). Because of this idiosyncrasy, UT–Pan American is excluded from the analysis.

10. The complete results are available upon request.

11. Alternative definitions of selectivity produce a similar pattern. Additionally, data from the years prior to the Top Ten Percent Law show no such discontinuity.

12. I index $\beta_{1,i}$ by i to emphasize that the parameter is allowed to vary.

13. Note that the discussion of average treatment effects assumes the treatment effect is homogeneous.

14. See Dale and Krueger (2002) for a discussion of selection on unobservables.

15. For example, see Imbens and Lemieux (2008); Angrist and Lavy (1999); Lee and Card (2008); Card and Shore-Sheppard (2004); and Hahn, Todd, and Van Der Klaauw (1999, 2001). Under certain conditions, the estimates produced from the two methods are numerically equivalent.

16. Note that previous versions of Cortes (2008) used distance from the nearest selective college as the instrument. The same discussion applies.

17. Cortes (2008) also implements a difference-in-difference regression. This approach gives a simple descriptive before/after analysis of top-decile students versus non-top-decile students. It does not identify the causal effect of the Top Ten Percent Law.

18. See Imbens and Lemieux (2008) for a discussion of "bandwidth selection." The results are robust to a number of different bandwidth specifications.

19. Based on the median values of *Test Score* shown in Table 2, this is a reasonable difference between a selective and unselective school.

20. Two-stage least squares (2SLS) estimates are often larger (in magnitude) than OLS. As discussed by Card (2001), one explanation for why this is true is that OLS estimates report the average effect for the whole population to whom the treatment is available, but the 2SLS estimates report the average effect for only the individuals whose behavior is affected by the treatment (thus, the instrument is an indicator for top decile of high school class rank). When not all of the individuals to whom the treatment is available elect to take the treatment, then the OLS estimates are in a sense diluted. In this case, only a certain percentage of the population to whom the treatment is available take the treatment, but because OLS measures the effect of the treatment on the entire population, the estimated effect is attenuated in the OLS estimates.

21. Note that in the regressions by year, *topten* is defined as equal to 1 if the individual was in the top decile of her or his high school class.

References

Alon, Sigal, and Marta Tienda. 2005. Assessing the "mismatch" hypothesis: Differences in college graduation rates by institutional selectivity. *Sociology of Education* 78 (4): 294-315.

Angrist, Joshua, and Victor Lavy. 1999. Using Maimonides' rule to estimate the effect of class size on student achievement. *Quarterly Journal of Economics* 114 (2): 533-75.

Bowen, William G., and Derek Bok. 1998. *The shape of the river: Long term consequences of considering race in college and university admissions*. Princeton, NJ: Princeton University Press.

Brewer, Dominic J., Eric R. Eide, and Ronald Ehrenberg. 1999. Does it pay to attend an elite college? Cross cohort evidence on the effects of college type on earnings. *Journal of Human Resources* 34 (1): 104-23.

Bucks, Brian 2002. The effects of Texas's top ten percent plan on college choice. Unpublished manuscript, Texas Schools Project, University of Texas at Dallas.

Card, David. 2001. Estimating the return to schooling: Progress on some persistent econometric problems. *Econometrica* 96 (5): 1127-60.

Card, David, and Lara Shore-Sheppard. 2004. Using discontinuous eligibility rules to identify the effects of the federal Medicaid expansions on low income children. *Review of Economics and Statistics* 86 (3): 752-66.

College Division of Barron's Educational Series. 2002. *Barron's Profiles of American Colleges: 25th Edition.* Hauppauge, NY: Barron's Educational Series, Inc.

Cortes, Kalena E. 2008. College quality and the Texas's top ten % plan: Implications for minority students. Working Paper, Texas Higher Education Opportunity Project, Princeton University, Princeton, NJ.

Dale, Stacy B., and Alan B. Krueger 2002. Estimating the payoff to attending a more selective college: An application of selection on observables and unobservables. *Quarterly Journal of Economics* 117 (4): 1491-1527.

Hahn, Jinyong, Petra Todd, and Wilbert Van Der Klaauw. 1999. Evaluating the effect of an antidiscrimination law using regression-discontinuity design. Working Paper 7131, National Bureau of Economic Research, Cambridge, MA.

Hahn, Jinyong, Petra Todd, and Wilbert Van Der Klaauw. 2001. Identification and estimation of treatment effects with a regression discontinuity design. *Econometrica* 69 (1): 201-9.

Imbens, Guido W., and Joshua D. Angrist. 1994. Identification and estimation of local average treatment effects. *Econometrica* 62 (2): 467-76.

Imbens, Guido W., and Thomas Lemieux. 2008. Regression discontinuity designs: A guide to practice. *Journal of Econometrics* 142 (2): 615-35.

Lee, David S., and David Card. 2008. Regression discontinuity inference with specification error. *Journal of Econometrics* 142 (2): 655-74.

Long, Mark C., and Marta Tienda. 2008. Changes in Texas's universities' applicant pools after the Hopwood decision. Working Paper, Texas Higher Education Opportunity Project, Princeton University, Princeton, NJ.

Niu, Sunny X., Teresa Sullivan, and Marta Tienda. 2008. Minority talent loss and the Texas top 10% law. *Social Science Quarterly* 89 (4): 831-45.

Niu, Sunny X., and Marta Tienda 2007. The impact of the Texas's top 10% law on college enrollment: A regression discontinuity approach. Working Paper, Texas Higher Education Opportunity Project, Princeton University, Princeton, NJ.

Niu, Sunny X., Marta Tienda, and Kalena E. Cortes. 2006. College selectivity and the Texas top 10% law. *Economics of Education Review* 25:259-72.

Rothstein, Jesse, and Albert Yoon. 2007. Mismatch in law school. Unpublished manuscript.

Why Are Men Falling Behind? Gender Gaps in College Performance and Persistence

By
DYLAN CONGER
and
MARK C. LONG

This article examines the male disadvantage in grade point average, credits earned, and persistence in college. Using data on enrollees in Florida and Texas four-year colleges to decompose gender differentials in the first semester, changes in the differentials between semesters, and persistence through college, we find that males earn lower GPAs and credits in their first semester of college largely because they arrive with lower high school grades. After the first semester, males fall further behind their female counterparts in grades and credits. Females' better high school grades explain some of the widened gender disparity in performance but differences in college course-taking and majors also explain gender gaps in credits, grades, persistence, and graduation.

Keywords: higher education; gender differences; human capital; college performance; college persistence

The gender gap in postsecondary education has taken a remarkable turn. Males' share of total college enrollment has fallen steadily from 71 percent in 1947 to 43 percent in 2005, with 1978 the last year that males held an advantage (see Figure 1 derived from data in Snyder, Dillow, and Hoffman 2008). Males also complete college at lower rates than females; 42 percent of bachelor's degrees went to men in 2005-06 despite males comprising 46 percent of freshmen in 2002. These data suggest that males fall behind even after they have made the initial decision to obtain a college diploma (Snyder, Dillow, and Hoffman 2008). Gender differences in college enrollment are problematic for college administrators, who seek gender-balanced student populations (see, e.g., Gibbs 2008). In addition, while males remain overrepresented in several high-wage occupations and industries (Blau 1998), the growing female advantage in college completion is likely to affect the labor market in new ways.

The empirical literature has not kept pace with this reversal in gender disparities at the postsecondary level. Only a few studies explore

DOI: 10.1177/0002716209348751

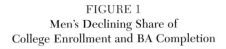

FIGURE 1
Men's Declining Share of
College Enrollment and BA Completion

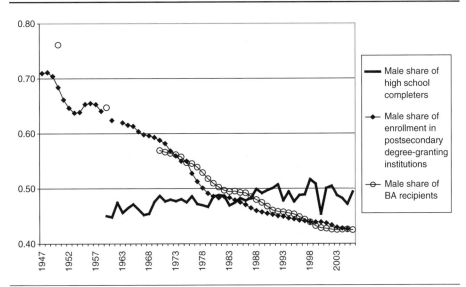

SOURCE: Digest of Education Statistics, 2007.

why males fall behind their female counterparts in college enrollment, and even fewer examine the completion disparity. All of the enrollment-gap studies document females' higher high school grades and reported postsecondary ambitions

Dylan Conger is an assistant professor in the Trachtenberg School of Public Policy and Public Administration at George Washington University. Her research concerns disadvantaged and minority youth with a focus on education policies and urban areas. Current projects concern the role that high school courses play in racial, socioeconomic, and gender disparities in educational outcomes; gender disparities in higher education; the public policies that influence English Language Learners ability to learn English; and the educational outcomes of immigrant students.

Mark C. Long is an associate professor of public affairs at the Daniel Evans School at the University of Washington. His research focuses on the effects of affirmative action and alternative college admissions policies on college entry; the effects of college financial aid on household savings; the effects of high school course-taking and school and college quality on test scores, educational attainment, labor market outcomes, family formation, and other behaviors; and the economics of nursing labor markets.

NOTE: We thank Marta Tienda, Eric Furstenberg, Eric Grodsky, and anonymous reviewers as well as participants at the Texas Higher Education Opportunity Project (THEOP) Research Workshop at Princeton University and The City University of New York Office of Academic Affairs for helpful comments. We are also grateful to the Florida Department of Education for making the Florida data available and to THEOP for making the Texas data available. Funding for this project was provided by the U.S. Department of Education's Institute of Education Sciences and by the Smith Richardson Foundation. Ana Karruz, Danielle Fumia, and Jason Williams provided excellent research assistance. All errors and oversights remain our responsibility.

(Jacob 2002; Peter and Horn 2005; Reynolds and Burge 2004; Riegle-Crumb 2007). High school grades tend to explain more of the enrollment gap than performance on academic proficiency exams, which have led some to conclude that females have higher non-cognitive skills, such as organization, dependability, and self-discipline (which are captured in grades once performance on academic exams is held constant), that increase their access to college (Jacob 2002). The completion gap research (which tends not to condition on the decision to enroll) points to gender differences in expected returns to a college diploma, where returns are sometimes defined broadly to include marriage markets (Charles and Luoh 2003; DiPrete and Buchmann 2006). Yet the persistent female advantage *conditional on college enrollment* suggests that expected premiums to a college degree can only partly explain completion disparities. Open questions remain regarding the relative contribution of family background, precollegiate preparation, and college experiences—university attended and courses selected, as examples—to gender differences in college performance and persistence.

This article aims to answer these questions. We use administrative data on enrollees in Florida and Texas four-year institutions to examine and explain gender differences in grade point averages (GPAs), college credits, and persistence. We find that males take fewer credits and earn lower grades than females in their first semester of enrollment. Male students are also less likely to persist and graduate from college, and they earn fewer cumulative credits and lower cumulative grades. The male–female differentials are not generally driven by differences in demographics, the quality of high schools and neighborhoods, high school test scores, or the selectivity of the university attended. In fact, many of these factors tend to favor male enrollees. Instead, male enrollees have lower high school grades upon college entry, and this single factor (controlling for test scores and other factors) explains more than three-fifths of the gender differential in credits earned and GPA in the freshman year. Males' disadvantages in the first semester of college, coupled with their higher propensity to take more difficult college courses, also explain a large share of their relatively poor performance in later semesters and their lower rates of persistence.

Prior Research on Gender Gaps in Postsecondary Education

Relatively little research has explored why men fall behind at the postsecondary level, and what research does exist focuses almost exclusively on college enrollment or college completion. Research on disparities in credits and grades earned along the way is sparse, despite evidence of additional labor-market responsiveness to grades and total credits, even conditional on completion (Jones and Jackson 1990; Kane and Rouse 1995). Prior studies of female advantages in college enrollment find that they have higher high school GPAs than men, are more likely to graduate from high school, and are more likely to take rigorous course loads while in high school (Peter and Horn 2005; Riegle-Crumb 2007). Prior research also finds that girls are advantaged in non-academic areas, such as parental, peer, and teacher expectations; as well as non-cognitive skills, such as organization, self-discipline, attentiveness, dependability, and seeking help from others (Reynolds and Burge 2004; Riegle-Crumb 2007; Jacob 2002). Some have used the more easily observed high school grades as a proxy for these non-cognitive advantages, once academic test scores are held constant (Jacob 2002). Of course, grades may reflect additional cognitive abilities that are not captured in achievement exams. In addition to increasing their likelihood of being accepted to a university, these advantages may also lower the psychic costs of schooling.

Standard human capital theory suggests that the ability of college students to perform well and persist though school is determined by a variety of costs and incentives, all of which may differ for male and female enrollees. For instance, males are less likely to enroll in college, but those who do enroll score higher on high school achievement tests and the Scholastic Aptitude Test (SAT) than females, and require less remediation in college-level mathematics (LoGerfo, Nichols, and Chaplin 2006; Long, Iatarola, and Conger 2009; Rothstein 2004). At the same time, females are less likely to major in subjects with strict grading standards, such as mathematics and engineering (Turner and Bowen 1999). Females also disproportionately attend colleges that have looser admissions requirements and higher admissions rates (Jacobs 1999). This partly reflects the fact that selective universities often have larger male-dominated engineering programs and are less likely to accept part-time students, who are disproportionately female (Jacobs 1999). The higher high school achievement scores of male entrants should lower the psychic costs of schooling relative to females, yet the less selective institutions and majors chosen by females should lower their psychic and direct costs (through lower tuition), rendering the net effect of these two forces indeterminate.

The handful of studies that have explored female advantages in college completion rates tend to find that incentives due to shifting female premiums on college degrees may also be at work. Yet the incentives are not due to an increase in the wage premium on a college degree for women relative to men; in fact, with the decline of the manufacturing sector, the wage premium associated with completing more years of education and with attending a higher-quality college has been rising faster for men than for women (Charles and Luoh 2003; Long forthcoming). Instead, Charles and Luoh (2003) suggest that greater variation in the returns to a college degree among men relative to women leads to greater uncertainty for men, which in turn lowers their educational attainment levels. Taking a slightly more social perspective, DiPrete and Buchmann (2006) suggest that the female advantage in college completion is more likely due to the male–female differential in what they refer to as "personal" returns to education, including a higher probability of marriage, a higher standard of living, and a lower probability of being poor. Neither the Charles and Luoh (2003) nor the DiPrete and Buchmann (2006) papers examine college completion among college enrollees. Therefore, the importance of expected labor market returns relative to costs (direct, psychic, or opportunity) may be overstated because the gender gaps in labor market incentives should be relatively small among college entrants. To elaborate, gender differences in knowledge of the labor market should be smaller among college entrants (all of whom have made an initial decision to obtain a college degree) than among middle school or high school students. Differences in the rates at which males and females complete college may be due to changes in these perceptions of the labor market (e.g., males' expectations of the returns to a college degree become more uncertain as they progress through college) or, more likely, to the unanticipated costs of college, both direct and psychic. By restricting an analysis of college completion to those who have decided to enroll, we can better isolate the contribution of the costs of college to gender gaps.

Given the shortage of research on the reversal in the gender postsecondary education gap, we have much to contribute. First, by examining several measures of college performance—GPAs, credits earned, and college completion rates—we shed light on whether gender gaps are constant, growing, or diminishing during the students' years of college enrollment. Second, we control for many important determinants of college achievement that prior studies have omitted, including demographic background, educational needs, high school quality, performance on high school achievement exams, high school grades, college quality, and college major. Finally, we analyze two complementary, administrative datasets that track the census of college students in two large states throughout their college careers.

Data

The first source of data comes from students who enrolled in one of Florida's eleven public four-year universities in 2002-2003 in the year immediately follow-ing their high school graduation. More specifically, the dataset consists of a cen-sus of Florida public eighth graders in 1997-1998 plus any other student who entered this cohort given normal progression (i.e., new ninth graders in 1998-1999 + new tenth graders in 1999-2000 + new eleventh graders in 2000-2001 + new twelfth graders in 2001-2002). Students are followed through the 2004-2005 school year, and we are able to follow students as they make movements across Florida's postsecondary public universities. For these students, we have complete high school and college transcript records, tenth-grade test scores, demographic information, and limited measures of employment while in college.[1] These data were supplied to the authors by the Florida Department of Education.

The second data source includes a census of enrollees at the following five Texas institutions: Rice University in 2000-2001; the University of Texas (UT) at Austin in 1999-2000; Texas Agricultural & Mechanical University (TAMU) in 1999-2000; UT–Pan American in 1999-2000; and TAMU-Kingsville in 1998-1999. Students at these universities are followed for six years (except for students at Rice and TAMU-Kingsville, who are followed for five years). For these students, we have records on college credits earned, GPA, declared major by term of enrollment, and college graduation. In addition, we have limited information collected on their college applications, including SAT and American College Testing (ACT) scores, high school class rank, high school identifiers, advanced placement (AP) test-taking and test-passing indicators (for UT-Austin), high school extracurricular activities (for TAMU and TAMU-Kingsville), mother's and father's education (for UT-Austin), and parents' income (for UT-Austin and TAMU-Kingsville). The Texas data were compiled and made available to the authors by the Texas Higher Education Opportunity Project (www.theop.princeton.edu).

These administrative datasets hold several important advantages over national survey data (e.g. National Educational Longitudinal Study). First, they offer large numbers of students attending individual postsecondary institutions, which allows us to conduct a more intensive probe than earlier studies, for instance, by including high school and university fixed effects. Second, since we observed students in each semester, we can evaluate how gender differentials evolve during the students' college careers. Third, these data provide insight into recent cohorts of college students, who are subject to current postsecondary and labor market conditions. The data are limited to just Florida and Texas, but 13 percent of U.S. freshmen enrollees in 2005 were located in these two states (Snyder, Dillow, and Hoffman 2008), making the results here relevant for discussions of gender gaps nationally. To be sure, each dataset has its limitations (for instance, our Florida postsecondary sample includes only students from public secondary institutions in Florida and our Texas data include a limited set of control variables), but together, they overcome several data weaknesses.

Estimation Strategy

The precise right-hand side variables differ slightly according to the dependent variable and the sample of universities, but the general estimation strategy is as follows:

$$Y_{ihj} = G_i\beta_1 + A_i\beta_2 + R_i\beta_3 + C_i\beta_4 + X_i\beta_5 + W_i\beta_6 + M_i\beta_7 + \alpha_j + v_h + \varepsilon_i. \tag{1}$$

Y_{ihj} is the outcome (GPA, credits earned, persistence to the junior year, and graduation) for student i from high school h in university j. G_i equals 1 if the student is male; A_i is a vector of high school achievement test scores; R_i is the student's high school class rank percentile; C_i is a vector of higher-level high school course-taking and/or performance variables; X_i is a vector of other pre-collegiate background characteristics, such as race/ethnicity and eligibility for free or reduced-price lunch; W_i is whether the student earned wages while in college; M_i is a vector of variables capturing the student's major or the types of postsecondary courses that the student attempted; α_j is a vector of college campus fixed effects; ε_h is a vector of high school fixed effects; and v_i is an error term. We estimate equation (1) with ordinary least squares when the dependent variable is hours or GPA earned and probit specification when the dependent variable is persistence or graduation.

Each of the variables in this equation is expected to measure some portion of the costs and incentives males and females face in college, although they are not easily categorized as such. For example, pre-collegiate characteristics (e.g., poverty, race) and preparation (e.g., high school test scores) measure students' ability to complete college-level material, the returns they expect, and the direct costs they face. In addition to capturing differences in the quality of the institutions students attend and the support they receive, the university fixed effects may also measure and control for some differences in the expected returns to the diploma. The same can be said for the postsecondary courses students choose. The residual in equation (1) captures the usual list of suspects. Major possibilities include measurement error (for instance, if high school test scores do not fully capture cognitive ability) and tastes for schooling or education. Differences in preferences for schooling between male and female college enrollees who are otherwise equal on all observables could be attributed to any number of differences, such as family resources and expectations, biology, socialization, peer support, faculty mentoring, and perceived labor market returns.

We then decompose the portion of the gender gaps that are explained by the sets of observed covariates shown in equation (1), such as the difference between men and women in high school rank percentile. We estimate equation (1) separately for males and females (without the male indicator variable) to determine the difference between men and women in how each right-hand side variable affects college outcomes. Assuming one vector of observable characteristics (Z), our general equation for the decomposition is:

$$\Delta\mu(_{M,W}) = [\mu(Z_M) - \mu(Z_W)]\beta_M + \mu(Z_W)[\beta_M - \beta_W], \qquad (2)$$

where $\Delta\mu(_{M,W})$ is the mean gap between men and women; $[\mu(Z_M) - \mu(Z_W)]\beta_M$ captures the portion of the mean gap that is due to differences between men and women in their observable characteristics, Z; and $\mu(Z_W)[\beta_M - \beta_W]$ measures the portion of the mean gap that is unexplained. Equation (2) uses the male coefficients, which tells us how much males would gain if they had the same observable characteristics as females yet kept the same estimated effect of each characteristic on the dependent variable. By substituting the female coefficients into equation (2), we learn how much of the gap would be altered if males had their own observable characteristics, but the same estimated effects as females. We estimate our decompositions using both male and female coefficients.

In order to learn more about the within-college gender differences, we then examine gender gaps for eight institutions from Florida and Texas that vary substantially in their degrees of selectivity and racial composition of their enrollment (see Appendix Table A1). For our Texas institutions, we are able to model whether the student completed college within five or six years in addition to the credits and GPA earned along the way. Our goal with these multiple dependent variables and institutions is to examine the full variation in the college gender gap, and its determinants, by university and state.

A Note on the Gender Gap in College Enrollment

In our Florida sample, roughly 49 percent of all 2002 high school graduates were male while only 40 percent of the fall semester 2002 four-year college entrants were male. Given the disproportionate share of females enrolling in college, one might be concerned that those males who do enroll may have some positive unobserved trait that prompts their enrollment. If so, and assuming this unobserved trait is positively correlated with college performance, then we would expect that the coefficient on Male from equation (1) (β_1) would be positive as it would absorb this latent positive male characteristic. When we estimate a probit model of college enrollment for the Florida graduating class of 2002, we were able to reduce the gender gap in enrollment to nearly zero when controlling for all of the observable pre-collegiate characteristics shown in equation (1)—specifically, tenth-grade achievement scores, high school class rank, high school courses, demographics, and high school fixed effects. The male coefficient in an enrollment model without any covariates is –.065; while in our more fully specified model with pre-collegiate covariates, the marginal effect of being male is reduced to just –.009. Most of the enrollment gap is due to female advantages on observable characteristics and little of the gender gap is based on differences in unobservables *conditional on observables*. Nevertheless, as stated above, there may still be some upwards bias on the male coefficient in our models.

Results

Table 1 shows the mean GPA, credit hours, and sixth-semester enrollment for students who enrolled in a Florida four-year public institution in fall 2002 ($N = 25,732$). The "overall sample" column refers to students who were enrolled in each semester, regardless of whether they were observed in previous or later semester (conditional on first-semester enrollment). In the first semester, females earn an average GPA of 2.85 and males 2.67, for a male–female differential of –.18. The female GPAs rise slightly over the following five semesters, and gender gaps widen by a small amount.[2] In addition to earning lower GPAs in each semester, males earn fewer credit hours and are less likely to remain enrolled; roughly 79 percent of the female freshmen persisted to the sixth semester compared with only 74 percent of the male freshmen. The credit hour gaps grow over time from –.37 in the first semester to –.78 by the last semester, for a differential of 6.40 in cumulative credits through spring 2005.

The next two columns in Table 1 show the differentials in GPA, hours earned, and persistence among the 18,367 students who were continuously enrolled in each of the six semesters. Among this subsample of persisters, the GPA and credit hour gender gap is very small in the first semester, and smaller in each semester than it is among the overall sample. Yet the increase in the male–female differential is much larger among the persisters than among the overall sample, and by the sixth semester, the GPA and credit hour differentials among those who

TABLE 1

Gender Differences in GPA, Credits Earned, and
Persistence, all 11 Four-Year Florida Public Universities

	Overall Sample		Continuously Enrolled Sample ($N = 18,364$)	
	Female Mean	Male–Female Difference	Female Mean	Male–Female Difference
GPA				
Fall 2002	2.85	−0.18***	3.07	−0.08***
Spring 2003	2.86	−0.20***	3.07	−0.11***
Fall 2003	2.89	−0.19***	3.02	−0.13***
Spring 2004	2.96	−0.20***	3.05	−0.16***
Fall 2004	3.03	−0.22***	3.08	−0.20***
Spring 2005	3.07	−0.22***	3.09	−0.21***
Cumulative through spring 2005	2.83	−0.25***	3.08	−0.14***
Credits earned				
Fall 2002	11.9	−0.37***	12.7	0.01
Spring 2003	11.6	−0.66***	12.4	−0.30***
Fall 2003	11.4	−0.58***	12.0	−0.35***
Spring 2004	11.4	−0.56***	11.8	−0.38***
Fall 2004	11.5	−0.92***	11.8	−0.84***
Spring 2005	11.6	−0.78***	11.7	−0.76***
Cumulative through spring 2005	68.1	−6.40***	80.7	−3.53***
% who reach 6th semester	79%	−5.0%***		

NOTE: Both samples include students who graduated from a Florida public high school in 2002 and who enrolled in a Florida state university in the fall of 2002. The overall sample refers to students who were enrolled in the respective semester, regardless of whether they were enrolled in previous or later semesters. In the fall of 2002, the overall sample included 25,732 students. The continuously enrolled sample consists of students who were enrolled in all 6 semesters. The cumulative figures include grades and credits earned in the summer terms.
*$p < .10$; **$p < .05$; ***$p < .01$.

are continuously enrolled reaches near parity with the differentials among the overall sample of students. This increased differential among the subset of students who do not drop out suggests that the disparities observed in the overall sample are not explained by males who arrive at school with a higher propensity for dropout. In fact, the relatively small differential in the first semester combined with the large increase in the differential among the persisters suggests that somewhere between the first and sixth semesters, males who arrive with equal ability and propensity to persist lose their relative standing.

Table 2 provides results from three separate analyses that together explain gender disparities in first-semester GPA. The first column shows the male–female differentials on all variables included on the right-hand side of the regressions (see Appendix Table A2 for the male and female means on these variables).

TABLE 2
Regression and Decomposition of First-Semester GPA, all Florida Public Universities

Grade Point Average: Females   2.85
Grade Point Average: Males   2.67
Raw Gender Gap =   −0.18***

	Male–Female Difference in Observables	Regressions			Total Explained	
					58.8%***	54.3%***
					Decomposition	
		Overall	Male	Female	Using Male Coefficients	Using Female Coefficients
Male		−0.082*** [0.011]				
First-semester credits attempted	0.082*	0.011*** [0.002]	0.012*** [0.003]	0.010*** [0.002]	−0.9%*	−1.0%*
Standardized 10th-grade math	0.192***	0.038*** [0.012]	0.012 [0.019]	0.058*** [0.015]	0.0%	−3.6%**
Standardized 10th-grade reading	−0.056***	0.096*** [0.012]	0.087*** [0.019]	0.098*** [0.014]	2.3%***	2.4%***
High school rank percentile	−4.56***	0.028*** [0.000]	0.028*** [0.001]	0.028*** [0.001]	68.0%***	68.6%***
High school AP/IB courses:						
Math	0.069***	0.101*** [0.014]	0.121*** [0.023]	0.083*** [0.017]	−2.1%	−1.6%
Science	0.056***	0.040*** [0.014]	0.050** [0.022]	0.041** [0.018]		
English	−0.066***	0.088*** [0.013]	0.087*** [0.024]	0.085*** [0.017]		

(continued)

TABLE 2 (continued)

Grade Point Average: Females	2.85	
Grade Point Average: Males	2.67	
Raw Gender Gap =	−0.18***	

		Regressions			Total Explained	
					58.8%***	54.3%***
					Decomposition	
	Male–Female Difference in Observables	Overall	Male	Female	Using Male Coefficients	Using Female Coefficients
Social studies	−0.004	0.086*** [0.013]	0.105*** [0.021]	0.069*** [0.016]		
Foreign language	−0.006	0.033*** [0.018]	0.052* [0.031]	0.022 [0.023]		
Race: Black	−0.047***	−0.021 [0.020]	−0.003 [0.035]	−0.027 [0.024]	1.7%*	1.5%**
Hispanic	0.000	−0.010 [0.019]	−0.002 [0.031]	−0.021 [0.025]		
Asian	0.010***	−0.009 [0.024]	0.022 [0.037]	−0.037 [0.031]		
Free or reduced-price lunch	−0.033***	−0.038** [0.015]	−0.011 [0.026]	−0.052*** [0.019]	−0.2%	−1.0%***
Foreign-born	0.003	0.051*** [0.019]	0.049 [0.032]	0.044* [0.024]	−0.1%	−0.1%
Age as of 2002	0.073***	0.018* [0.011]	0.023 [0.018]	0.018 [0.014]	−0.9%	−1.0%*
LEP	0.000	0.061*** [0.023]	0.105*** [0.039]	0.035 [0.030]	0.0%	0.0%
Non-gifted exceptionality	0.020***	0.000 [0.032]	−0.018 [0.046]	0.022 [0.046]	0.5%	0.0%
University fixed effect					−1.9%**	−3.4%***
High school fixed effect					−7.6%***	−6.4%***
Number of observations		25,732	10,292	15,440		

*p < .10. **p < .05. ***p < .01.

The next three columns provide the results of GPA regressions for all students, then separately for males and females. The last two columns provide the results of our decomposition analysis.

We condition the first-semester GPA regressions on the number of credits *attempted* in the first semester. Interestingly, males attempt slightly *more* credits in the first semester. Thus, the gender gap in the number of credits *earned* reflects a gender gap in completing courses with a passing grade. Looking back to their high school experiences reveals that male enrollees have higher tenth-grade math achievement scores, but lower tenth-grade reading achievement scores, and they are nearly five percentage points lower in their high school class rank distribution. Male enrollees are more likely to have taken advanced placement (AP) or international baccalaureate (IB) classes in math and science, but less likely to have taken an AP/IB English course. Finally, on demographics, males are more likely to be Asian (or white as shown in Appendix Table A2) and less likely to be black, are less likely to have received free or reduced-price lunch during high school, but are more likely to be older and to have some form of disability (i.e., "non-gifted exceptionality"). In combination, the gender gaps in these characteristics do not provide a clear pattern of advantage for female students as several characteristics would seem to suggest male advantages (for instance, higher tenth-grade math achievement scores and advanced math course-taking).

The next three columns in Table 2 provide regression results. With all controls, the gender gap drops by 59 percent to a differential of –.082.[3] The coefficients on the college-level determinants suggest that students who attempt more credits earn higher GPAs. All the high school and demographic variables have the expected influences on freshman GPA; for instance, high achievement scores, good grades, and more advanced courses associates with higher GPA, while free or reduced-price lunch eligibility associates with lower GPA. Yet the influence of these determinants of college performance differ for males and females. For example, the male and female coefficients on high school reading achievement scores, class rank percentile, and course-taking are comparable, while the positive relation between math achievement scores and college grades only holds for females. Receipt of free or reduced-price lunch was negatively related to GPA for females, but not for males. Also, males who were deemed limited English proficient at some point during high school earn *higher* college GPAs, while this relation does not hold for females.

The final two columns in Table 2 (the decomposition results) reveal that a single factor, gender gaps in high school class rank percentile, explains most of the gap in first-semester GPA. If men earned the same grades as women in high school, the male–female differential in first-semester GPA would decrease by 68 percent (using male coefficients). If men earned the same high school grades and converted those into college grades in the same way women do, the gap would shrink by 68.6 percent.

Male college enrollees come from high schools whose students earn higher GPAs in college. That is, male college enrollees are *advantaged* by the high schools that they attended relative to their female college classmates.[4] If male college enrollees attended the same high school as female college enrollees, we would expect the first-semester GPA gender gap to widen by 7.6 percent (using male coefficients).

Most of the other factors that we examined either had small effects on the college GPA gender gap or favored males. For example, high school course-taking modestly favors males and would widen the gender gap by an insignificant 2.1 percent (using male coefficients). Males' advantage on math achievement scores does not explain the first-semester GPA gender gap using male coefficients (since the coefficient on math scores for males is essentially zero). However, if males enjoyed the same return to math scores as females, the gender gap would widen by 3.6 percent if the gender gap in tenth grade math scores were eliminated. Put differently, if females catch up to their male high school classmates on math scores, we would expect female college grades to improve and the college GPA gap to widen.

Together, these male–female differences on observables explain between 54 percent and 59 percent of the male–female differential in GPA (depending on whether male or female coefficients are used). The residual could be due to any number of uncontrolled factors, such as preferences for leisure time, family circumstances, amount of financial aid, hours of employment, types of classes taken in the first semester, and motivation to earn good grades in college.

We next evaluate the factors explaining gaps in cumulative credits earned through the sixth semester. The results are shown in Table 3 (results for other dependent variables will be summarized in Tables 4 and 5 to simplify the presentation). Data limitations prevented us from evaluating students' progress in Florida universities past three years. However, cumulative credits through three years is likely to be highly correlated with the student eventually graduating from college; for the Texas universities that we discuss later, we find that gaps in cumulative credits through three years are mostly mirrored by gaps in graduation.

In this analysis, we condition on credits earned in the first semester and the share of credits earned in various subjects as a proxy for college major. Not surprisingly, there is a strong relation between the number of credits earned in the first semester and cumulative credits earned through six semesters; an additional credit earned in the first semester would predict an increase of 2.6 credits earned through six semesters. Moreover, nearly one-sixth of the gender gap in cumulative credits can be explained by the gender gap in first semester credits earned. Gaps in high school class rank contribute an additional 23 percent.[5]

Interestingly, students with higher tenth-grade math achievement scores earn *fewer* cumulative credits, and this relationship is true for both males and females. Thus, males' advantage on math scores predicts fewer cumulative credits for males and partially explains the gender gap (8.8 percent using male coefficients). Students with higher tenth-grade reading achievement scores also earn fewer cumulative credits, but the relationship is weaker. It is possible that students with high math ability leave Florida colleges in response to labor market incentives, or that they exit for higher quality private schools.

The remainder of Table 3 shows gender gaps in college course-taking. Males take more of their college credits in Business, Engineering/Computer

TABLE 3
Regression and Decomposition of Cumulative Credits
through Spring 2005 ("Sixth" Semester), all Florida Public Universities

Credits Earned: Females:	68.1
Credits Earned: Males:	61.7
Raw Gender Gap =	−6.4°°°

	Male−Female Difference in Observables	Regressions			Total Explained	
		Overall	Male	Female	79.6%°°°	65.1%°°°
					Decomposition	
					Using Male Coefficients	Using Female Coefficients
Male		−2.4°°°				
		[0.3]				
First-semester credits earned	−0.37°°°	2.6°°°	2.7°°°	2.5°°°	15.9%°°°	15.1%°°°
		[0.0]	[0.1]	[0.1]		
Standardized 10th-grade math	0.192°°°	−1.98°°°	−2.88°°°	−1.31°°°	8.8%°°°	4.2%°°°
		[0.33]	[0.53]	[0.42]		
Standardized 10th-grade reading	−0.056°°°	−0.43	−0.59	−0.29	−0.6%	−0.4%
		[0.30]	[0.48]	[0.38]		
High school rank percentile	−4.56°°°	0.33°°°	0.34°°°	0.33°°°	23.3%°°°	22.4%°°°
		[0.01]	[0.02]	[0.02]		
Share of college credits in:					33.5%°°°	23.0%°°°
Agriculture	−0.001	18.0°°°	23.2°°	12.7°		
		[5.4]	[9.7]	[6.8]		
Architecture	0.000	11.1°°°	9.5°	14.6°°°		
		[3.3]	[5.5]	[4.2]		
Business	0.015°°°	25.6°°°	31.4°°°	21.9°°°		
		[2.5]	[3.8]	[3.4]		

(continued)

197

TABLE 3 (continued)

Credits Earned: Females:	68.1
Credits Earned: Males:	61.7
Raw Gender Gap =	-6.4***

	Male–Female Difference in Observables	Regressions			Total Explained	
					79.6%***	65.1%***
					Decomposition	
		Overall	Male	Female	Using Male Coefficients	Using Female Coefficients
Education	-0.025***	39.7***	56.8***	37.8***		
		[2.8]	[6.8]	[3.6]		
Engineering/computer science	0.048***	16.1***	22.4***	9.2**		
		[2.7]	[3.9]	[4.2]		
Fine arts	-0.002	-3.9	-6.0	-1.3		
		[2.7]	[4.0]	[3.7]		
Health	-0.028***	31.7***	48.3***	2.0***		
		[3.0]	[6.2]	[3.8]		
Humanities	-0.010***	-24.2***	-20.4***	-24.9***		
		[2.6]	[3.9]	[3.5]		
Natural/physical sciences	0.028***	-7.6***	-8.8**	-6.0*		
		[2.5]	[3.7]	[3.5]		
Social sciences	-0.012***	-2.9	-3.5	-2.4		
		[2.6]	[3.9]	[3.5]		
Social work	-0.007***	33.3***	71.3***	29.3***		
		[4.7]	[12.3]	[5.4]		
Technical/vocational	0.000	45.9***	53.1***	43.5***		
		[3.2]	[5.4]	[4.1]		
Communications	-0.008*	36.9***	40.1***	37.0***		
		[3.3]	[5.6]	[4.2]		
Number of observations		25,732	10,292	15,440		

NOTE.: Regressions and decompositions also include: student's high school course-taking, race, and age; indicators of the student's free or reduced-price lunch status, foreign born, limited English proficiency, non-gifted exceptionality, and worked during the years 2002–2003 to 2004–2005; and high school and university fixed effects. Full results are available from the authors.
*p < .10. **p < .05. ***p < .01.

Science, and Natural/Physical Sciences; while females take more of their credits in Education, Health, Humanities, Social Sciences, Social Work, and Communications.[6] The largest gender gaps are in Education, Health, Engineering/ Computer Science, and Natural/Physical Sciences. Interpreting the regression coefficients in this table is somewhat challenging. As an example, suppose a student switched 100 percent of his credits from the omitted category (Other) to Education. We would expect this student to earn 39.7 additional credits. Now, compare this coefficient on Education (39.7) to those on Health (31.7), Engineering/Computer Science (16.1), and Natural/Physical Sciences (–7.6). Clearly, the subjects in which males concentrate produce fewer cumulative credits than the subjects in which females concentrate. This could be because students in these majors are required to take fewer credits in order to graduate: for example, at the University of Florida, Education majors are required to take more credits than Liberal Arts and Sciences majors.[7] Another possibility is that the material in some courses (e.g. those in Engineering/Computer Science and Natural/Physical Sciences) is so strenuous that students who take these courses are less likely to earn a passing grade. Overall, gender gaps in college course-taking subjects explain 33.5 percent of the cumulative credit gender gap using male coefficients (or 23 percent using female coefficients).

We have omitted from Table 3 other variables that were controlled for, including student's high school course-taking, race, and age; indicators of the student's free or reduced-price lunch status, foreign-born, limited English proficiency, non-gifted exceptionality, worked during the academic years 2002-2003 to 2004-2005; and high school and university fixed effects. These factors contributed little; high school fixed effects had the largest effect, predicting a 2 percent widening of the cumulative credit gender gap if male and female college enrollees attended the same high schools. In total, these factors shown in the table and those not shown explain 65 percent to 80 percent of the cumulative credit gender gap.

In our final analysis, we examine all dependent variables separately across institutions from Texas and Florida. The purpose of this analysis is to explore the variation in the magnitude and predictors of the gender gaps across institutions of differing quality, size, and characteristics. We focus less on testing hypotheses and comparing magnitudes than on identifying larger patterns that might lay the foundation for further research on the institutional determinants of postsecondary gender gaps. From Florida, we select the two flagship institutions, University of Florida (UF) and Florida State University (FSU), and Florida A&M University (FAMU), a historically black university. From Texas, we focus on the two flagship institutions UT and TAMU, as well as two less selective public institutions (UT–Pan American and TAMU-Kingsville), and Rice University, a private and extremely selective institution with an average freshman SAT of around 1,400. UT–Pan American is located along the Mexican border and designated as a Hispanic-Serving Institution.

Table 4a provides the first-semester gender gaps at each institution in addition to the portion of the total gaps that are explained by various factors shown in Table 4b. The percentages reveal the amount by which the gender gap would change if males had the same characteristics as females but if the effect of each characteristic on the dependent variable remained the same (in other words, the

TABLE 4A
Share of First-Semester Gender Gaps Explained
at Select Florida And Texas Universities

	N	Female Mean	Male Mean	Difference	Total Explained
First-semester grade point average					
All Florida public Us	25,732	2.85	2.67	−0.18°°°	59%°°°
Rice Univ.	613	3.37	3.28	−0.09°	25%
Univ. of Florida	5,119	3.24	3.13	−0.11°°°	51%°°°
UT-Austin	7,222	3.04	2.89	−0.15°°°	8%
Florida State Univ.	4,624	2.87	2.66	−0.21°°°	47%°°°
Texas A&M Univ.	6,561	2.89	2.73	−0.16°°°	62%°°°
Florida A&M Univ.	1,454	2.42	2.18	−0.25°°°	63%°°°
UT-Pan American	1,537	2.22	2.00	−0.22°°°	49%°°°
Texas A&M-Kingsville	1,092	2.53	2.23	−0.29°°°	43%°°
First-semester credits earned					
All Florida public Us	25,732	11.89	11.51	−0.37°°°	96%°°°
Rice Univ.	613	14.75	14.80	0.05	—
Univ. of Florida	5,119	11.51	11.31	−0.20°°°	46%°
UT-Austin	7,222	16.55	16.57	0.02	—
Florida State Univ.	4,624	15.11	15.11	0.00	—
Texas A&M Univ.	6,561	12.25	11.81	−0.44°°°	40%°°°
Florida A&M Univ.	1,454	11.90	11.01	−0.89°°°	65%°°°
UT-Pan American	1,537	6.81	6.49	−0.32°	12%
Texas A&M-Kingsville	1,092	10.37	11.51	1.14°°°	27%°°

NOTE: Decompositions use the male coefficients.
°$p < .10$. °°$p < .05$. °°°$p < .01$.

decompositions use the male coefficients). Despite the vast differences across these eight institutions in their selectivity, the gender gaps in first-semester grades are remarkably similar, ranging from .09 at the University of Florida to .29 at TAMU-Kingsville. To some degree it appears that more selective institutions have smaller first-semester GPA gender gaps. With the exceptions of Rice and UT, we are able to explain 43 percent to 62 percent of these gaps using first-semester credits attempted and pre-collegiate observable characteristics. For Rice and UT, these factors are not collectively able to significantly explain first-semester GPA gender gaps.

For first-semester credits, we see variance in gender gaps across institutions; significant female advantages are found at half of the institutions, while there are insignificant gender differences at Rice, UT, and FSU, and significant male advantages in credits earned at TAMU-Kingsville. Excluding UT–Pan American, we are able to explain 27 percent to 65 percent of these gaps using pre-collegiate observable characteristics. For UT–Pan American, these factors are not collectively able to significantly explain first-semester credits earned gender gaps.

In Table 4b, we present the decomposition results for these outcomes. Notably, gaps in high school class rank percentile significantly explain gaps in

TABLE 4B
Share of First-Semester Gender Gaps Explained at Select Florida and Texas Universities

	Share Explained by Gender Gaps in:							
	Credits Attempted (FL) or Earned (TX) in First Semester	SAT/ACT Score	10th-Grade Math FCAT Score	10th-Grade Reading FCAT Score	High School Class Rank Percentile	High School Courses	High School Characteristics (or HS Fixed Effect for All FL Us)	University Fixed Effect
First-semester grade point average								
All Florida public Us	−1%*		0%	2%***	68%***	−2%	−8%***	−2%**
Rice Univ.	−5%*	−4%			31%**		7%	
Univ. of Florida	3%*	−26%***	−12%**	3%*	85%***	−20%***	−8%	
UT-Austin	0%		4%	3%	54%***	−7%**	−11%***	
Florida State Univ.	−5%*		4%	3%	46%***	2%	0%	
Texas A&M Univ.	42%***	−12%***			27%***		1%	
Florida A&M Univ.	4%		0%	3%	59%***	6%	−8%	
UT-Pan American	5%	−2%			43%***		3%	
Texas A&M–Kingsville	−12%*	3%			41%***		6%	

(continued)

TABLE 4B (continued)

First-semester credits earned	Credits Attempted (FL) or Earned (TX) in First Semester	Share Explained by Gender Gaps in:						
		SAT/ACT Score	10th-Grade Math FCAT Score	10th-Grade Reading FCAT Score	High School Class Rank Percentile	High School Courses	High School Characteristics (or HS Fixed Effect for All FL Us)	University Fixed Effect
All Florida Public Us			−18%***	2%	109%***	−16%***	−8%	15%**
Univ. of Florida			−32%***	4%	116%***	−36%***	−12%	
Texas A&M Univ.		−11%***			43%***		−1%	
Florida A&M Univ.			0%	2%	63%***	2%	−9%	
UT–Pan American		−9%			32%**		−9%	
Texas A&M–Kingsville		7%*			−4%		0%	

NOTE: Decompositions use the male coefficients. Rice University, UT-Austin, and Florida State are omitted from the First-Semester Credits Earned decompositions as there were not significant gender gaps in first-semester credits earned at these universities. Regressions and decompositions also control for high school extracurricular activities (for Texas A&M and Texas A&M–Kingsville); student's race; parent's income (for UT-Austin and Texas A&M–Kingsville); parent's education (for UT-Austin); and student's free or reduced-price lunch status, foreign-born status, age, limited English proficiency, and non-gifted exceptionality (for Florida universities). Full results are available from the authors.
*p < .10. **p < .05. ***p < .01.

first-semester GPA, with a range of 27 percent at TAMU to 85 percent at UF. Likewise, with the exception of TAMU-Kingsville, where males earned more credits in the first semester than females, gaps in high school class rank explain 32 percent to 116 percent of gender gaps in credits earned.

No other student characteristic has this strong or consistent a relationship with gender gaps. However, there are some interesting individual results. For example, male advantages in tenth-grade math achievement scores and high school courses for students at UF substantially lessen gender gaps in GPA. Likewise, male advantages on SAT/ACT scores lessen gender gaps in GPA at UT and TAMU. Finally, at TAMU, 42 percent of the gender gap in first-semester GPA can be explained by females earning more credits in the first semester. We have omitted from Table 4b the results for high school extracurricular activities (for TAMU and TAMU-Kingsville), student's race, parents' income (for UT and TAMU-Kingsville), parents' education (for UT), student's free or reduced-price lunch status, foreign-born status, age, limited English proficiency, and non-gifted exceptionality (for Florida universities). These factors have mostly small and/or insignificant effects on gender gaps.

In Table 5a, we show gender gaps in cumulative GPA and credits through three years, persistence (i.e., attending during the spring of the third year), and graduation for the Texas universities. Again we see significant female advantages in cumulative GPA ranging from .08 to .33 and credits ranging from .99 to 6.44. The gaps in cumulative credits were again insignificant at Rice and UT, but significant gaps in credits emerged after the first semester at FSU. At TAMU-Kingsville, we find that the male advantage in first-semester credits disappears and becomes a significant male disadvantage by the end of three years. Additionally, we find significant female advantages in persistence at each of the Florida universities (ranging from 2.6 percent to 7.0 percent points) and graduation at each of the Texas universities (ranging from 5.4 percent to 11.1 percent points).[8]

Table 5b shows the decomposition results for these outcomes. Gaps in cumulative GPA are largely explained by gaps in first-semester GPA for each institution ranging from 12 percent to 89 percent. Gaps in cumulative credits attempted also significantly explain gaps in cumulative GPA at six of the eight universities, and explain 52 percent of the gap in cumulative GPA at TAMU. Students' college course-taking or major choice significantly explain gaps in cumulative GPA at five of the eight universities, while gaps in high school class rank explain gaps in cumulative GPA at seven of the universities. This latter result is important: gender gaps in high school performance significantly presage gender gaps in college performance that arise *after* the first semester. Finally, differences in test scores explain very little of cumulative GPA gaps at these universities. We also control for a variety of other factors including whether the student worked for wages during the first three years of college (see the notes at the bottom of Table 5b). None of these other factors substantially explained gender gaps in cumulative GPA.

With the exception of TAMU-Kingsville, the results for cumulative credits through three years are consistent with those for cumulative GPA and are perhaps more striking. Gaps in credits earned in the first semester account for 0

TABLE 5A
Share of Later Gender Gaps Explained at
Select Florida and Texas Universities

	N	Female Mean	Male Mean	Difference	Total Explained
Cumulative grade point average through three years					
All Florida public Us	25,732	2.83	2.59	−0.25°°°	75%°°°
Rice Univ.	613	3.42	3.34	−0.08°°	97%°°
Univ. of Florida	5,119	3.25	3.05	−0.19°°°	73%°°°
UT-Austin	7,222	3.01	2.80	−0.22°°°	64%°°°
Florida State Univ.	4,624	2.91	2.62	−0.28°°°	67%°°°
Texas A&M Univ.	6,561	2.96	2.75	−0.21°°°	76%°°°
Florida A&M Univ.	1,454	2.30	2.01	−0.29°°°	66%°°°
UT-Pan American	1,537	2.19	2.03	−0.16°°°	113%°°°
Texas A&M-Kingsville	1,092	2.42	2.09	−0.33°°°	72%°°°
Cumulative credits earned through three years					
All Florida public Us	25,732	68.12	61.72	−6.40°°°	80%°°°
Rice Univ.	613	84.34	83.34	−1.00	—
Univ. of Florida	5,119	78.24	72.50	−5.74°°°	68%°°°
UT-Austin	7,222	75.94	74.95	−0.99	—
Florida State Univ.	4,624	78.01	72.68	−5.33°°°	77%°°°
Texas A&M Univ.	6,561	73.34	67.73	−5.62°°°	59%°°°
Florida A&M Univ.	1,454	65.74	59.29	−6.44°°°	132%°°°
UT-Pan American	1,537	25.84	22.55	−3.29°°°	131%°°°
Texas A&M-Kingsville	1,092	50.07	44.00	−6.07°°°	−24%
Attended any Florida public four-year college in spring 2005 ("sixth" semester)					
All Florida public Us	25,732	78.6%	73.6%	−5.0%°°°	110%°°°
Univ. of Florida	5,119	91.0%	88.5%	−2.6%°°°	65%°°
Florida State Univ.	4,624	83.1%	78.1%	−5.0%°°°	104%°°°
Florida A&M Univ.	1,454	76.7%	69.6%	−7.0%°°°	138%°°°
Graduated at this college within six years (five years for Rice and Texas A&M-Kingsville)					
Rice Univ.	613	95.1%	89.0%	−6.1%°°°	5%
Univ. of Texas	7,222	73.5%	64.2%	−9.3%°°°	45%°°°
Texas A&M Univ.	6,561	83.4%	77.0%	−6.4%°°°	25%°°
UT-Pan American	1,537	16.4%	10.9%	−5.4%°°°	90%°°°
Texas A&M-Kingsville	1,092	30.1%	19.0%	−11.1%°°°	23%

NOTE: Decompositions use the male coefficients.
°°$p < .05.$ °°°$p < .01.$

Share of Later Gender Gaps Explained at Select Florida and Texas Universities

		Share Explained by Gender Gaps in					
	GPA in First Semester	Credits Earned in First Semester	Cumulative Credits Attempted (FL) or Earned (TX) Through Three Years	Florida: Share of Courses in Major Areas; Texas: Major	SAT/ACT Score	10th-Grade Math FCAT Score	10th-Grade Reading FCAT Score	High School Class Rank Percentile
Cumulative grade point average through three years								
All Florida public Us	39%°°°		15%°°°	12%°°°		0%	1%°°°	14%°°°
Rice Univ.	69%°		6%	26%°°	-2%			6%
Univ. of Florida	30%°°°		13%°°°	24%°°°		-3%	0%	14%°°°
UT–Austin	38%°°°		3%	13%°°°	6%°°°			11%°°°
Florida State Univ.	39%°°°		11%°°°	17%°°°		0%	0%	7%°°°
Texas A&M Univ.	34%°°°		52%°°°	7%°°°	-5%°°°			10%°°°
Florida A&M Univ.	37%°°°		13%°°	-9%		0%	6%°°	24%°°°
UT–Pan American	89%°°°		11%°°	4%	-3%			12%°°
Texas A&M–Kingsville	12%°°°		12%°°°	10%	-3%			14%°°°
Cumulative credits earned through three years								
All Florida public Us		16%°°°		34%°°°		9%°°°	-1%	23%°°°
Univ. of Florida		12%°°°		43%°°°		3%	-1%°	16%°°°
Florida State Univ.		0%		38%°°°		18%°°°	-2%	15%°°°
Texas A&M Univ.		26%°°°		29%°°°	-4%°°			10%°°°
Florida A&M Univ.		37%°°°		62%°°°		0%	-4%	28%°°°
UT–Pan American		25%°		56%°°	1%			45%°°°
Texas A&M–Kingsville		-37%°°°		-17%	-6%			20%°°

(continued)

TABLE 5B (continued)

	GPA in First Semester	Credits Earned in First Semester	Cumulative Credits Attempted (FL) or Earned (TX) Through Three Years	Florida: Share of Courses in Major Areas; Texas: Major	SAT/ACT Score	10th-Grade Math FCAT Score	10th-Grade Reading FCAT Score	High School Class Rank Percentile
				Share Explained by Gender Gaps in				
Attended any Florida public four-year college in spring 2005 ("sixth" semester)								
All Florida public Us				29%°°°		13%°°°	0%	57%°°°
Univ. of Florida				33%		–6%	–5%	61%°°°
Florida State Univ.				33%		25%°°°	4%	40%°°°
Florida A&M Univ.				86%°°°		–1%	–9%	31%°°
Graduated at this college within six years (five years for Rice and Texas A&M–Kingsville)								
Rice Univ.				–9%	9%			9%
UT-Austin				27%°°°	15%°°°			25%°°°
Texas A&M Univ.				2%	1%			30%°°°
UT–Pan American				34%°	0%			51%°°°
Texas A&M–Kingsville				–4%	–8%			17%°°

NOTE: Decompositions use the male coefficients. Rice University and UT-Austin are omitted from the Cumulative Credits Earned through Three Years decompositions as there were not significant gender gaps in cumulative credits earned at these universities. Regressions and decompositions also control for university and high school fixed effects (for all Florida public Us); high school characteristics (for individual universities); high school courses (for Florida universities and the Univ. of Texas); high school extracurricular activities (for Texas A&M and Texas A&M–Kingsville); student's race; parent's income (for UT-Austin and Texas A&M–Kingsville); parent's education (for UT-Austin); and student's free or reduced-price lunch status, foreign-born status, age, limited English proficiency, non-gifted exceptionality, and an indicator for whether the student worked during the first three years after college entry (for Florida universities). Full results are available from the authors.

°p < .10. °°p < .05. °°°p < .01.

206

percent (FSU) to 37 percent (FAMU) of gaps in cumulative credits. Differences in college course-taking and major choice contain sizable predictive power, explaining 29 percent to 63 percent of gender gaps in cumulative credits. Gaps in high school GPA again contribute 10 percent to 45 percent of these gaps. Cumulatively, the factors that we control explain 59 percent to 132 percent of the gaps in cumulative GPA (see Table 5a). TAMU-Kingsville is notably different from the other institutions, as was previously noted, as males took more credits than their female classmates in the first semester.

For persistence at the Florida colleges, differences in college course-taking explain 33 percent to 86 percent and gaps in high school class rank explain 31 percent to 61 percent of gaps in persistence. At FSU, controlling for other factors, tenth-grade math scores are negatively related to persistence and thus male advantages in tenth-grade math scores explain 25 percent of the gender gap in persistence.

For graduation at the Texas colleges, differences in college major have strong explanatory power at UT and UT–Pan American, but do not explain gaps in graduation at Rice, TAMU, or TAMU-Kingsville. Gaps in high school class rank significantly explain 17 percent to 51 percent of gaps in graduation at four of the five Texas universities, Rice being the exception. At UT, controlling for other factors, higher SAT/ACT scores are associated with *lower* likelihood of graduation. Thus, the male advantage in SAT/ACT scores at UT explains 15 percent of the gender gap in graduation.

To summarize, our analysis of gender gaps across eight institutions of differing quality, characteristics, and in two different states suggests two major findings: females outpace males in nearly all institutions and, with some exceptions, the drivers of the gaps are remarkably similar.

Conclusion

After decades of research aimed at explaining why girls are less likely to enroll in college than boys, the attention has recently shifted to the relatively dismal performance of boys at the postsecondary level. The female advantage persists after enrollment, with females now graduating from college at higher rates than males. In this article, we have examined what happens when boys and girls of equal prior preparation and family background reach the same college, where boys fall behind, and why. Specifically, we used administrative data on postsecondary entrants in two of the largest states in the nation—Texas and Florida—both to quantify gender gaps in college performance and to provide some explanations.

Given that females are more likely than males to enroll in college and, consequently, more likely to be drawn from lower levels of the unobserved motivation or ability distribution, it is not clear that females should still outperform males once in college. Our data suggest that, indeed, they do. Across all eleven public four-year institutions in Florida, for instance, males earn .37 fewer credits than females in their first semester and even fewer credits in later semesters, such that by the end of their sixth semester, males have a cumulative disadvantage of

6.4 credits. Males also earn lower grades than females in each year of college, with a gender GPA gap for Florida entrants of approximately .20 in each semester. In the five Texas universities that we examined for which college completion could be determined, males are also less likely to graduate.

To explain these differential outcomes, we estimated a series of regressions of gender gaps in outcomes for all of the Florida entrants and entrants into individual institutions. We began our discussion with the factors that appear *not* to be driving the gaps. Among Florida entrants, we find that the gaps are mostly robust to controls for demographics (e.g. race/ethnicity) and educational needs (LEP and exceptionality), high school fixed effects, tenth-grade achievement scores, and advanced high school course-taking. In fact, differences in tenth-grade achievement scores and the high schools attended currently advantage males in college. In addition, the gaps are remarkably unaltered by the addition of college campus fixed effects.

Instead, what single-handedly substantially reduces the gap at all of these institutions are the gender gaps in high school class rank percentiles, a measure of their grades relative to their high school peers. Females earn higher high school grades and class ranks, and these rankings are far more predictive of credits and collegiate GPA than any other variable in the model, including high school achievement scores. High school grades also substantially predict college-level cumulative grades and credits, controlling for first-semester grades and credits. This finding is consistent with other research that points to the tremendous importance of high school grades and, more generally, non-cognitive abilities in predicting success in postsecondary institutions and the labor market (Bowen and Bok 1998; Heckman and Krueger 2005).

We also find that males are disadvantaged by choosing majors associated with lower GPAs, lower credits, and lower rates of persistence. For instance, the courses male college entrants in Florida tend to take (Business, Engineering/Computer Science, and Natural and Physical Sciences) explain 12 percent of their lower cumulative GPAs, 34 percent of their lower cumulative credits, and 29 percent of their lower likelihood of persistence, conditional on first-semester performance. Finally, though we reduce the gaps substantially with our observables, we are unable to reduce them to zero in most cases. Thus, despite controls for backgrounds, educational needs, high school quality and performance, and college quality and major, males are still falling behind. There are several remaining explanations that we have not addressed. For instance, there is some evidence that females are more likely to apply for, receive, and respond to tuition and other postsecondary supports, which lowers the cost of school and may increase their probability of graduation (Angrist, Lang, and Oreopoulos 2006; Dynarski 2007). Others find that females have greater incentives to do well in college given male–female differentials in the stability or quality of the returns to a college degree (Charles and Luoh 2003; DiPrete and Buchmann 2006). Our findings suggest either that our measure of high school grades does not fully hold these factors constant or that they grow over time. Put differently, females' non-cognitive advantages (e.g. applying for financial aid) and incentives to attain may increase as they progress through school.

APPENDIX

TABLE A1
Selectivity of Florida and Texas Universities

University	Barron's Guide Year	College Admissions Selector	Median SAT Critical Reading	Median SAT Math	Median Composite ACT	Percentage of Applicants Accepted	Percentage White	Percentage African American	Percentage Hispanic	Percentage Asian American	Balance: Percentage Not Listed
Rice Univ.	1999	Most competitive				27	80				20
	2005	Most competitive				24	53		11	15	21
Univ. of Florida	1999	Highly competitive	614	630	27	54	77				23
	2005	Most competitive	625	642	27	48	76		13		11
UT-Austin	1999	Very competitive	595	617	25	78	66		13	11	10
	2005	Highly competitive	600	630	25	47	59		13	14	14
Florida. State Univ	1999	Very competitive				73	76	11			13
	2005	Highly competitive	590	600	25	59	71	12			17
Texas A&M Univ.	1999	Very competitive	570	600		73	80		11		9
	2005	Highly competitive	580	610	25	67	76				24

(continued)

TABLE A1 (continued)

University	Barron's Guide Year	College Admissions Selector	Median SAT Critical Reading	Median SAT Math	Median Composite ACT	Percentage of Applicants Accepted	Percentage White	Percentage African American	Percentage Hispanic	Percentage Asian American	Balance: Percentage Not Listed
Florida A&M Univ.	1999	Competitive			20	67	10	86			4
	2005	Competitive						94			6
UT–Pan American	1999	Noncompetitive				71			87		13
	2005	Less competitive			18	72			87		13
Texas A&M–Kingsville	1999	Less competitive			17	69	29		62		9
	2005	Less competitive					29		62		9

SOURCE: 1999 and 2005 Barron's Profiles of American Colleges.
NOTE: Mean SAT scores shown for UT-Austin for 1999.

Differences in Mean Characteristics of Florida High School Graduates
and Enrollees at Florida Public Universities

	High School Graduates			FL Public Univ. Enrollees		
	Male	Female	Sig. Diff.	Male	Female	Sig. Diff.
White	57.4%	55.3%	°°°	66.7%	62.7%	°°°
Black	21.2%	23.2%	°°°	13.8%	18.5%	°°°
Hispanic	17.7%	17.8%		12.7%	12.7%	°°°
Asian	2.5%	2.4%	°°	5.3%	4.3%	°°°
Received free or reduced-price lunch	39.7%	40.3%	°°°	19.2%	22.5%	°°°
Age in 2002	18.72	18.54	°°	18.38	18.31	
Foreign born	12.5%	12.9%		10.2%	9.9%	
Limited English proficient	14.5%	14.4%		8.4%	8.4%	
Non-gifted exceptionality	17.1%	8.8%	°°°	3.8%	1.9%	°°°
Standardized 10th-grade math score	0.271	0.211	°°°	0.958	0.766	°°°
Standardized 10th-grade reading score	0.133	0.312	°°°	0.772	0.828	°°°
High school class rank percentile	62.8	71.3	°°°	79.2	83.8	°°°
Took AP/IB math course	8.0%	8.6%	°°°	31.5%	24.5%	°°°
Took AP/IB English course	8.1%	9.2%	°°°	31.7%	38.3%	°°°
Took AP/IB science course	8.7%	14.7%	°°°	29.5%	23.9%	°°°
Took AP/IB social studies course	10.9%	15.2%	°°°	38.7%	39.1%	
Took AP/IB foreign language course	4.3%	6.7%	°°°	13.0%	13.6%	
PSE credits: Agriculture				0.5%	0.6%	
PSE credits: Architecture				0.6%	0.6%	
PSE credits: Business				7.5%	6.0%	°°°
PSE credits: Education				0.8%	3.3%	°°°
PSE credits: Engineering & computer sci.				7.2%	2.4%	°°°
PSE credits: Art				6.2%	6.4%	

(continued)

211

TABLE A2 (continued)

	High School Graduates			FL Public Univ. Enrollees		
	Male	Female	Sig. Diff.	Male	Female	Sig. Diff.
PSE credits: Health				1.5%	4.2%	°°°
PSE credits: Humanities				21.6%	22.6%	°°°
PSE credits: Math and science				28.4%	25.6%	°°°
PSE credits: Social science				18.0%	19.2%	°°°
PSE credits: Social work				0.2%	0.9%	°°°
PSE credits: Technical & vocational				1.3%	1.3%	
PSE credits: Communications				2.5%	3.4%	°
Worked during first year in PSE				70.8%	70.7%	
Worked during first three years in PSE				89.3%	88.9%	
High school's percent FRPL	44.4%	44.7%	°°°	43.0%	39.1%	°°°
High school's mean 10th-grade math score	0.018	0.022	°°	0.189	0.150	°°°
High school's mean 10th-grade reading score	0.014	0.020	°°°	0.182	0.142	°°°
Florida A&M University				6.0%	5.2%	°°°
Florida Atlantic University				6.0%	6.0%	
Florida Gulf Coast University				2.6%	2.5%	
Florida International University				7.7%	7.6%	
Florida State University				18.3%	17.5%	
University of Central Florida				15.9%	19.0%	°°°
University of Florida				19.6%	20.4%	
University of North Florida				5.9%	5.8%	
University of South Florida				15.2%	13.3%	°°°
University of West Florida				2.4%	2.4%	
New College of Florida				0.4%	0.3%	°

NOTE: AP/IB refers to advanced placement or international baccalaureate. "PSE credits" is share of cumulative credits through the 6th semester. Missing data for the high school graduates sample has not been imputed, while missing data for the Florida public university enrollees sample has been imputed, as discussed in the text.

°$p < .10$. °°$p < .05$. °°°$p < .01$.

Notes

1. We do not have tenth-grade test scores for students who entered the Florida secondary system after the tenth grade (7 percent of students). A very small percentage of students (less than 1 percent) are missing data on high school rank percentile, age, or foreign-born status. We impute all missing values using multiple imputations by chained equations, creating five multiply imputed datasets. We also have limited high school course-records for those students who were not observed in all four years of high school (for instance, those who entered the Florida secondary system in the eleventh grade).

2. Note that, for the overall sample, cumulative GPAs for females and males through spring 2005 are lower than GPAs in any individual semester. This result occurs since students who have lower GPAs in a given semester attend college for fewer terms. Thus, when we include students who ever attended a four-year Florida public university during the 2002-2003, 2003-2004, or 2004-2005 school years, the cumulative GPA for these students is lower than the GPAs observed for the subsample of students who attend in a particular term.

3. Since differences in observable characteristics favor female enrollees, and given their higher rate of enrollment in postsecondary institutions, we conducted a different thought experiment. Suppose that males and females with similar observable characteristics enrolled in four-year, in-state, public colleges at the same rates. What would the gender gap in first year GPA be under this scenario? To address this question, we ran a first-stage probit predicting the likelihood of enrolling in a Florida public four-year institution conditional on pre-collegiate variables (A_i, R_i, C_i, X_i) and high school fixed effects (v_h). We then matched each male that attended college with a female (without replacement) based on their likelihood of enrolling. The matched sample consists of 10,292 male and 10,292 female students. For this matched sample, the gender gap in first semester GPA is –.14 (2.81 for females versus 2.67 for males). That is, the gender gap is reduced 23 percent (1–.14/.18) when matching on the likelihood of enrollment.

4. Male college entrants are, in fact, drawn from schools with lower shares of poor students, and higher test scores and graduation rates than female college entrants. Smaller gender disparities exist among the universe of high school graduates (see Appendix B). Either college-going males disproportionately select into good high schools, or more likely, males need to attend good high schools in order to overcome their deficiencies on other observable characteristics in order to be motivated to attend college.

5. In results that are shown in Table 4b, and discussed subsequently, we show that the gender gap in high school class rank explains 109 percent of the gap in first semester credits earned (using male coefficients; 93 percent using female coefficients). Thus, the *total* contribution of gaps in high school class rank to gaps in cumulative credits is roughly 41 percent (i.e., 23 percent + 109 percent ° 16 percent).

6. The omitted category includes courses that could not be classified into these primary majors, such as physical education courses, military education courses, and library and information studies courses. There was no substantial gender difference for this omitted category, which accounted for 3.8 percent of males' courses and 3.6 percent of females' courses, respectively.

7. University of Florida 2002-2003 Undergraduate Catalog (http://www.registrar.ufl.edu/catalog.html).

8. In results not shown, with the exception of Rice, we find gaps in persistence at the Texas universities ranging from 1.6 percent to 8.8 percent. At Rice, we find males are slightly more likely to persist (0.8 percent) but significantly less likely to graduate within five years (6.1 percent).

References

Angrist, Joshua, Daniel Lang, and Philip Oreopoulos. 2006. Lead them to water and pay them to drink: An experiment with services and incentives for college achievement. Working Paper 12790, National Bureau of Economic Research, Cambridge, MA.

Blau, Francine D. 1998. Trends in the well-being of American women, 1970-1995. *Journal of Economic Literature* 36 (March): 112-65.

Bowen, William G., and Derek C. Bok. 1998. *The shape of the river: Long-term consequences of considering race in college and university admissions.* Princeton, NJ: Princeton University Press.

Charles, Kerwin K., and Ming-Ching Luoh. 2003. Gender differences in completed schooling. *Review of Economics and Statistics* 85 (3): 559-77.

DiPrete, Thomas, and Claudia Buchmann. 2006. Gender-specific trends in the value of education and the emerging gender gap in college completion. *Demography* 43 (1): 1-24.

Gibbs, Nancy. 2008. Affirmative action for boys. *Time Magazine*, April 3.

Heckman, James J., and Alan B. Krueger. 2005. *Inequality in America: What role for human capital policies?* Cambridge, MA: MIT Press.

Jacob, Brian A. 2002. Where the boys aren't: Non-cognitive skills, returns to school and the gender gap in higher education. *Economics of Education Review* 21 (6): 589-98.

Jacobs, Jerry A. 1999. Gender and the stratification of colleges. *Journal of Higher Education* 70 (2): 161-87.

Jones, Ethel B., and John D. Jackson. 1990. College grades and labor market rewards. *Journal of Human Resources* 25 (2): 253-66.

Kane, Thomas J., and Cecilia E. Rouse. 1995. Labor market returns to two- and four-year colleges. *American Economic Review* 85 (3): 600-614.

LoGerfo, Laura, Austin Nichols, and Duncan Chaplin. 2006. *Gender gaps in math and reading gains during elementary and high school by race and ethnicity.* Washington, DC: Urban Institute. http://www.urban.org/publications/411428.html.

Long, Mark C. Forthcoming. Changes in the returns to education and college quality. *Economics of Education Review.*

Long, Mark, Patrice Iatarola, and Dylan Conger. 2009. Explaining gaps in readiness for college-level math: The role of high school courses. *Education Finance and Policy* 4 (1): 1-33.

Peter, Katharin, and Laura Horn. 2005. *Gender differences in participation and completion of undergraduate education and how they have changed over time.* NCES 2005-169. Washington, DC: National Center for Education Statistics, U.S. Department of Education.

Reynolds, John R., and Stephanie W. Burge. 2004. Gender-related changes in educational expectations: The roles of family, school, and race/ethnicity. Working paper. http://garnet.acns.fsu.edu/~jreynold/socofed-submitted.pdf.

Riegle-Crumb, Catherine. 2007. More girls go to college: Academic and social factors behind the female postsecondary advantage. Working paper. http://theop.princeton.edu/workingpapers.html.

Rothstein, Jesse M. 2004. College performance predictions and the SAT. *Journal of Econometrics* 121 (1-2): 297-314.

Snyder, Thomas D., Sally A. Dillow, and Charlene M. Hoffman. 2008. *Digest of education statistics 2007.* NCES 2008-022. Washington, DC: National Center for Education Statistics, Institute of Education Sciences, U.S. Department of Education.

Turner, Sarah, and William Bowen. 1999. Choice of major: The changing (unchanging) gender gap. *Industrial Labor Relations Review* 52 (2): 289-313.

PART FIVE

Conclusion

What Have We Learned?

The use of preferences for racial or ethnic groups has spurred a lively debate about the merits of such policies. As underscored by this volume, however, most of the discussion about these issues has neglected a key point: students' decisions play an important role in determining the outcomes we observe in higher education. In other words, affirmative action, or lack thereof, will not alone determine whether our colleges and universities are racially and ethnically diverse. Students' decisions about where to apply to college and, if admitted, whether to attend result in the educational patterns one observes; and while an existing policy may influence students' behavior and institutions' admissions decisions, ultimately student actions drive the observed result.

Beyond institutional admissions criteria and related policies, many factors influence students' application and attendance decisions. Among the determinants of college-decision making, researchers have considered the role of academic preparation, finances, expectations, and information along with how parents, schools, and neighborhoods influence these key factors. Relatively little research has applied these types of analyses to the context of affirmative action policy. One reason has been a lack of data. The studies in this volume make use of a rich dataset that includes administrative records

Beyond Admissions: Reflections and Future Considerations

By
BRIDGET TERRY LONG

Bridget Terry Long is a professor of education and economics at the Harvard Graduate School of Education. Her interests in the economics of education include the transition from high school to higher education and beyond, with a focus on college access and choice, factors that influence student outcomes, and the behavior of postsecondary institutions. She is a faculty research associate of the National Bureau of Economic Research (NBER) and a research affiliate of the National Center for Postsecondary Research (NCPR).

DOI: 10.1177/0002716209348752

and student surveys, offering a fresh perspective on how race-conscious and race-neutral policies influence the decision-making process.

With the important role of student decision-making in mind, the articles in this volume detail several important facts. First, the educational pipeline from high school to college begins far before an application is submitted. As discussed in the first section, students form their expectations about whether they will attend and then decide where to apply. These decisions vary greatly by background and, as emphasized in the second part of the volume, by high school. Persisting race and income differences along the educational pipeline imply substantial gaps in college access even in the face of racial preferences. In addition, because students' decisions, behavior, and access to resources and opportunities are also important determinants of campus racial and ethnic composition, postsecondary institutions require more than race-conscious policies to diversify their campuses.

Another important point highlighted by this volume concerns the importance of examining not only college access but also longer-term student success. Only half of students who enter college complete a baccalaureate degree by age 25 (Mortenson 2002). Therefore, discussions of diversity must move from a singular focus on access rates to devoting some attention to diversity among successful students and college graduates. If enrollment rate gaps are narrowed but graduation rates have widened over time, then the ultimate goal of a diverse postsecondary system will not be met. Several of the later articles acknowledge this point by considering college major choice, grades, and graduation.

Additional Issues to Consider

This volume sheds considerable light on many of the issues related to student access and success, but several additional points deserve consideration. First, beyond the factors that influence student decision-making reviewed in this volume, there are many other decision points, policies, and issues that ultimately influence whether a student has the opportunity to attend a four-year institution. College affordability, academic preparation, and information all play important roles in the attendance decision. Additionally, I review several factors that influence college persistence. Although several articles in this volume note differences in college outcomes by observable student characteristics, it bears emphasis that multiple factors influence whether a student is successful in higher education, including unobservable student traits (e.g., effort, motivation, and confidence) and the policies, programs, and cultures of the colleges and universities that students attend. Similar to the college enrollment decision, the likelihood that a student completes a college degree is the result of a complex process of many interacting issues. I close with a short discussion on the degree to which results based on Texas have external validity for the rest of the country.

The role of financial aid in student decisions

Cost has long been known to influence college enrollment and choice decisions, and declining affordability is one factor responsible for the persistent gaps
in college access by race and income. From 1976 to 2005, the average cost of a
public, four-year institution increased from $617 to $5,491, a multiple of 2.7
times in real terms (College Board 2006a). Median family income did not keep
pace, rising only 23 percent in real terms during the same period (U.S. Census
Bureau 2005). Based on these divergent trends, the federal Commission on the
Future of Higher Education, which was appointed by the secretary of education,
concluded, "There is no issue that worries the American public more about
higher education than the soaring cost of attending college" (2006, 19).

Although billions of dollars are spent each year on financial aid to address concerns about college cost, current expenditures are insufficient. Pell Grants constitute the primary federal need-based aid program, but their value has eroded over
time. In real terms, the maximum Pell Grant in 1975-76 was $5,064; it was only
$4,050 by 2005-06, a 20 percent decrease after accounting for inflation (College
Board 2006b). At the state level, although more money is allocated to need-based
programs, spending on non-need based programs, such as the merit-based
Georgia HOPE Scholarship, grew 348 percent during the past decade (National
Association of State Student Grant and Aid Programs [NASSGAP] 2006). Many
colleges and universities have also shifted their focus from need to merit as part
of enrollment management strategies. The structure of institutional merit aid
includes a range of preferential packages that vary from scholarships and grants
based on standardized test scores to programs rewarding activities most likely to
be found in affluent high schools.

The implication of trends in financial aid programs is that many students have
significant unmet financial need even after accounting for all aid resources. Long
and Riley (2007) document the significant amount of unmet need, particularly
among students from low-income backgrounds and students of color. Furthermore,
many others, including Davis (2003), argue that institutional tuition discounting in
the form of preferential packaging and merit aid have decreased college access
among those least able to afford higher education. Thus, partially funded students
are left with the dilemma of making up the difference between their available
resources (including aid packages and family contributions) and the costs of their
educations. Trends in unmet need are particularly alarming because affordability
and financial aid are very influential in college decisions, especially among low-
income students and students of color (Leslie and Brinkman 1998; Dynarski 2000;
Kane 2003; Long 2008). Several studies also establish the connection between
student persistence and financial aid (e.g., Cabrera, Nora, and Castañeda 1993;
Bettinger 2004).

To better understand changes in Texas higher education, the role of financial
aid must be considered. Even if an admission policy change increases access to
students at a wider range of high schools, it is worthless to the many students who
are unable to pay the costs of such institutions. In the context of large income

disparities, admissions policy must also be coupled with financial aid policy. The implementation of the Top Ten Percent Law in 1998 occurred during a time when federal aid to middle-income families was increasing, with changes to the federal need analysis formula, the expansion of the unsubsidized Stafford Loan Program, and the creation of the federal Higher Education Tax Credits. As federal aid for needy students (the Pell Grant) continued to stagnate, Texas introduced aid for low-income students. For example, the Texas Grant, which was created in 2000, provides funds to academically prepared low-income students who attend institutions within Texas. However, it is unclear if this aid policy was sufficient to encourage students to make different college enrollment decisions. This issue warrants further evaluation in future studies about admissions policy.

Academic preparation and college remediation

Another relevant factor in students' decisions about higher education is their level of academic preparation, which both deters access for many students and predicts success in college. Adelman (1999, 2006b), for instance, finds that a student's academic background is the most critical factor in determining college enrollment and success. Several of the articles in this volume acknowledge this fact by accounting for differences in precollege academic achievement when comparing the decisions and outcomes of students. Unfortunately, many students finish high school below grade-level competency. Greene and Foster (2003) estimate that only 32 percent of all students leave high school ready to study college-level material. The proportion academically prepared for higher education is even smaller among black and Hispanic students (20 and 16 percent, respectively).[1] Similar to the discussion of financial aid, concerns about academic preparation might limit access for racial and ethnic minorities to public universities in Texas, particularly those who graduate from underperforming high schools.

Many underprepared students do not attempt to go to college, but those who do enroll encounter significant barriers. As mentioned briefly by Fletcher and Tienda in this volume, the most common institutional response to underpreparation is placement in remedial or developmental courses. In 2001, colleges required nearly one-third of first-year students to take remedial courses in reading, writing, or mathematics (National Center for Education Statistics 2003), but more recent administrative data suggests this percentage is underestimated (Bettinger and Long 2007). Low-income students and students of color are much more likely to be placed into remedial or developmental courses (Bettinger and Long 2007). Differences in the rigor and quality of high school classes, as measured by the resources of a school district, also translate into differences in remedial placement. High-poverty districts and urban districts have more students placed into college remediation than other districts (Ohio Board of Regents [OBR] 2002). Therefore, high school of origin is related to not only college application but also the ability to successfully enter college-level courses.

While the hope is that postsecondary remediation programs can compensate for differences in the preparation of students from different backgrounds, the evidence suggests otherwise. Martorell and McFarlin (2008) examine the impact of remediation on student outcomes in Texas using state administrative data. The study exploits information on two- and four-year college students' remedial placement exam scores to compare students just above and below the placement cutoff. They find that participation in remediation had little effect on a wide range of educational outcomes; hence students were no better off for having taken the courses. Studies of remediation in other states have found more promising results. Focusing on Florida, Calcagno and Long's (2008) analysis of the impact of developmental education suggests that remediation might promote early persistence in college, but it does not necessarily improve students' long-term progress towards a degree. Results based on a study of Ohio students show more positive results. Bettinger and Long (2009a) find that remedial students were more likely to persist in college and to complete a bachelor's degree compared to students with similar test scores and backgrounds who were not required to take the courses. Moreover, Bettinger and Long (2005b) find that community college students placed in math remediation were 15 percent more likely to transfer to a four-year college and to take 10 more credit hours than students with similar test scores and better high school preparation. Overall, these three studies indicate that remediation programs could have positive effects on collegiate outcomes, but these are not assured.

Gaps in academic preparation are difficult and expensive to overcome, and admissions policies will always be limited in their impact by the number of students academically prepared to enter top institutions. Furthermore, students who do gain admission must still pass placement exams or risk being deferred to remedial or developmental programs. Given the large percentage of students placed in such programs, their effect on college success warrants additional attention. Even under the best circumstances, being placed in remediation lengthens the time it takes to complete a degree. The repercussions of insufficient academic preparation go beyond access, carrying over to student persistence and performance.

Would a change in policy actually influence decisions? The role of information

Another major impediment to higher education for many students, particularly those from low-income families or families with no prior experience with college, is the complexity of the college admissions process and financial aid systems, as well as a lack of accurate information about higher education costs. College attendance is the culmination of a series of steps and benchmarks, and the current landscape is too complex and difficult for many families to navigate. As noted by Grodsky and Riegle-Crumb in this volume, students must first aspire to attend college or derive aspirations from their parents, teachers, and/or mentors. Additionally, students must prepare academically for college by taking the required classes, carrying a sufficiently high grade point average (GPA) and registering for the Scholastic Aptitude Test (SAT) or American College Testing

(ACT) admissions exam. They should meet with their guidance counselors and visit college campuses. Finally, they must fulfill the requirements for high school graduation.

The likelihood that students have engaged in these activities differs by background. Kane and Avery (2004) document major differences by high school in meeting the milestones necessary to prepare for entry into a four-year college. Low-income high school students in their sample possessed little understanding about how to handle the admissions process. The Commission on the Future of Higher Education acknowledged these problems, concluding that some students "don't enter college because of inadequate information and rising costs, combined with a confusing financial aid system" (2006, 7). Therefore, in addition to cost and academic preparation, information gaps also pose formidable hurdles for college access and persistence. Having early information about higher education may influence whether a student even bothers to prepare academically or financially for college.

The important role of information has several implications in the context of college admissions. First, as documented by this volume, application behavior differs by background, which is partly due to gaps in information and lack of guidance navigating through the process. Another implication is that a policy change may not have the expected impact if students are not aware of the change or are unsure about how to take advantage of it. College access programs may be necessary to enable the enrollment of low-income students, but they are insufficient by themselves. The visibility and design of the program or policy also matters. Like other social programs (Currie 2004), research suggests college access policies are most successful when they are well-publicized and relatively easy to understand and access (Dynarski 2000, 2002; Cornwell, Mustard, and Sridhar 2006).

As noted by Long, Saenz, and Tienda in this volume, the Top Ten Percent Law created a transparent admissions policy. They find that this decreased the concentration of enrollees at the public flagships from a limited set of high schools as other high schools began to send graduates to the University of Texas at Austin. This underscores the positive impact that clear information can have in broadening access, but it warrants emphasizing that not all groups responded to the policy equally. As with other programs, students differed in their access to clear and accurate information about the policy, which could limit its impact. Moreover, student perceptions about campus climate, whether accurate or not, also influence their behavior. The lesson is that researchers and policymakers must take the perspective of prospective students—in terms of what they know and understand—to understand whether a policy will be effective.

From access to college success: What is the role of the postsecondary institutions?

College access and enrollment are insufficient indicators to establish whether a policy aimed at increasing postsecondary diversity has been a success because stark differences in college persistence exist by race. Among first-time, full-time, degree-seeking undergraduates entering four-year institutions in 1998, graduation rates were highest for Asian students (65 percent) followed by whites (58 percent). Black and Hispanic students in this cohort graduated at much lower rates—40 and 46 percent, respectively (Knapp, Kelly-Reid, and Whitmore 2006). By 2004, only 12 percent of Hispanics and 18 percent of blacks over the age of 25 had obtained a bachelor's degree (U.S. Census Bureau 2006).

Differences in academic preparation are most frequently summoned to explain these outcomes, but as the above discussion about remediation highlights, such gaps do not fully explain differences in completion. Even after taking into account academic preparation, college attrition is particularly problematic among low-income students. Among college-qualified students, as defined by their high school GPA and test scores, only 36 percent of low-income students completed a bachelor's degree within 8 years, while 81 percent of high-income students did so (Adelman 2006a). The observable characteristics of students, such as their preparation, are but one part of the puzzle; unobservable student traits are also important.

One issue neglected in the discussion of college success concerns the role of institutions and, in particular, how their practices promote or undermine the success of their students. Research about student engagement is instructive about this question. Analysts of student engagement distinguish among three dimensions: academic integration, social integration, and institutional commitment. Students who feel academically and/or socially connected to their institution are more likely to stay enrolled than those who feel disconnected. Many students withdraw from college when their commitments to the institution falter (Tinto 1975; Kuh et al. 1991; Astin 1993). Involvement in campus organizations also increases students' benefits from college by fostering networks and personal skills. Level of engagement partly depends on students, but the programs, policies, and norms of an institution are also likely to encourage or discourage such involvement. For example, many colleges and universities have implemented first-year programs to engage with college freshmen.

Within the classroom, postsecondary institutions can also influence students' continuation decisions. Using the basic framework of an educational production function, institutions supply inputs such as faculty, class size, and student supports, which help determine the educational process and resulting outcomes of students. Past work has established the important role of faculty, and different types of instructors may be more or less effective in helping students learn (Bettinger and Long forthcoming; Hoffman and Oreopoulos 2009; Ehrenberg and Zhang 2005). Particularly for minorities, the race or gender of an instructor may influence course selection and major choice, particularly in fields in which students of color and women are underrepresented (Bettinger and Long 2005a). The size of classes and lectures also influences student outcomes. Bettinger and Long (2009b) show that an increase in collegiate class size is associated with higher dropout rates. These studies all underscore the fact that institutional resources and programs influence student collegiate outcomes.

Given these points, another aspect of the discussion concerning college access and success should focus on the role of institutions. In the wake of changes to admissions policies, how did colleges and universities adapt their policies and programs to the changing profile of students? What practices were most effective? What lessons can other institutions learn about how to maximize student success regardless of background? These are key questions that cannot be ignored if one is to fully understand students' responsiveness to changes in admission policy and whether or not they succeed in college.

Beyond Texas

Given the rich data resource afforded by the Texas Higher Education Opportunity Project (THEOP), these studies provide insight into postsecondary experiences in Texas. Also, the policy changes and court decisions of the time provided the opportunity to study the effects of admissions policies in the state. These are valuable contributions to our understanding of student decisions and outcomes, but are they generalizable to the larger population? Would one expect to see the same results in other states or for other populations? This is a key issue considering the continued debate about admissions preferences in many parts of the country.

When debating external validity, it is first worth asking if one has identified the true cause of an observed change in outcomes. Is the change due to the policy, or is there something about the particular context or environment that influenced the results? Would a particular initiative have the same effects elsewhere? Learning about the particular context is essential to understanding the implications of a result. In the case of Texas, there are clear parallels to the populations of states such as California and Florida, but the degree of the match should also be judged based on the similarity of postsecondary systems and college-age populations. Therefore, the results from these studies should not be applied elsewhere without careful consideration of the similarities and differences in these attributes.

Still, the analysis on how students make decisions corresponds to national trends. Family background and high school influence the determination of college attendance, and postsecondary success has not been realized equally for all groups. These trends are especially disturbing given the changing demographics of the country. The proportion of American college students who are racial or ethnic minorities has steadily increased over the past several decades, from 15 percent in 1976 to 31 percent in 2005 (Snyder, Dillow, and Hoffman 2007). Based on U.S. Census Bureau projections, Swail (2002) estimates that a majority of the 18- to 24-year-olds will be minorities by 2050. Therefore, the outcomes of students of color will increasingly determine the nation's skill level and standard of living.

Fortunately, with the expansion of state data sources, much more research is being done on the behavior and outcomes of students, particularly racial and ethnic minorities and those from low-income background. With state administrative data that tracks students along the educational pipeline, more information is becoming available about the leaks that need to be addressed. These data sources also allow for the examination of how other state policies have affected college applications, admissions, persistence, and graduation. Hopefully, this volume will be followed by a great deal of work on other states and contexts.

Note

1. Greene and Foster (2003) define being minimally "college ready" as (1) graduating from high school; (2) having taken 4 years of English; 3 years of math; and 2 years of science, social science, and foreign language; and (3) demonstrating basic literacy skills by scoring at least 265 on the reading National Assessment of Education Progress (NAEP).

References

Adelman, Clifford. 1999. *Answers in the toolbox: Academic intensity, attendance patterns, and bachelor's degree attainment*. Washington, DC: U.S. Department of Education, Office of Educational Research and Improvement.

Adelman, Clifford. 2006a. *Internal analysis*. Washington, DC: U.S. Department of Education.

Adelman, Clifford. 2006b. *The toolbox revisited: Paths to degree completion from high school through college*. Washington, DC: U.S. Department of Education.

Astin, Alexander W. 1993. *What matters in college: Four critical years revisited*. San Francisco: Jossey-Bass.

Bettinger, Eric. 2004. How financial aid affects persistence in college. In College Choices: The Economics of Which College,When College, and How to Pay For It, ed. by Caroline M. Hoxby. Chicago: University of Chicago Press.

Bettinger, Eric, and Bridget T. Long. 2005a. Do faculty members serve as role models? The impact of faculty gender on female students. *American Economic Review* 95 (2): 152-57.

Bettinger, Eric, and Bridget T. Long. 2005b. Remediation at the community college: Student participation and outcomes. *New Directions for Community Colleges* 129 (1): 17-26.

Bettinger, Eric, and Bridget T. Long. 2007. Institutional responses to reduce inequalities in college outcomes: Remedial and developmental courses in higher education. In *Economic inequality and higher education: Access, persistence, and success*, ed. Stacy Dickert-Conlin and Ross Rubenstein, 94-133. New York: Russell Sage Foundation.

Bettinger, Eric, and Bridget T. Long. 2009a. Addressing the needs of under-prepared college students: Does college remediation work? *Journal of Human Resources*.

Bettinger, Eric, and Bridget T. Long. 2009b. Mass instruction or higher learning? The impact of class size in higher education. Unpublished manuscript.

Bettinger, Eric, and Bridget T. Long. Forthcoming. Does cheaper mean better? The impact of using adjunct instructors on student outcomes. *Review of Economics and Statistics*.

Calcagno, Juan Carlos, and Bridget Terry Long. 2008. The impact of postsecondary remediation using a regression discontinuity approach: Addressing endogenous sorting and noncompliance. Working Paper 14194, National Bureau of Economic Research, Cambridge, MA.

Cabrera, A.F., Nora, A., & Casteneda, M.B. (1992). The role of finances in the persistence process: A structural model. *Research in Higher Education* 33(5): 571-93.

Commission on the Future of Higher Education. 2006. *A test of leadership: Charting the future of U.S. higher education*. Washington, DC: U.S. Department of Education.

College Board. 2006a. *Trends in college pricing*. New York: Sandy Baum and Kathleen Payea.

College Board. 2006b. *Trends in student aid*. New York: Sandy Baum and Kathleen Payea.

Cornwell, Christopher, David B. Mustard, and Deepa J. Sridhar. 2006. The enrollment effects of merit-based financial aid: Evidence from Georgia's HOPE program. *Journal of Labor Economics* 24 (4): 761-86.

Currie, Janet. 2004. The take up of social benefits. Working Paper 10488, National Bureau of Economic Research, Cambridge, MA. http://www.nber.org/papers/w10488.pdf.

Davis, Jerry. 2003. "Unintended Consequences." *National CrossTalk.* Summer.

Dynarski, Susan. 2000. Hope for whom? Financial aid for the middle class and its impact on college attendance. *National Tax Journal* 53 (3): 629-61.

Dynarski, Susan. 2002. The behavioral and distributional implications of aid for college. *American Economic Review* 92 (2): 279–85.

Ehrenberg, Ronald G., and Liang Zhang. 2005. Do tenured and tenure-track faculty matter? *Journal of Human Resources* 40 (3): 647-59.

Greene, Jay, and Greg Forster. 2003. Public high school graduation and college readiness rates in the United States. Education Working Paper no. 3, Manhattan Institute, Center for Civic Information, New York.

Hoffman, Florian, and Philip Oreopoulos. 2009. Professor qualities and student achievement. *Review of Economics and Statistics* 91 (1): 83-92.

Kane, Thomas J. 2003. A quasi-experimental estimate of the impact of financial aid on college-going. National Bureau of Economic Research Working Paper No. 9703, Cambridge, MA.

Kane, Thomas J., and Christopher Avery. 2004. Student perceptions of college opportunities: The Boston COACH program. In *College decisions: The new economics of choosing, attending and completing college*, ed. Caroline Hoxby, 355-91. Chicago: University of Chicago Press.

Knapp, Laura G., Janice E. Kelly-Reid, and Roy W. Whitmore. 2006. Enrollment in postsecondary institutions, fall 2004; graduation rates, 1998 and 2001 cohorts; and financial statistics, fiscal year 2004. Report no. 2006-155, National Center for Education Statistics, U.S. Department of Education, Washington, DC.

Kuh, George D., John H. Schuh, Elizabeth J. Whitt, and Associates. 1991. *Involving colleges*. San Francisco: Jossey-Bass.

Leslie, L., & Brinkman, P. 1987. Student price response in higher education. *Journal of Higher Education* 58:181-204.

Long, Bridget T. 2004. How have college decisions changed overtime? An application of the conditional logistic choice model. *Journal of Econometrics* 121(1-2): 271-296.

Long, Bridget T., and Erin K. Riley. 2007. Financial aid: A broken bridge to college access? *Harvard Educational Review* 77 (1): 32-63.

Martorell, Paco, and Isaac McFarlin. 2008. Help or hindrance? The effects of college remediation on academic and labor market outcomes. Unpublished manuscript.

Mortenson, Thomas. 2002. Institutional graduation rates by control, academic selectivity and degree level 1983 to 2001. *Postsecondary Opportunity*, March.

National Association of State Student Grant and Aid Programs (NAASSGAP). 2006. *36th annual survey report on state sponsored student financial aid: 2004-05 academic year*. Washington, DC: NASSGAP.

National Center for Education Statistics. 2003. *Remedial education at degree granting postsecondary institutions in fall 2000*. Washington, DC: U.S. Department of Education.

Ohio Board of Regents. 2002. Making the transition from high school to college in Ohio.

Snyder, Thomas D., Sally A. Dillow, and Charlene M. Hoffman. 2007. *Digest of education statistics 2006*. NCES 2007-017. Washington, DC: Government Printing Office.

Swail, Watson S. 2002. Higher education and the new demographics. *Change*, 15-23 July/August.

Tinto, Vincent. 1975. Dropout from higher education: A theoretical synthesis of recent research. *Review of Educational Research* 45:89-125.

U.S. Census Bureau. 2005. Current population survey, annual social and economic supplements. Table F-6. Regions—Families (all races) by median and mean income: 1953 to 2004.

U.S. Census Bureau. 2006. Current population survey 1994 and 2004, Tables 10, 12, 14. Washington, DC: U.S. Census Bureau.